Social History in Perspective
General Editor: Jeremy Black

Social History in Perspective is a series of in-depth studies of the
many topics in social, cultural and religious history for students. They
also give the student clear surveys of the subject and present
the most recent research in an accessible way.

PUBLISHED

John Belchem *Popular Radicalism in Nineteenth-
Century Britain*
Tim Hitchcock *English Sexualities, 1700–1800*
Sybil Jack *Towns in Tudor and Stuart Britain*
Hugh McLeod *Religion and Society in England, 1850–1914*
N. L. Tranter *British Population in the Twentieth Century*
Ian D. Whyte *Scotland's Society and Economy in Transition, c.1500–c.1760*

FORTHCOMING

Eric Acheson *Late Medieval Economy and Society*
Ian Archer *Rebellion and Riot in England, 1360–1660*
Jonathan Barry *Religion and Society in England, 1603–1760*
A. L. Beier *Early Modern London*
Sue Bruley *Women's Century of Change*
Andrew Charlesworth *Popular Protest in Britain and Ireland, 1650–1870*
Richard Connors *The Growth of Welfare in Hanoverian England,
1723–1793*
Geoffrey Crossick *A History of London from 1800–1939*
Alistair Davies *Culture and Society, 1900–1995*
Simon Dentith *Culture and Society in Nineteenth-Century England*
Martin Durham *The Permissive Society*
Peter Fleming *Medieval Family and Household in England*
David Fowler *Youth Culture in the Twentieth Century*
Malcolm Gaskill *Witchcraft in England, 1560–1760*
Peter Gosden *Education in the Twentieth Century*
Harry Goulbourne *British Race Relations in Historical Perspective*
S. J. D. Green *Religion and the Decline of Christianity
in Modern Britain, 1880–1980*
Paul Griffiths *English Social Structure and the Social Order, 1500–1750*
Anne Hardy *Health and Medicine since 1860*
Steve Hindle *The Poorer Sort of People in Seventeenth-Century England*
David Hirst *Welfare and Society, 1832–1939*
Helen Jewell *Education in Early Modern Britain*
Anne Kettle *Social Structure in the Middle Ages*
Alan Kidd *The State and the Poor, 1834–1914*
Peter Kirby and S. A. King *British Living Standards, 1700–1870*
Arthur J. McIvor *Working in Britain 1880–1950*

Titles continued overleaf

List continued from previous page

Christopher Marsh *Popular Religion in the Sixteenth Century*
Anthony Milton *Church and Religion in England, 1603-1642*
Michael Mullett *Early Modern British Catholics, 1559–1829*
Christine Peters *Women in Early Modern Britain, 1690–1800*
Barry Reay *Rural Workers, 1830–1930*
Richard Rex *Heresy and Dissent in England, 1360–1560*
John Rule *Labour and the State, 1700–1875*
Pamela Sharpe *British Population in the Long Eighteenth Century, 1680–1900*
Malcolm Smuts *Culture and Power in England*
John Spurr *English Puritanism, 1603–1689*
W. B. Stephens *Education in Industrial Society: Britain 1780–1902*
Heather Swanson *Medieval British Towns*
David Taylor *Crime, Policing and Punishment*
Benjamin Thompson *Feudalism or Lordship and Politics in Medieval England*
R. E. Tyson *Population in Pre-Industrial Britain, 1500–1750*
Garthine Walker *Crime, Law and Society in Early Modern England*
Andy Wood *The Crowd and Popular Politics in Early Modern England*

Please note that a sister series, *British History in Perspective*, is available which covers all the key topics in British political history.

English Sexualities, 1700–1800

Tim Hitchcock

Senior Lecturer in Early Modern History
University of North London

St. Martin's Press
New York

ENGLISH SEXUALITIES 1700–1800
Copyright © 1997 by Tim Hitchcock

St. Martin's Press, Scholarly and Reference Division, 175 Fifth Avenue, New York, N.Y. 10010

First published in the United States of America in 1997

This book is printed on paper suitable for recycling and made from fully managed and sustained forest sources.

Printed in Hong Kong

ISBN 0–312–16573–0 (cloth)
ISBN 0–312–16574–9 (paperback)

Library of Congress Cataloging-in-Publication Data
Hitchcock, Tim, 1957–
English sexualities, 1700–1800 / Tim Hitchcock.
p.   cm. — (Social history in perspective)
Includes bibliographical references and index.
ISBN 0–312–16573–0 (cloth). — ISBN 0–312–16574–9 (pbk.)
1. Sex—England—History.   2. Sex customs—England—History.
3. Sexual orientation—England—History.   4. Sex differences–
-England—History.   I. Title.   II. Series.
HQ615.H57   1997
306.7'0942—dc20   96–34976
                                                                CIP

Dedicated with love and respect to
Jim and Florence Hitchcock

Contents

Preface and Acknowledgements   viii

1 Introduction: Sex Before Discourse   1
2 The Public Cultures of Sex   8
3 'The Surest Way of Wooing': Marriage, Courtship
   and Sexuality   24
4 The Body, Medicine and Sexual Difference   42
5 Subcultures and Sodomites: the Development of
   Homosexuality   58
6 Tribades, Cross-Dressers and Romantic Friendship   76
7 Sexual Fear and the Regulation of Society   93
8 Conclusions   110

Notes   115

Further Reading   146

Index   167

Preface and Acknowledgements

This is a synthetic book which attempts to bring together and make accessible a complex historiography. In the process it does come to conclusions which are new, and does add the results of original research to the work of others. But fundamentally, this book seeks to comprehend the rapidly growing and changing literature on eighteenth-century sexualities. In this, of course, it cannot be entirely successful. Indeed, as it goes to press, new and exciting work on sexuality is appearing almost every month which modifies the conclusions developed here. Similarly, it cannot fully succeed because the topic is possessed of few known boundaries. Some readers will look in vain for topics which I have excluded, and others will be confounded by the inclusion of those I have chosen to discuss. I have excluded, for example, any extended analysis of religious discourses around sex and sexuality. Similarly, I have avoided any conclusion about the relative pleasure derived from sex in different historical circumstances. At the same time, I have included discussions of the history of medicine and social policy. The limitations these choices reflect are inevitable in a book of this sort, and to that extent do not warrant an authorial apology. But they do indicate that this work can be little more than a very selective introduction to a much broader topic – the ramifications of which can be seen in almost every aspect of social and cultural history.

Even in the process of writing a book of this length the number of debts one accumulates is large. First, I would like to thank Jeremy Black. I can think of no greater privilege than to be asked to write a book on a subject of one's own choosing. I would also like to thank Kelly Boyd, Rohan McWilliam, John Tosh, Tim Wales, Laura Gowing, John Broad, Robert Shoemaker, Pamela Sharpe and John Kortum for commenting on the manuscript. Their advice has made this a much better book. I would also like to thank Tim Wales and Mary Fissell for suggesting, quite independently of each other, that John Cannon's autobiography would be of interest to me. My greatest debt, however, is to Professor Penelope Corfield whose support and advice have been invaluable. Beyond these, I would like to thank Richard Dunn, John Black, Anthony Henderson, Kathy Castle, Sheila McElligott, Arthur

Burns, Julian Hoppitt and Thomas Laqueur for their encouragement, enthusiasm, example and simple common sense. Finally, I must record a profound debt to Sonia Constantinou, who was the first to read the manuscript and whose good judgement I value enormously, and to my son, Nicholas, who constantly (and loudly) reminded me that sex and reproduction are intimately connected.

1 Introduction: Sex before Discourse

On the morning of 16 November 1707, Elizabeth Gray entered the Sardinian Chapel in Duke Street, London, where she stripped off her clothes and ran naked to the altar. 'She appeared in several Strange . . . Postures, and . . . did hold forth in a Powerful manner; and could by no means be prevailed upon to desist; but . . . told them she was come to Reform the people, and bring them to a right understanding.' It was a full fifteen minutes before she could be prevailed upon to stop talking, dress and leave.[1]

For the Roman Catholics attending chapel that day, her naked body was a powerful religious symbol. Both Elizabeth Gray, a prominent member of the French Prophets, and her audience understood her actions as a reminder of the nakedness of Adam and Eve in the Garden of Eden before the fall, and as a commentary on the false hierarchies and idolatrous content of contemporary religion. And while Elizabeth Gray's audience was certainly shocked, the radicalism of her religious message was the cause.

A little over a hundred years later a group of naked male swimmers became the object of a vigorous and well publicised campaign. The shopkeepers and small businessmen of Chelsea decided they could not tolerate nude men swimming in the Thames, believing their very bodies represented a powerful affront to the innocence of English women. For ten years between 1815 and 1825, swimmers were regularly brought to court on a charge of indecent exposure. Indeed the campaign was only brought to an end when Thomas Clutterbuck succeeded in having the law overturned in 1825, after he had been prosecuted by a Chelsea baker. The court concluded that, in order to be prosecuted, the naked body had to be 'wilfully' displayed with 'intent to insult any female'. The very existence and popularity of the campaign, however, demonstrates the extent to which the body in all its guises had become a site of almost exclusively sexual meaning.[2]

Between Elizabeth Gray and Thomas Clutterbuck lies a century of profound development in social attitudes towards sexuality, reproduction and the body. This book explores this transformation by looking at public debates and discussion around sex, at courtship and reproduc-

1

tion, medicine, popular belief, homosexuality, lesbianism, and social policy. It argues that eighteenth-century England witnessed a 'sexual revolution' which transformed attitudes, creating a phallocentric and increasingly heterosexual culture which saw forms of behaviour beyond the bounds of penetrative heterosexuality as 'unnatural'. Of course, this does not mean that men and women having penetrative sex together was in any way new in the eighteenth century; rather it suggests that a new way of conceptualising that process arose in which a clearer set of boundaries between the 'natural', i.e. penetrative and heterosexual, and the 'unnatural' were promulgated to a wide audience. This 'sexual revolution' was not a liberation, but a part of the process of creating a 'natural', biological understanding of the world which was at the heart of Enlightenment thinking, and which in turn was used to label any alternative form of behaviour or belief as 'unnatural', its adherents, as 'other'. In the process this study describes and condenses the rapidly expanding literature on the history of Western, and in particular eighteenth-century English sexuality, and places its overall argument in the context of the work of others.

* * *

The writing of the history of sexuality has been intimately intertwined with the modern creation of the ideas of a sexual 'identity' and of sexual politics since the late nineteenth century. In part, the origin of the sub-discipline can be traced back to the rise of professional sexologists such as Havelock Ellis, and the development of Freud's psychoanalysis. Certainly, the sexologists created the typologies with which the modern history of sexuality is concerned. Homosexuality, lesbianism and hetero-sexuality are all categories created and problematised in that period.[3]

But if the late nineteenth century named the categories and sub-divisions which characterise the history of sexuality, it has only been in the last thirty years that the beginnings of a coherent story of the development of Western sexuality has begun to emerge. From the amalgam of the history of the family, the histories of homosexuality and lesbianism, of pornography, demography, of the body, gender and medicine, disciplines which were themselves coming to maturity in this period, a history of Western sexuality is being created.

And while the high-flown and increasingly scientific writings of nineteenth-century sexologists provide one starting point, the most obvious origins of this history of sexuality lie in writing on the development of pornography. In the self-consciously academic work of literary historians like David Foxon, and the later work of writers such as Peter Wagner and, from a feminist perspective, Lynn Hunt, the ever-increasing amount and specialisation of written and visual porn has been charted.[4] In the process these historical accounts, and the content of Western pornography itself, has formed the basis for what might be characterised as the 'liberation' school of the history of sexuality. Throughout the 1960s and 1970s it is this approach, in which an increasing number of accounts of sexual pleasure are taken to reflect an ever-increasing level of satisfaction, which dominates the historiography. One of the main characteristics of this approach was the belief that extreme repression and intolerance had been a traditional attribute of Western society, that this was in sharp contrast with non-Western and ancient societies, and that this extreme repression was gradually undermined from the seventeenth century onwards, facing only a temporary reversal during the height of Victorian prudery.

It is not only in relation to pornography that this kind of 'liberation' has been charted. Other literatures have also, either consciously or unconsciously, tended to adopt this approach. In the history of the family, and in particular in Lawrence Stone's *Family, Sex and Marriage* (1977) and his more recent *Road to Divorce* (1990), a rise in sentimental attachment between men and women within marriage and, by extension, a greater degree of love in relation to sex have been described. Stone has posited the development of a Western 'companionate marriage' in the late seventeenth century. When this literature is combined with the results of the work of the Cambridge Group for the History of Population and Social Structure, which has demonstrated a demographic transition towards earlier and more fecund marriages in the mid eighteenth century, an increasingly whiggish model of growing sexual pleasure and emotional intimacy can be depicted.[5] Indeed, this story of growing sexual satisfaction can be seen as one facet of the broader phenomenon of 'whig' history in general, in which it is assumed that history proceeds in an orderly manner from barbarity to civilisation, from the backward to the developed.

Historians of the Western experience have used this background to argue further that the process of increasing sexual pleasure and sophistication was continued and refined in the nineteenth and twentieth centuries – pointing to the work of the sexologists and psychoanalysts as evidence.[6]

Perhaps the most ardent statement of this 'liberationist', and hence whig, approach can be found in the work of Edward Shorter. In a series of articles and books published between the early 1970s and mid 1980s, Shorter argued that the eighteenth century witnessed a general

European 'sexual revolution' in which women, and plebeian women in particular, gained a greater sense of individual economic freedom which they in turn used actively to pursue sexual pleasure. Newly independent urban working women, naturally, in Shorter's view, found the opportunities for sex irresistible, resulting in both more sex and a growing population.[7]

This whiggish analysis of the sexual experience of our foreparents has, however, been gradually replaced by a more nuanced view. Certainly Shorter has been roundly condemned by a number of critics who have pointed out that the demographic models do not support his peculiarly urban transition and, more importantly, that he is dependent on an essentialist construction of the character of sexual desire in which desire is a biological given, an 'essential' element of human make-up. In a very real sense what Shorter and other 'liberationists' have assumed is that there is an unlimited human need for sex which is separate from the cultural construction of desire. By assuming that sexual desire is a biological imperative these historians create heterosexual lust as an ahistorical phenomenon – a universal factor. There could be no history of sexual desire itself because that was a constant. As a result, historians in this tradition have tended to emphasise the characteristics of past societies which prevented the 'natural' expression of an entirely 'natural' libido. In Shorter's view all that was needed to create a sexual revolution was opportunity – which for early-modern Europe was provided by growing urbanisation and economic well-being.

With the increasing intellectual importance of the history of mentalities and, in an anglophone context, the linguistic turn, through which the importance of language and culture have been reasserted, this essentialism has generally fallen out of favour. It is not that a 'liberationist' history has been entirely overturned, but rather that it has been modified through the work of Michel Foucault, the historians of medicine and the body, and a more sophisticated approach to the nature of sexual desire derived to a large extent from the history of homosexuality.

Perhaps the greatest single influence can be found in Michel Foucault's incomplete writings on the topic. In the three volumes of his *History of Sexuality* (English translations 1979, 1985, 1986) completed before his death, Foucault suggested that the very rise of discourses around sexuality, along with the apparent increase in the repression of sexual behaviour which seemed to characterise a Western experience in the nineteenth century, itself created and reflected a whole new preoccupation with sex.[8] In other words where Shorter saw a gradual decline in the repression of sex, Foucault saw the gradual growth of discourses around sexuality and hence the creation of a growing number of sites of sexual definition and behaviour. By reformulating the history of sexuality, Foucault in effect allowed historians to see sexual desire itself as a product of a particular moment and a particular culture. In the process he transformed a story of liberation into one of creation, and at the same time fundamentally challenged the essentialist basis of the ways in which sex and sexuality had been defined since the late nineteenth century. He did not, however, entirely supplant the historical agenda relating to sex. Just as with earlier historians, Foucault's work emphasised a range of modern developments – analysing the growing mountain of sexual reference of the eighteenth and nineteenth centuries, and leaving largely unexplored the silence which came before. In part this was a result of Foucault's own untimely death, but it has had the effect of creating in Foucault's work a mirror of the concerns and agenda of the 'liberationists'.

Foucault's influence has been profound and universal, and, when combined with the growing literatures on the histories of homosexuality and the body, has, during the 1980s and 1990s, created a relatively clear new trajectory for the history of sexuality. In sum, this literature suggests that the West inherited an amorphous set of sexual categories, which, although making sharp distinctions between the characteristics associated with men and women, assumed that sexual desire could be directed towards a wide range of objects. Non-heterosexual sex outside the context of marriage was certainly a heinous sin, but it was not a perversion of 'nature', nor a psychological illness. In this view the sodomite, adulterer and masturbator were all examples of a broader category of sinner in which almost everyone was counted. And while sodomy and lesser sins like pride or gluttony were certainly not treated in the same manner – pride attracted the gentle admonition of one's neighbours at the same time as sodomy could readily result in execution – all sin was part of a continuum of transgressions of which each individual man and woman necessarily partook. In other words, it was not that everyone was equal in their sinfulness, but that they were all equally subject to the same sinful desires. With the decline of humoural or Galenic medicine over the course of the period 1670–1820, and the rise of the idea of a 'natural' sexual differentiation in the late eighteenth century, heterosexuality was gradually defined and imposed on both plebeian and elite cultures. 'Normal' men and women from this period onwards were assumed to find each other 'naturally' attractive. And anyone whose sexual desires led down other paths could now be viewed as 'unnatural', a freak against whom those identified with the newly created category of heterosexual could define themselves.

This process of the naturalisation of heterosexuality reached its apotheosis with the medicalisation of sexual desire at the end of the nineteenth century. And as a result of the central role of sex in psychoanalysis and its variants, the process has been extended in the twentieth century to include the creation of powerful normative models for sexual desire, any variation from which has generally been viewed as an illness.

But as it currently stands this story continues to direct our attention to the agenda developed by 'liberationist' historians. The legal and social treatment of variant sexuality, of prostitution and pornography, of medical and social policy discourses around sex, are from either theoretical perspective the significant sites of historical change. As a result the transformation from a 'liberationist' to 'creationist' approach has had less impact than one might at first expect. More than this, either approach directs our attention to a fundamental transformation in social attitudes towards sex and sexuality firmly sited in the eighteenth century – a transformation which was itself a significant part of the broader development in power relationships and social organisation associated with the Enlightenment.

* * *

This study provides a detailed description of the evidence and literature which support the conclusions outlined above. It reviews the current historiography of pornography, courtship and marriage, demography, homosexuality and lesbianism. But it likewise seeks to question the teleological assumptions which underlie much of the work on the history of sexuality, the assumption that sex in some way became 'better'. In particular, this book will argue that rather than looking for a straightforward developmental process characterised by either a 'liberation' or a 'creation', we need to question more rigorously the definitions and categories we use to define sexuality; we need to be more alive to the world views of early-modern people, to their assumptions and expectations. Most of our measures of sexual behaviour, and of sexuality itself, are focused on things which can be described using the language of a modern 'naturalised' sexuality. In other words, there is a tendency for historians to look for homosexuals, lesbians and heterosexuals, where early-modern people would see only sinners. In order to understand early-modern sexuality and the changes it underwent, we need to take more seriously the categories and concerns of the individuals involved.

More than this, we need to question more rigorously the silence which preceded the development of a language of sexuality. We need to look again at the unrecorded sexual behaviour which came before the rise of mandatory heterosexuality and 'natural' sexual difference. One purpose of this book will be to argue for the existence of sex before discourse; to suggest that the absence of modern forms of sexuality does not make early-modern sexualities less complex, or less important or less real.

2 *The Public Cultures of Sex*

A handsome smock to be run for by women this day, a mile and a
half, the best of three heats, at the Cow and Calf, by Chelsea
Common. The start at four o'clock. No less than four to start. The
two noted Welsh Girls come to run against the Earl's Court Girls.

4 August 1755[1]

Running races in which young women necessarily exposed their legs to
a mixed crowd of drunken onlookers form just one aspect of the public
culture of sex which characterised eighteenth-century England. At the
other end of the spectrum were the libertine clubs and explicit pornography of the elite. When the, admittedly Scottish, Beggar's Benison
held its semi-annual meetings, the all-male, elite participants dressed in
monkish gowns, greeted each other by rubbing their erect penises
together and collectively masturbated into a ceremonial cup.[2] On most
occasions a young woman from the local village would be paid to
expose her genitals to the assembled crowd, before the reading of
explicit stories or medical accounts of various sexual phenomena.[3]
Between these extremes of both taste and class was a panoply of public
sexual activity and explicit writing. In joke books, trial reports, medical
literature, and wildly extended and metaphorical treatments of sex, a
public culture of sexual reference was played out which formed a
fundamental part of the growing print culture which characterised the
eighteenth century. To some extent its variety can be accounted for by
the social class of the various audiences. French language pornography
(the most common sort) obviously found its readership among the
educated elite, while the relative paucity of English equivalents suggests
that the market for this type of thing among the middling sort was less
widespread. At the same time the frequently vicious and explicit
humour of the chapbooks suggests that the primarily plebeian audience
for this material had an entirely different attitude towards sex. Likewise,
the variety, metaphorical nature and crude humour of much of the
more expensive English language materials suggests a different attitude
again among its audience – an appreciation of sexual humour, combined with a status-conscious prudery – the kind of prudery which

8

means that it is inappropriate to say 'fuck', but entirely acceptable to ⟩ retail a dirty joke which has sex as its central point.

This chapter will look in detail at the whole range of sexually explicit works produced, and try to relate the various genres to their intended audiences. It will also look at the development and importance of the highly self-conscious libertinism which characterised a portion of upper-class male society, and which perhaps forms the most studied of eighteenth-century public cultures of sex.

The least developed modern literature on eighteenth-century sex is that related to the labouring poor. We have had innumerable articles and books treating the importance of a work like Cleland's *Memoirs of a Woman of Pleasure*, but there is no single work which treats the public aspect of plebeian sexuality. What we do know, however, is that it was various, robust and frequently explicit. Games such as 'lip frog' or leap frog, played largely by people in their late teens and early twenties, was, in the eighteenth century, considered an ideal opportunity for sexual display in an era before underwear. It also gave numerous occasions for highly sexualised physical contact between the sexes. As has already been mentioned, running races had their sexual elements, while the general atmosphere of alehouse culture was conducive to both bawdy humour and a degree of controlled sexual behaviour.[4]

Perhaps the most obvious centre of plebeian public sexuality was the various fairs, both the hiring fairs and others.[5] In 1743 John Cannon recorded his memories of a local fair some thirty years earlier:

> ... being at a little paltry fair at Babcary always held the 14th of September, I singled out Mary the eldest daughter of Henry Chapman of East Lidford, a comely modest girl & of good behaviour, & Nathaniel Withers picked on Mary, eldest daughter of Thomas Addams of the same place. She was a brown handsome girl, very talkative yet modest. These were our companions and with these we took our pleasure & acquaintance in the fair & accompanied them home to the house of the former where we passed the night in good entertainment & civil mirth. These amours was continued by me sometimes with one of these Marys & sometimes with the other yet in a civil way & might have had in either of them a wife agreeable.[6]

John Cannon was almost always prudential in his courting practices, but the rough and tumble sexuality of fairs and alehouses could frequently lead to less controlled behaviour. Francis Place reported that in the late eighteenth century, London youth felt under very little constraint.[7] He later recorded having witnessed scenes of relative freedom at the Easter Greenwich Fair, with 'lads and lasses making their way to the Hill hand in hand playing at thread-the-needle. Other groups were intensely occupied at Kiss-in-the-ring. Others playing at leapfrog in a long train of twenty or more.'[8] As well as the fairs, urban inhabitants had numerous opportunities for public courting in alehouses, which were very much the centre of plebeian social life.[9] In London at least, these institutions provided both places to meet and drink, and the opportunity of renting a room if so desired. The frequently tragic result was pregnancy, as in the case of Rebecca Clements, of Chelsea, who started courting John Coustos in 1746: '. . . he had carnal knowledge of her body for the first time . . . at the Angel Inn behind St. Clement's Church . . . and several times after at the said Inn – and particularly about eight months ago at a house known by the sign of the Cheshire Cheese near the creek adjoining to Chelsea.'[10] Rebecca eventually gave birth to a bastard child in the parish work-house.

Our access to the sexual relationships which occurred in these public spaces is limited, but we do have chapbook and popular print sources which at least give us an idea of what the people partaking of these social occasions found worth reading. Margaret Spufford has done the most detailed study of the content of early-modern English chapbooks.[11] Her work is primarily directed towards the seventeenth century, but many of her conclusions hold good for the first half of the eighteenth as well. She suggests that while much of this inexpensive and accessible literature is highly sexualised, with a substantial proportion being directly concerned with courting and reproduction, there are sub-genres within this material. Spufford argues that many compliment books and slightly risqué stories were intended for and enjoyed by a female plebeian audience, and that, at the same time, a male audience was being fed a less nuanced style of humour, in which the sex is brief and uninspired. The most important point she makes, however, is that both men and women enjoyed a rude sense of humour, that women, and widows in particular, were expected to enjoy and seek out sex, and that a bawdy banter was a normal form of interchange between the sexes.[12]

The attitude towards women's sexuality, and that of widows in particular, is reflected in a speech by a widow from 'Cupid's Court of Salutations':

A thousand bashful Coxcombs might have come and I should have dasht them out of all countenance, but thou hast hit the nail on the head, and hadst thou not tired me with tedious Wooing, thou hadst never got me, but now be as brief to procure a Licence speedily (that shall be your charge) for tomorrow I must be wedded, and bedded, or I am gone again.[13]

The nature of this material is difficult to assess. It is both explicit and innocent. The reader is obviously expected to find the situations and speeches funny, but at the same time somehow titillating. And while it is certain there are sexual differences in the response readers made to this material, it is also certain that both sexes shared an appreciation of it. But perhaps it is the resolutely collective nature of this material, and the sexual lives of plebeians in general, which sets it most firmly apart. This was not, to use J.-J. Rousseau's expression, literature meant to be 'read with one hand'.[14] Instead, it was part of a shared and mutually policed sexual culture, in which a large range of sexual activity was available to the group – but from which the sexually active couple, or indeed individual masturbator, would find it extremely difficult to separate themselves.

These tensions are perhaps best drawn out by a story which appeared in *Poor Robin's Intelligence* (1691), a cheap humorous paper probably intended for a plebeian or artisanal audience:

From Holborn, we have this love intrigue transmitted, that a pair of pleasing amorists being desirous greatly to try what charms loves power contained beyond the smiling glances of the soul surprising eyes, and softest touches of a fragrant kiss; . . . they wrapped in shades, enter the damsel's master's warehouse, . . . and being placed decently against several bales of goods that stood piled in the middle of that place . . . , [she prepared] to receive the kind embraces of her vigorous lover, who came on with such a fury, as overturned the pyramid which did support this charming Venus, which falling, overwhelmed . . . [an] apprentice, who being drunk, had reposed himself behind it to sleep himself into a sober mood, who waking in a great amazement, supposing that he was entombed alive, and loudly did begin to bawl for help, crying murther, murther, for the lords sake help; which sudden noise surprised our amorists at such a rate, that they . . . fled with coats and britches, cravat and handker-chief in a confused manner, rampled and about their heels, so that being met before they could compose themselves, the whole intrigue [was] revealed and the bashful lovers were forced to compound for silence, whilst all the while the youth lay breathing out his last at both ends, unable to relieve himself, until some pitying hand gave him an anticipated resurrection, by unloading of his accidental burthen.[15]

The humour of this piece lies not in the sexual goings on of the couple, but the fact that they were discovered by their peer group. Here was both the sexual content of plebeian culture, and one of the main policing methods which kept individual behaviour in check.

* * *

Many of the things which have been said about plebeian public sexuality are also true of the rather more private sexuality of the middling sort. Indeed, there can be no well defined line of demarcation between the two. Chapbooks melded into more expensive forms of sexually explicit literature. And while one can identify a series of genres in which the language used, price asked and content make it clear that the labouring poor were not its intended audience, it is uncertain that the chapbooks and song sheets did not themselves have an audience among the middling sort. In other words, any attempt to draw a line between the readership of the various genres is bound to result in a degree of misrepresentation. Nevertheless, genres such as trial reports, many forms of medical literature, sexually explicit metaphor, and what one might call Grub Street sexual humour certainly contained a different set of assumptions about their audience than did the inexpensive chapbooks sold up and down the country.

Perhaps the most peculiarly English of these literatures is the extended sexual metaphor.[16] This tradition can be traced back to Shakespeare, John Donne and the metaphysical poets, but had its first extended use in *Erotopolis: The Present State of Betty-land* (1684), and was brought to a high degree of sophistication in a series of works by Thomas Stretser, or Stretzer, published in the 1730s and 1740s. In a series of works, ranging from single sheets to pamphlets of forty or fifty pages, Stretser used both geographic and botanical metaphors as an excuse for the detailed description of both male and female genitalia. *The Natural History of the Arborvitae, Tree of Life* (1732) gave an extended description of the penis, a short extract from which should give a good idea of the style of these works:

The tree is slow of growth, and requires time to bring it to perfection, rarely seeding to any purpose before the fifteenth year; when the fruits coming to good maturity, yield a viscous juice of balmy *succus*, which being from time to time discharged at the pistillum, is mostly bestowed upon the open Calyx's of the *fruitex vulvaria* . . .[17]

The combination of highly florid and Latinate expressions with the self-conscious adoption of the rather pretentious style of contemporary scientific writing is entirely typical of this genre, and to this extent betrays the audience at which it is directed.

Perhaps the best indication of how the producers of this material expected it to be received can be found in Stretser's *Merryland Displayed: or, Plagiarism, Ignorance and Impudence, Detected* (1741). In this volume Stretser dissects the content of his own extended geographical metaphor on women's genitalia, *The New Description of Merryland*, fulminating against his own bawdy humour. In *Merryland Displayed* Stretser mockingly recounts the reception of his earlier work:

> I am sorry to find that some of the fair-sex, as well as the men, have too freely testified their approbation of this pretty pamphlet, as they call it, and that over a tea-table some of them make no more scruple of mentioning Merryland, than any other part of the creation: It seems they like this book, because (as they pretend) there is not a baudy word in it . . .[18]

Perhaps the reference to the tea-table is more telling than the author's assumption that women were discussing his pamphlet – certainly it suggests the class of readership Stretser was aiming at. From here the author goes on to point out all of the sources of quotations and information contained in the earlier pamphlet. He suggests that most of the anatomical detail (which, in terms of eighteenth-century medicine, is both detailed and up to date) came from public exhibitions of waxwork models of anatomised women. Beyond this, *The New Description of Merryland* is exposed as a hodge-podge of the advertisements of quacks and a smattering of classical and Latin quotes, combined with four or five recent travel books and expedition accounts. Perhaps the most interesting element of this pamphlet is the extent to which it relied on London-based public displays and advertisements. While Richard Manningham's wax models, or 'artificial matrix', and his lectures on midwifery are frequently referred to,[19] Stretser also makes use of 'Two Quack Advertisements of the Royal Beautifying Fluid' and 'Dr Cam's Electuarium Mirabile'.[20] All of this suggests that these pamphlets were part and parcel of a more widespread, urban, middling-sort culture of sex which contained both private and public elements.

Nor, oddly, was this culture and genre restricted to sex. It was a useful weapon in the more serious debate about gender. The idea of an extended metaphor or simile was used to good effect in works such as *The Simile: or Woman a Cloud. A Poem* (1748), in which the supposed characteristics of women are painstakingly dissected. Perhaps even closer to Stretser's work is the similar material focused on scatological humour – works such as *Flos Ingenii vel Evacuatio Discriptionis. Being an Exact Description of Epsam, and Epsam Wells* (1674), the opening lines of which provide an insight into the tenor of the whole work: 'It is a sorry town, Shituate in a good aire, naturally bounded with Bumsteed downs on the east, and arsteed on the south . . .'.[21]

None of these works were by any definition pornographic; instead they seem to have reflected a shared culture of sexual reference and humour in which genitals were funny. And while adolescents may well have masturbated while reading about the *fruitex vulvaria* and *arbor vitae*, this provides evidence for the power of childhood imagination rather than the intent of the authors of these works. In sum, this kind of material suggests that sex was to some extent a shared joke, and that while it was increasingly being recounted over the tea-table, it was, throughout most of the eighteenth century, still capable of going out of doors.

Other genres played on a similar shared interest in sex. Two that have gained a deal of attention are the sex manual and anti-masturbatory diatribe. These works will be dealt with at greater length in a later chapter, but here it is important to note that historians such as Peter Wagner have suggested that these genres were highly voyeuristic and intended to produce a sexual response. He has argued that the personal accounts of the experience of masturbators in works such as *Onania, or, The Heinous Sin of Self-Pollution, and All its Frightful Consequences in Both Sexes* (1708) were in themselves meant to arouse the reader.[22] Wagner has similarly argued that *Aristotle's Masterpiece* and Venette's *Secrets of Conjugal Love* had equivalent functions.[23] And indeed there can be no doubt that many adolescent readers found this kind of relatively explicit material sexually exciting – certainly John Cannon regularly masturbated with the aid of a midwifery manual in the early 1700s, until his mother took the book away and hid it.[24] But it is unwarranted to extrapolate from this kind of evidence a single role for this material. While it was certainly part of the public world of eighteenth-century sex, its primary role, as Roy Porter has argued in a series of articles and books, was as a source of serious, pro-natal information (in the case of the sex manuals) and serious, if wrong, beliefs about the harmfulness of masturbation (in the case of *Onania*, the works of Tissot and James Graham).[25]

While Peter Wagner perhaps overstates the erotic or pornographic content of medical works, he is certainly correct in his contention that trial reports and accounts of divorce proceedings were read in part for their sexual elements.[26]

From the republication of the *Tryal and Condemnation of Mervin, Lord Audley Earl of Castlehaven* (1699) 'real life' sexual dramas became an increasing part of the eighteenth-century scene. With sodomy, cross-class sex, rape and the added pull of aristocracy, the trial of the Earl of Castlehaven was a natural success – made all the more palatable by the certain knowledge that the principals had been executed over sixty years earlier.[27] But equally popular, if more legalistic and seldom quite as racy, were the *Old Bailey Sessions Papers* which became more detailed over the course of the first half of the century, and the *Ordinary of Newgate, His Account of the Behaviour, Confession and Dying Words of the Malefactors who were Executed at Tyburn*, which, like the Sessions Papers, came out in serial form throughout the century.[28]

The *Sessions Papers* and the Ordinary's *Account* combined sex and crime in a new way, and under the guise of the moral purpose of reporting legal proceedings provided what seems to have been an inexhaustible demand for their product. To describe them as porno-graphic would be inaccurate, but it was certainly the case that they were intended to raise the blood of the reader. And more importantly, their inclusion of sexually explicit accounts of rape, sodomy and sexual activities associated with theft formed a prominent site for the discussion of sex in eighteenth-century public culture. Certainly, the vast majority of men and women would feel it appropriate to read this material, and while men may have done so at the coffee house and women at home, the kinds of brutal detail contained in these accounts were certainly the common coin of everyday conversation for both sexes.

A sense of the content of these accounts can be gained from the published report of the trial of Colonel Francis Charteris who was charged with raping a servant in his house, Ann Bond, in 1729. The court insisted on cross-questioning the victim as to the details of the rape. The evidence was then duly reported to the public as follows:

> Being asked whether the Prisoner [Charteris] had his cloathes on? She [Ann Bond] reply'd, he was in his night gown. – Being asked whether she had not her petticoats on? She reply'd, yes; but he took them up, and held her down upon the couch – Being asked, whether

she was sure, and how she knew he had carnal knowledge of her? She reply'd, she was sure he had, and that he laid himself down upon her, and entered her body. – She was also asked how it was afterwards? She reply'd that there was a great deal of wet . . .[29]

Charteris was convicted, sentenced to death and then pardoned.

Even more explicit and gratuitous were legal accounts associated with divorce and adultery, or criminal conversation suits. The decline of the Church Courts in the late seventeenth century, and the transferral of matrimonial suits to the civil courts provided a new opportunity for the reporting of the sexual goings on of the elite.[30] The publication of the trial of the Earl of Castlehaven has already been noted, but this was followed by a series of reports of proceedings for criminal conversation, i.e. suits for damages brought to court, usually by a husband against his wife's lover, or a father against his daughter's seducer. By mid-century a successful crim.con. suit was usually deemed necessary in order to mount a successful parliamentary divorce. These criminal proceedings brought into the public domain all the lurid evidence provided by servants and principals. The details of who did what to whom, where, when and how, were paraded in open court, and frequently retailed at 1s 6d on the street corner. Throughout most of the first three quarters of the century these reports were printed as one-off pamphlets, but by the 1780s whole sets of crim.con. accounts were becoming available. In 1789 Francis Plowden published his twelve-volume *Crim.Con. Biography: or Celebrated Trials in the Ecclesiastical and Civil Courts for Adultery*, while four years later the even more explicit *Cuckold's Chronicle* appeared, reproducing only the salacious elements of the trials and saving the reader the need to plow through the legal formalities.[31] One German visitor to London commented on the popularity of these works:

> . . . the most scandalous literature in London consists of the reports of Crim. Con. and Divorce Cases which are printed without expurgation. No book is asked for so frequently in the lending library, and the editions, reprints and extracts from them prove their popularity.[32]

The widespread consumption of this sort of material is again reflective of a public culture of sex. There was no dearth of sexually explicit descriptions. What is perhaps noteworthy, however, is that the vast majority of this material was contained within a series of masking discourses – the jargon of law and medicine, or poetic metaphor forming an excuse for talking about and reading about sex. And again, as with the material on metaphorical sex and medical sex, these trial reports were more about the public discussion of sexual matters than they were aids to masturbation.

The range of eighteenth-century literatures in which sex formed a prominent part is extensive. To those literatures discussed above could be added numerous novels and plays – there is no doubt, for instance, that an eighteenth-century audience would have understood Lovelace's intent when writing his poem to Clarissa's muff.[33] But more than the literature which has come down to us, there was a wide variety of other sub-genres which brought sex into a public and printed domain. To take but one currently disregarded example, a broadside like *The Counterfeit Bridegroom* contained both humour and explicit sexual references. Indeed the whole work, the account of the disappointments of an eighteen-year-old inadvertently married to a cross-dressed woman, seems designed to encourage coffee house and tea-table discussion.[34]

* * *

While the genres which have been discussed thus far were fundamentally about public interaction, a range of literatures meant to be consumed in private was also available. This literature was essentially pornographic in intent and content. The word 'pornography' was not coined in English until 1857, and literally means 'whore's story'. Eighteenth-century pornography was, in many cases, most notably *Memoirs of a Woman of Pleasure*, literally a prostitute's story. But more than this, the genre can be identified by the seriousness with which it takes itself, its explicitness and its apparent intent to arouse a sexual response.[35] Eighteenth-century pornography was not meant to be read aloud, or to a crowded alehouse audience. Instead, it was an aid to masturbation, which, even in the eighteenth century, was a largely private affair.

The other aspect of eighteenth-century English pornography of which one must be aware is that, with one notable exception, it was generally either French or Italian. And while many French and Italian works appeared rapidly enough in English translations, they were almost invariably set in distant or unusual locations.

This is not the place to retail the history of individual works of pornography. There are numerous studies which trace works such as *The School of Venus* and the *Fifteen Plagues of a Maidenhead*. Volumes by Peter Wagner, David Foxon and Lynn Hunt provide a more detailed and better guide to this literature than can be produced in this short space. It is worthwhile, however, looking briefly at this material and trying to set it in some kind of historical context.

The first and most important pornographic work to influence the English-speaking world was that of sixteenth-century author Aretino. Both in the original Italian and in various free translations, his *Ragionamenti* and the collection of 'postures' which were published under his name (although not by him) form the starting point for most studies of pornography. Aretino wrote dialogues between prostitutes in which an experienced woman gradually introduces a novice to the intricacies of sex. The first crude English translation appeared in 1658 under the title *The Crafty Whore, or the Mistery and Iniquity of Bawdy Houses Laid Open* . . . and the 'whore's dialogue' became perhaps the most popular of all pornographic forms – and was extended to include dialogues between the simply enthusiastic as well as the professional.[36]

While Aretino remained popular throughout the eighteenth century, Latin works such as Nicolas Chorier's *Satyra Sotadica* also became available.[37] Again, free translations were made and distributed. But the source and language of preference for pornography was undoubtedly French. From the 1680s a wide variety of works, including *L'Escole des filles*, *Vénus dans le cloître* and *Histoire de Dom B . . . portier des Chartreux*, was imported and distributed.[38]

A steady stream of similar works rolled off the presses throughout the following century, and among foreign language works and their translations there were few substantive developments. Obviously, at the end of the century, the violence, cruelty and sheer perversity of De Sade added a new twist to this tradition, but throughout, French pornography remained wedded to the dialogue and marked by its anti-clerical and anti-aristocratic content.

In the work of Robert Darnton and Lynn Hunt, a relatively clear story is now developing which suggests that the nature of these works was very much about the structure of the *Ancien Regime* and of the *Monde* and *Demi-Monde*. Darnton, in particular, argues that French pornography was generally written by aspiring or failed philosophes, who, having been encouraged by the success of early Enlightenment figures, had sought their fortunes through the use of their pens in Paris. More than this, he suggests that the disillusion of these men with the highly structured and elitist Parisian literary scene led them to use their pornography as a political weapon, both during the *Ancien Regime* itself and during the Revolution. Darnton argues that scenes of nuns and clerics partaking of sexual libertinism, and of aristocrats (particularly the various Queens of France) partaking of outrageous sexual stunts, were part and parcel of the Enlightenment itself – a form of sophisticated social critique.[39]

Unfortunately this scenario does not really work in an English context. What appears radical and subversive in France became conservative and reactionary in England. Citing the sexual libertinism of foreign aristocrats and Catholic clergy merely had the effect of reinforcing the already bigoted opinions of English readers. So, while this literature may be part of the French Enlightenment, it is not part of the English equivalent (if indeed England can be said to have had an Enlightenment at all).

While there may not have been an alternative English tradition, there were notable examples of English pornography. The works of the Earl of Rochester can be considered obscene at least, if not particularly pornographic, while, of course, the great pornographic classic of the century was written in English – Cleland's *Memoirs of a Woman of Pleasure.*

More ink has been spent on John Cleland and his one great book than on any other equivalent figure in the history of pornography. A full biography has been written, as well as innumerable articles.[40] But the significance of the work lies in the extent to which it broke out of the literary conventions of contemporary pornography, and instead adopted those of the newly popular novel. Published in 1749, *Memoirs of a Woman of Pleasure* or *Fanny Hill* was the pornographic equivalent of a domestic romantic novel, in which the travails of courtship and adventure inevitably end with the heroine settling down to live happily ever after with the hero. Written in the epistolary style of Richardson's *Pamela*, it ends with Fanny, the heroine, settling down with her one true love, Charles, the man to whom she lost her virginity. That a variety of explicit sexual scenes were shoe-horned into this genre says more about the form of the novel than it does about Cleland or pornography. But, taken in relation to the analysis of French pornography, briefly described above, the existence of *Fanny Hill* reflects the extent to which pornography looked profoundly conservative from an English perspective. If in France one of its roles was to encourage political dissent, its primary role in England seems to have been to encourage domestic contentment – albeit a contentment based on the assumption of male promiscuity and the availability of commercial sex.

Beyond Cleland's works there is almost nothing worth noting in English pornography. Works such as the *Essay on Woman*, generally, if inaccurately, attributed to Wilkes, is simply an obscene parody of earlier literary work. At the same time the various sub-genres of pornography, at the cusp between masturbatory aid and public entertainment, are interesting primarily as a set of markers for this boundary. In this category one must put serial publications like the *Bon Ton Magazine: or a Microscope of Fashion and Folly* (1791–5), *Harris's List of Covent Garden Ladies* (1761, 1788–93) and *The Rambler's Magazine* (1783–90). But, however unimaginative or French eighteenth-century pornography was, these writings did have an audience, and it is to the nature of this audience, and the commercial interests which sought to pander to it, that we must now turn.

Lawrence Stone has recently argued that the readership of eighteenth-century pornography might have been much broader than has traditionally been assumed. On the basis of one case in Norwich in 1707, he has argued that at least a portion of the middling sort were familiar with pornographic writing originally aimed at an elite audience, and, more importantly, were willing to take it as a source of inspiration in relation to sexual behaviour.[41] Whether or not the burghers of Norwich were reading dirty books is less important than where, how and for what reason people in general did. On this point, however, there is relatively little information. Perhaps the most commonly cited instance of the use of pornography is the story of Pepys' use of *L'Escole des filles* as a masturbatory aid, before burning his once-read and recently purchased copy.[42] But more telling, of both the audience and uses to which pornography was put, are the nine copies of the *Memoirs of a Woman of Pleasure* which were recorded amongst the baggage of Arthur Wellesley, future Duke of Wellington, on his setting out for an extended posting in India.[43] Considering the long sea voyage and the single men's quarters at his destination, there can be little doubt as to his intended personal use for this material, while the number of volumes involved suggests a possible role for pornography as an appropriate gift for male friends.

Besides serving as a masturbatory aid for English upper-class men, the other role for pornography seems to have been in the brothel. There are few accounts or images of the interior of an eighteenth-century brothel that do not include either written or visual pornography. The extent to which these are depictions of reality is difficult to assess, but it is almost certain that the readers of this material were both moneyed and male, and that they were part of a peculiarly homosocial world of upper-class men.

While it is not a new observation that most upper-class English men masturbated regularly, this material at least suggests that pornography of the sort described above was largely restricted to the elite. When this evidence is combined with the fact that many works circulated widely in their original French or Latin, the class, or at least educational, bias in the readership of pornography seems largely self-evident.

What is more difficult to assess is the relationship between this material and the more popular and public sexual humour and accounts which were described in the first part of this chapter. Indeed, if one looks at the publishing history of these materials it is very difficult to find a clear distinction between pornography and other types of sexually explicit literature – they all tended to be published by the same people. Edmund Curll has become synonymous with eighteenth-century pornography. His role as the defendant in the 1727 trial directed at the suppression of *Venus in the Cloister; or the Nun in her Smock* has ensured that historians remember his name.[44] But perhaps more typical of eighteenth-century pornographers was Ralph Griffiths, the publisher of *Fanny Hill.*[45] The *Eighteenth-Century Short Title Catalogue* lists him as the publisher of over four hundred items, covering a huge variety of topics. Besides the *Memoirs*, he produced works on Jacobitism, medicine, child rearing, popular humour, distilling, Creek Indians' accounts of fires, satires on town life, an epistolary novel, histories and sermons. He also published a dictionary of love and the literary memoirs of Laetitia Pilkington.

Within this corpus are most of the genres which characterised mid-eighteenth-century printing, and that *Memoirs of a Woman of Pleasure* found a place in this list should provide a strong reminder that modern divisions between pornography and other literatures are just that, modern.

* * *

Despite the permeability of the boundaries between pornography and other genres, there is one distinction the eighteenth century would have recognised – the boundary that lies between what would have been described as libertine behaviour and everything else. In almost every sense – in the prominent role of prostitutes, the emphasis on female virginity and its loss, and the valorisation of male sexual pleasure – pornography gave voice to the ideals of contemporary male libertinism.

Much has been written about libertinism – indeed, it is in part upon the existence of an elite libertine culture that the traditional view of the eighteenth century as a period of extreme bawdiness is based.[46] But it is important to realise both the limited nature of self-conscious libertinism – it was restricted to a small group of elite men – and the rather sad and absurd content of libertinism as a philosophy and social activity. I have already described the ridiculous activities of the Beggar's Benison, with its pseudo-Masonic culture of collective masturbation. But this is just an extreme example of the kind of libertine culture available in a number of clubs up and down the country.[47] Indeed, while groups like the Medmenham Monks occasionally met with women willing to play nun to their monk, these societies seem resolutely male in character and masturbatory in habit.[48] Indeed, there is no evidence that heterosexual sex actually occurred at the meetings of any of these clubs. More likely were the reading of obscene poems like *An Essay on Woman* or the hiring of an eighteenth-century equivalent of a stripper. 'Posture Nan' was a popular figure in this regard, being a character adopted by several women in succession. The woman playing 'Nan' would enter a room, strip and, possibly with the aid of a mirror, show her genitals to the assembled audience. There was no movement involved, and the whole process seems to have been markedly clinical.[49] An alternative activity reported from a number of sources is described in *The Memoirs of Sally Salisbury* (1723). Sally is described:

> . . . standing upright upon a bed, but reversed, her head being in that place where her heels should be, she was honoured with having two Peers for her supporters, each holding and extending a well shaped leg: thus every admirer pleased with the sight, pulled out his gold, and with the greatest alacrity pursued the agreeable diversion [of throwing coins at Sally's crotch].[50]

While the psychological significance of these kinds of activities is at best opaque, they certainly reflect an entirely homosocial world, where collective masturbation, rather than sex itself, seems to have been the main point. And while the rhetoric of libertinism, with its aggressive and predatory sexuality, suggests a justification for promiscuity and a new attitude to sex itself, the reality of libertine clubs provides evidence only for the prudery, sexual and emotional immaturity, and general social incompetence of the participants. The ritualised structures, the gowns and ceremonies, reflect the growing impact of the clubs and voluntary societies which increasingly characterised eighteenth-century sociability. But their brand of sociability was more akin to train-spotting than to the easy-going sexuality sometimes claimed for them.

* * *

This chapter has been about the public face of eighteenth-century sexuality – the forms of sexual behaviour and discourse which could escape the bedroom and show their faces at the fair or tea-table. And what these discourses demonstrate most starkly is the extent to which sex was a shared joke for most people – that only pornography abandoned humour in favour of a voyeuristic and clinical view of sexuality. Sexually explicit visual material would likewise confirm this conclusion. A quick look through the works of Cruikshank or Rowlandson, or any of the visual artists producing sexual images in the eighteenth century, would reveal a great deal of explicit sex, but very little that is unleavened by humour.

What one also finds in this material is a domestic and conservative sub-text. Despite the association of radicalism with pornography in the early nineteenth century, and the undoubted political role of pornography in a French context, eighteenth-century English sexual humour and pornography seem resolutely directed towards reinforcing social norms rather than attacking them.[51] In plebeian culture most sexual humour reinforced the policing role of the peer group, while in the case of pornography the adoption of a novelistic form domesticated both libertinism and prostitution in a new way.

Perhaps the peculiarity, domesticity and conservatism of English discourses about sex can best be summed up by comparing English and French writings about Tahiti. After Bougainville visited the island in 1778 he published a popular account in which Tahiti is described as a sexual utopia. In other words, he used the island, and his perception of the inhabitants' sexuality, as an exemplar of Enlightenment ideals. For Bougainville, and later Diderot, the Tahitians were noble savages who had learned to live in nature, and for whom sex was demystified, joyous and free of guilt. When Cook visited the island during the course of the 1770s he came to a very different conclusion. He saw in Tahitian society many of the characteristics of home. For him the islanders were monogamous, property owning and domestic – lacking only the patina of Christianity to make them the South Sea equivalent of English men and women.[52]

3 'The Surest Way of Wooing': Marriage, Courtship and Sexuality[1]

This night I had another dream but much more fantastical methought
on a sudden I am wth one of the daughters of one Grace Hole at
Lidford at the backdoore of her house who tells me she had gotten at
her own charge a Licence to be married to me and so by her allure
ments the ceremony was performed. . . . My supposed Bride & her
sisters insisted . . . [I] go to bed wth my bride the bed being pre pared
in one corner of a chamber but not withstanding I thought I was yet
unmarried & single, being conscious to my self I was engaged to
another I grew into a perplexity & requested to be excused that night,
but promised to come the next following having thought to go home
to consult my parents . . . however she persisted on my stay[ing] & so
in veighed me & told me she expected carnality wth me as the duty
of a new married couple to wch I seemingly consented by grasping
her about, methought I felt her privities and at the same time I
demanded of her the Licence To which she answered she had none
but only a trick of hers to make me believe she had one to obtain her
ends . . .[2]

John Cannon, a financially improvident excise officer and charity
school master, had this dream at the age of fifty-four. He had been
married for twenty-five years, and was the father of five children. Yet
even he could not dream of a sexual encounter without unconsciously
linking it to courtship and marriage. In a series of erotic dreams he
records in his voluminous memoirs, Cannon consistently links sex and
marriage, and is frequently stricken down by uncertainty about his
ability to contract a valid dream marriage.

This equation of sex, courtship and marriage in John Cannon's
mind is emblematic of the extent to which the vast majority of
plebeian and middling-sort English people in first half of the eighteenth century invested their sexuality in the process of family
formation. The desire for sex is certainly there, but it is strictly
controlled within an ideological framework which saw sex, including

24

both penetrative and non-penetrative varieties, as part and parcel of the broader social process of marriage and procreation, rather than as a discrete activity.

The interrelationship between the categories of sex, marriage and parenthood, which to a modern mind seem relatively distinct, has left historians of eighteenth-century sexuality with a fundamental conundrum. From the late 1970s it has been amply apparent from the work of demographic historians, and most notably those working in association with the Cambridge Group for the History of Population and Social Structure, that the eighteenth century witnessed a marked transition in many of the indicators associated with family formation, the assumptions surrounding marriage and, by extension, attitudes towards and practices relating to sex.[3] Few adequate attempts have been made to explain these changes but their existence is now beyond doubt.

At the end of the seventeenth century the population of England was essentially stagnant, following a period of relatively rapid growth which had ended in the middle of the century. This period of population stagnation, between approximately 1650 and 1750, was most fundamentally characterised by late age at marriage. Men married at a mean age of approximately twenty-eight years and women at around twenty-seven years. This tendency to marry at a very late age, the European marriage pattern, was unique to Western Europe and the early-modern period (reaching an extreme in late-seventeenth-century England), and ensured that the overall fertility rate for the population was relatively low. By delaying female marriage over ten years past the onset of puberty, the number of children any one woman was likely to produce was dramatically lessened. This tendency to lower fertility based on age at marriage was then reinforced in England in the late seventeenth century by a number of other factors. A large proportion of both men and women never married and never produced any children. Indeed, it has been argued that it was this high rate of celibacy which was most important in maintaining population stability in the early eighteenth century.[4] In one relatively small sample, some 22.9 per cent of people between forty and forty-four years old remained unmarried.[5] These two factors were then combined with an extraordinarily low rate of bastardy and of premarital pregnancy – the illegitimacy ratio being 1.779 per cent[6] and the percentage of women pregnant at marriage being approximately 15 per cent.[7] And while the demographic history of the second half of the seventeenth and early eighteenth centuries may in some ways represent a blip in a larger pattern of population growth, it is clear that our period begins with a demographic regime in which many people remained celibate throughout their lives, perhaps only 80 per cent ever marrying, while only a tiny proportion were having penetrative sex outside the confines of courtship or marriage.

Equally apparent from the work of these same historians is that these factors did not remain constant. Primarily as a result of changes in fertility, rather than mortality, the population of England and Wales grew from 5.058 millions in 1701 to 8.664 millions in 1801.[8] By the early nineteenth century the age at marriage had dropped to 25.5 for men and 23.7 for women; the percentage of people remaining unmarried had fallen from perhaps 22 per cent to less than 9 per cent; the bastardy rate had soared to 5 per cent of all known births; and finally the percentage of first births occurring within eight months of marriage rose to between 33 and 37 per cent of the total.[9]

The transition between these extremes of stagnation and growth has been located in the first half of the century, with the upswing in population first becoming apparent around 1750, while changes to age of and proportion of the population marrying can be identified in the preceding twenty or so years.

While historians have been remarkably successful at describing these transitions they have had much less success explaining them. The demographers themselves point to economic models to account for these changes. Historians such as E.A. Wrigley suggest that rising real wages in the last half of the seventeenth century allowed a higher proportion of the population to marry, and to do so at a younger age – in other words, suggesting that the urge to marry was natural, and that it was the preventive check of poverty which created the low fertility pattern typical of the late seventeenth century.[10] Other economic factors, such as the rise of proto-industrialisation, the decline of apprenticeship and changing structures of rural labour, have all been identified as possible contributory factors in the demographic transition. None of these explanations have remained unchallenged, and none fit the demographic evidence very well.[11] There is a forty-year time lag between the rise in real wages and the drop in marriage age, and although this has been explained in terms of parental attitudes, and hence generational factors, the disparity in the chronology of these transitions remains. Changes in age at marriage, bastardy rates and proportion marrying occurred both in villages affected by industrial change and in other types of communities at about the same time. And the developments in apprenticeship and forms of rural labour do not tie in sufficiently well to the chronology of demographic change to suggest they were significant factors.[12]

While economic and demographic historians have been remarkably unsuccessful in explaining the demographic transition, qualitative historians have been equally frustrated. Writers such as Edward Shorter, Lawrence Stone and most recently Tom Laqueur and Henry Abelove have examined the cultural content of the transition, with a sharp eye for the rise of 'sentiment' and desire in sexual activity. Edward Shorter, for instance, argued in the mid 1970s that rising fertility and bastardy rates reflected a new attitude towards sex on the part of plebeian women. He suggested that with the growth of urbanisation and the increasing incorporation of young women into the moneyed economy, they chose to participate in penetrative sex more frequently – that, in other words, there was a 'sexual revolution' in female desire which was made possible by economic change. Shorter has been roundly condemned by a number of commentators. And his argument has largely fallen on the discovery that changes in sexual behaviour were equally apparent in rural and urban areas.[13]

A more measured case has been made by Lawrence Stone. He argues that the period between 1660 and 1800 witnessed the rise of a 'companionate' model of marriage in which love and affection became more significant, and which replaced the more austere puritan family of the previous century. Romance and the rise of the novel, the ability of children to choose their own partners and the influence of the law all, in Stone's view, ensured that a new pattern of marriage would become established.[14] Certainly, Stone's chronology has been questioned, and the rather unfocused relationship he suggests between these changes and the demographic transition has been criticised. Likewise, he has been taken to task for concentrating on the experiences of the elite at the expense of the poor majority of the population.[15] But, nevertheless, most historians would accept Stone's view that some form of change in sentiment occurred, even if they cannot agree as to its actual content or timing.

Most recently, historians Henry Abelove and Thomas Laqueur have each suggested a link between sentiment and desire as it relates to sex, and to broader cultural and economic shifts which characterised the eighteenth century. While both studiously avoid the reductionism of Edward Shorter, they agree that there was a change in the fundamental experience of sexual activity which owed its content to changing patterns and discourses of consumption and production. Abelove, for instance, suggested that just as industrial production grew in cultural significance as part of the industrial revolution, so the popularity of penetrative sex grew.[16] In a similar, if more complex way, Laqueur located the changing pattern of sexual behaviour within a wide variety of eighteenth-century discourses – those about reading, medicine, gender and capitalism in particular – and further suggested that the transition in sexual behaviour must be seen as an integral part of the cultural and production revolutions associated with the eighteenth century.[17]

Stone, Abelove and Laqueur all made valid and defensible points, but what each failed to identify is the effective mechanism for the transition of sentiment into action. While it is relatively easy to agree that changes in attitude occurred, it is more difficult to identify when and how these affected individuals. In order to examine these questions we have to turn to the historical record itself, and to a different body of literature – that on courtship, illegitimacy and the nuts and bolts of marriage.

Unfortunately, qualitative evidence for plebeian and middling-sort sexual behaviour is fragmentary. Although sex between heterosexual working people comprised the vast majority of all sexual activity, its very ubiquity has ensured its relative invisibility. While we know a great deal about elite courtship and libertinism, and even a fair amount about homosexual sex, heterosexual plebeian activities remain largely unexplored. There are Church Court and criminal records which do provide some insight into these areas of activity, but even these provide accounts of individual scenes, rather than fully contextualised stories, and are likely to represent the unusual rather than the norm.

One notable exception to the silence of the historical record is provided by John Cannon's 'Memoirs', quoted at the beginning of this chapter. In over seven hundred pages of closely written manuscript he recounts sixty years of experience as child, youth and adult – as student, farm labourer, excise officer and charity school master. As part of the details of this life, he gives a unique, first-hand account of courtship and marriage in the eighteenth century. And while he cannot himself be easily pigeon-holed amongst either plebeians or the middling sort, he certainly, at different times, courted women who would have fitted either description. In part because of the unusual details provided, but also because Cannon's experience fits beautifully with other evidence of popular sexuality, it is worthwhile looking at his career in some detail.

Born in 1684, John Cannon came from a lower-middling-sort family of small yeomen and petty traders in North Somerset. Until the age of thirteen he was kept at school, receiving a relatively thorough education, but was then sent into farm service with an uncle. Later he became an excise officer, and later still a charity school master, but at no time during his life did he earn more than £60 or £70 per annum and generally he earned much less than this.[18] His career as a sexually active child and young adult spanned the eighteen years between 1696 and 1714, and gives us an insight into both his sexuality and that of the women he dealt with.

He learned to masturbate from a seventeen-year-old school friend and cousin in 1696. He was twelve years old at the time, and he and a group of friends were swimming together after school. In a relatively formal scene, his friend took this occasion to show the younger boys:

> what he could do if he had a female in place, and withall took his privy member in his hand rubbing it up & down till it was erected & in short followed emission. The same as he said in copulation, & withall advised more of the boys to do the same, telling them that altho' the first act would be attended with pain yet by frequent use they would find a deal of pleasure on wch several attempted and found as he said.[19]

While Cannon was quick to condemn masturbation when he wrote up the memoirs at the end of his life, he took his cousin's advice and indeed found pleasure by frequent use. More than this, the dating and nature of these events are significant. That Cannon was masturbating from the age of twelve, and continued to do so throughout his adolescence, reflects the extent to which the desire for sexual pleasure was a normal part of growing up in the eighteenth century, even if penetrative sex was not. Also, the public and collective nature of Cannon's sexual discovery reinforces the view presented by historians such as John Gillis that early-modern courtship and the sexual activity which went with it was strongly controlled by the peer group.[20]

In the succeeding years Cannon uses most of the opportunities presented to him in order to discover more about sex. He was thrilled by reading *Aristotle's Master-piece* and Culpeper's *Midwifery* which he saw as allowing him insight into the 'secrets of nature', and which he avidly studied until his mother caught him masturbating with the latter and took away the book.[21] At about the same time, when he was sixteen, he drilled holes in the privy wall in order to allow him to look at the genitals of a female servant living in the house.[22]

The homosocial and at times anti-social elements of this adolescent male's experience were finally broken at the age of about twenty, when, always in the company of a group of male friends, Cannon began to visit and socialise with women of his own age. One Sunday, while visiting a nearby church with a group of young male bell-ringers, a plan to visit a near relation of one of the boys was set on foot. Three of the bell-ringers, including John Cannon, set off to visit Mary Withers, who, by prior arrangement, had two companions staying with her – one of whom was a young widow named Hester.

Mary Withers' mother had died some years earlier, and her father was away (a fact known by the three young men), so this party of six young men and women had complete run of the house and complete privacy. They spent the evening 'till near midnight in eating & drinking & pretend courtship'.[23] From here the whole party decided to accompany the young widow, Hester, to her home in a nearby village, during which journey John became very excited about carrying the three women across a stream. They spent the rest of the night in Hester's house, continuing their 'pretend courtship' until first light.

What is remarkable about this scene is the total lack of adult oversight. There was not a married person in sight, and the widow seems to have been seen much more as a possible sexual temptress than a restraining influence. Indeed, Cannon's assessment of the evening was that if he and his two male companions had 'been as forward as our females seemed to be we might have had our will and pleasure'. And while this smacks of the kind of self-serving reminiscences of lost sexual opportunities people in later life tend to indulge in, Cannon very quickly expressed alarm when the widow Hester became more serious. When Cannon subsequently visited Hester on his own, he was made aware that any more serious sexual activity would lead to marriage. Hester solicited Cannon 'to be in earnest' and to seriously consider marriage; and 'by her motions she would yield to anything', which 'forwardness in her caused me to break off'. In other words, the minute penetrative sex seemed to be possible Cannon ran a mile, certain that anything likely to lead to pregnancy would similarly lead to marriage. At this stage in his life it is obvious that Cannon was playing at courtship rather than courting, and that he had seriously miscalculated the intentions of his female companions who were more intent on the real thing. Indeed, Mary Withers, the host for the evening, very soon after became pregnant. The father refused to marry her ('notwithstanding vows & promises'), and she was then married to another, although she was at the same time sleeping with a third. Cannon also reports that she and her husband went on to have 'many Children' and that they were living happily 'at Castle Cary in 1740 . . .'.[24]

As a record of adolescent female sexuality the memoirs of an elderly man can seldom be relied upon, but Cannon's account is indicative of

the degree of freedom allowed eighteenth-century women and girls, and
makes it very clear that penetrative sex and pregnancy existed in the
minds of both men and women as a facet of courtship and a step
towards marriage. The fact that Cannon refused to pursue the widow
Hester into bed, and that Mary Withers did agree to sleep with at least
two of the men courting her, reflects attitudes towards sex which
allowed men to be largely passive and women to use the offer and
reality of sex as an integral part of their behaviour towards men.

These same facets of male and female behaviour are evident on
several occasions during the course of Cannon's other courtships, and
indeed resulted in his refusal to sleep with anyone he seriously considered marrying, although at least one of his amours expressed a
willingness to do so.

Until his early twenties Cannon's courting was essentially frivolous. It
was done entirely within the purview of his peers, tended to be
conducted at fairs, and was described by himself as consisting of nothing
more than 'cupboard love'.[25] In other words, Cannon was partaking of
the essentially playful sexual activity that was a part of the lives of most
people of the poorer and middling sort during the period of demographic stagnation between 1650 and 1750. His experience suggests
that while both men and women certainly did put off marriage until
their mid to late twenties, their late teens and early twenties were likely
to be filled with highly sexualised encounters. The nature of this culture
of non-penetrative sexual activity was largely controlled by the peer
group and was most likely to take place within the direct oversight of
other young people. As John Gillis has amply demonstrated, this culture
certainly contained a large degree of regional and class variation, but
the essential elements of sexual play and deferral of marriage were
common throughout England.

The nature of this culture of adolescent experiment changed significantly when the individuals involved became more serious. For John
Cannon his entry into more directed courting occurred in 1704, when 'by
the directions of my friends [i.e. relatives]', Cannon 'made addresses to
Mary only daughter of Widow Brown'. It did not come to anything
because Cannon quickly discovered that his prospective bride was possessed of 'a peevish temper' and was 'naturally covetous'. But these events
marked the start of a new phase in John Cannon's courting career, and
provide evidence for the existence of a tension between peer and family
control of courting. In Cannon's case, independent action and peer
opinion remained most important, but his parents and relatives obviously felt they should have a say, and in particular felt they should have

some oversight of any courting activity that was likely to lead to marriage. The cupboard love of Cannon's adolescence gave way to the courting activities of a young adult when his parents indicated that it would be appropriate for him to consider marriage.

Cannon did not follow his parents' advice, but from 1704 he began a process of much more directed courtships, any one of which might well have led to marriage. In the same year that he turned down his parents' choice, Cannon fell in love with a servant named Mary Rose – who was largely unsuitable, and from whom his parents did much to separate him. The courtship continued for almost ten years, and was only really broken off when Cannon married another woman. But in the process of courting Mary, Cannon considered himself to have gone at least part of the way towards an irrevocable commitment. The whole process started with 'amorous talks & quaint glances, kissing & toying when together in private'. Very quickly John and Mary progressed to mutual caressing, and 'by degrees a more close familiarity even to a plane discovery of such matters & concerns wch modesty teaches me to omit'.[26] Considering his lack of 'modesty' in relation to other aspects of his sexual behaviour, one can only assume that these comments refer to mutual masturbation (other possibilities such as oral sex seem notably absent from most accounts of eighteenth-century sexual behaviour).[27]

The opportunities for Mary and John to meet seem to have been relatively frequent and their activities quite widely known.

> Seldom a night passed but she passing through my bedchamber to her own came to my bedside & after some amorous whisperings we bid each other good night by tender and loving kisses. This I confess to be odd doings & somewhat difficult to be kept long a secret by reason of the boy my bedfellow, although we never acted any other than above mentioned wch might bring us disgrace.[28]

As might be expected, this inappropriate affair did not go unnoticed by Cannon's uncle and Mary's master, and resulted in Cannon's eventual removal from his uncle's household and his loss of a possible inheritance. Less care was taken about Mary, who remained employed in the house for the next ten years and eventually married a fellow servant.

The conflict created by John and Mary's behaviour was profound. John and his uncle actually came to blows, and his cousin Rebecca, who lived in the same house, actively plotted to break up the relationship. And it is relatively easy to see why. On the one hand, by conducting this courtship within the household Cannon removed the element of peer oversight. On the other, he refused the advice of his relations. In contracting to Mary he failed to follow either of the <u>two possible courses of legitimate courting.</u>

This profound disapproval did not lessen John and Mary's zeal, and perhaps led the couple to make the solemn commitment to each other which was to cause John a great deal of remorse and self-condemnation. They agreed to meet late one evening on the common in 1706, where they found a private place under a hedgerow:

> ... having sat here sometimes caressing each other I drew out of my pocket two papers ... wherein was contain'd strong resolutions severe & binding promises & a compact part & counter part to be constant to each other in life & death as it were binding in the presence of the all seeing God & who only we made our witness neither to transgress or forsake each other till death & further promising matrimony as soon as god would please to vouchsafe a favourable opportunity & for confirmation thereof we bow'd & broke in pieces an English shilling & I kept one part & Mary the other & she made two bags & shove'd this contract & piece of silver in one for herself & the other for me never to be opened till we had consummated matrimony. This action at first was shocking to us both but our ardent love dissipated the dreads on our spirits ...[29]

To break or bend a shilling as a signifier of marriage was a common popular practice throughout the early-modern period, and while the future tense in the promise to marry ensured that Cannon's undertaking would not be legally binding at common law, both he and Mary were 'man & wife, wanting the ceremony of marriage' in the eyes of the local community.[30] Perhaps more telling than the actual ritual is John Cannon's retrospective attitude towards it. He spent several pages justifying his behaviour, assuring the reader that he and Mary never had penetrative sex, and claiming that Mary in effect broke off the engagement by courting a fellow servant at a later date. This reflects the extent to which the couple's behaviour did, in the eyes of both the participants and the community, constitute a partially binding contract of marriage. Popular marriage ritual makes it clear that, far from being a single act or ceremony, eighteenth-century marriage was a process which lasted from courting, to betrothal, to the public declaration (either with banns or the more private licence), through the church service and penetrative consummation, culminating in the birth of the first child. These elements did not have a precise order, but each needed to be in place to secure a marriage. While it seems reasonable to assume that betrothal generally preceded consummation, it is likewise clear that the birth of the first child frequently came before the church service. What John and Mary had done was courted and betrothed themselves to each other – both actions as important in their eyes as the formal ceremony in church.

The relationship with Mary began to break up when John received a commission as an excise officer in 1707 and was forced to move to Berkshire, but the seriousness with which both he and Mary took their vows ensured that they continued to correspond until John's marriage in 1714.

As an example of normal, rural courtship among plebeian and middling-sort people, John and Mary's behaviour, while not entirely typical, highlights a number of significant factors. The seriousness with which they took apparently informal vows, the highly physical but non-penetrative sex, and the roles of both peer group and relations all seem to create a range of behavioural checks which would allow the extreme deferral of marriage which we have seen is characteristic of English society in the early eighteenth century. The demographic evidence suggesting that early-eighteenth-century England was a society in which penetrative sex, and hence pregnancy, was under strict control is amply supported by Cannon's experience. But more than this, what his memoirs suggest is that this control was in part a result of ready access to non-penetrative sexual activity, which was itself possible as a result of the internalised check created in both men and women by the role of penetration in making a marriage. Finally the memoirs reflect the power and desire of both peer group and relations to oversee courtship.

If this was a common rural pattern of courtship, it was also only one of several patterns available to Cannon.[31] His later courtship activities brought him into contact with a variety of less restricted styles of gender relations in which penetrative sex was more common, and which were to become more popular in the latter half of the century.

By becoming an excise officer and moving first to Reading and then Watlington in Oxfordshire, Cannon's sexual activities took on a new form. He was increasingly thrown in with other young men in a homosocial community with few of the structures of family and household with which Cannon was familiar. He also found himself with a fair amount of money, and forced to live in inns and lodgings which brought him into contact with a wide range of people.

From 1707 most of John's courting was a result of drink, and was described by himself as 'folly'. In the following seven years he became involved with three different women, lost his virginity and finally married. In 1709, 'somewhat intoxicated in liquor', Cannon made an attempt on a young student he was tutoring. He succeeded in putting his hand up her dress to her knees, at which point she began to resist his advances. What happened next is indicative of a very different attitude towards penetrative sex on the part of Joanna, John's new amour, than that held by Mary. Joanna, an eighteen-year-old virgin by John's account, turned to him and said 'Sir, if you will be constant to me above all others & in due time make me your lawful wife you shall have absolute command over me.' While this seems a surprising statement on the part of an eighteen-year-old girl, John's reaction is perhaps more surprising. First, he engaged to marry her, 'And then I used my lustfull freedom as I did frequently afterwards, but no otherwise [than] by handling for the thoughts of our vows & the hopes she had of being my wife kept us from any attempt at carnality.'[32] The very connection of sex with marriage seemingly ensured that John would studiously avoid any form of sexual activity that could be construed as reinforcing his commitment.

Given appropriate assurances, Mary obviously had a rather more positive view of sex leading to pregnancy and marriage. Indeed, later, when she discovered that John had been accused of fathering a bastard child, she 'urged me to fix a time to end our matter lawfully, wishing again that it had been her fortune [to become pregnant] ... for then she was sure I should not deny her ....'.[33]

That John's apparent refusal to penetrate anyone was associated specifically with marriage is further reinforced by his one premarital relationship in which penetrative sex actually occurred. While at Watlington, and while still engaged to both Mary and Joanna, Cannon also became involved with a servant named Anne Heister.[34] In this instance he makes no promise of marriage, and yet she is the one woman he is willing to sleep with. At the same time he expresses deep contempt for her, almost never referring to her by her proper name but calling her 'Lais' – a barbed Latin reference, implying she was a whore or prostitute.

After returning late one night he found Anne sitting up by the fire. And although there was no previous relationship between them, he 'slipt [his] ... hand under her coats to her knee wch she not resisted, ... boldly ventured higher, she suffring it patiently, laying aside modesty & shame, consented to whatsoever I did ...'. Cannon was obviously shocked by his apparent sexual power, and did no more on this occasion than the usual 'handling'. But on the following Sunday he and Anne had sex on his bed while the rest of the family was out. On this occasion John claims they were disturbed part of the way through, and that this resulted in Anne's complaint that 'she had not her full desire'.[35]

Cannon is remorseful about this and subsequent sexual encounters, but in this instance he did not see sexual penetration as an element of marriage – his moral sense had been anaesthetised by the lack of a promise. This distinction was lost on Anne Heister, however, as when she later became pregnant she unsuccessfully demanded that Cannon marry her.

The period during which Cannon was actively courting corresponds very well with the demographic transition in which a much higher proportion of people begin to marry, and in which premarital sexual activity becomes more common. While John Cannon's experiences with Mary, Joanna and Anne cannot be seen as part of a chronologically precise historical process, they do seem to represent the varying ways of wooing available to early-eighteenth-century men and women. Each is similar in terms of the double standard contained within them, but each is likewise distinct in terms of the roles for sex and sexual play they encompass. The most sexually controlled was certainly the model ascribed to by Mary and John, in which marriage is expected to follow betrothal without the surety of penetrative sex and subsequent pregnancy. The least controlled was that partaken of by Anne, who seems to have believed that sex was essentially separate from marriage, except when linked by pregnancy. And finally, a middle ground was represented by Joanna's belief that sex and pregnancy were a normal part of courting, and an insurance against male inconstancy.

Cannon's account of his sexual experiences was made long after the events described, and inevitably reflects the biases and self-delusions of an elderly man remembering the joys of his youth, but there can be little doubt as to the outline of the experiences of the principals involved in this story. And what is overwhelmingly apparent about the behaviour of these four is that sexual activity short of penetration was commonplace and accepted by young men and women. In a society where sexual reputation was fundamental to the lives of women in particular, the willingness of Cannon's partners to participate in long drawn out sexual play suggests that sex was not a problem, but that penetration was.[36] When discussing a pre-birth-control society this is perhaps a commonsensical conclusion. But the nature of the sexual culture of the early eighteenth century is not necessarily what one would expect. There seems to have been a level of active experimentation based on trust between men and women which is at the least surprising, and which seems very much at odds with the common historical view that sex in some way became 'better' (and presumably more likely to involve penetration) in the latter part of the century, and that the experiences of plebeian and middling-sort people prior to the late eighteenth century were either non-existent or fumbling.[37]

John Cannon's memoirs provide substantial evidence for one further element of plebeian and middling-sort sexual relations – the role of the marriage ceremony itself. While Cannon was still juggling with the affections of Anne, Joanna and Mary, he became involved with a fourth person, Susannah Deane, whom he finally married in 1714. The relationship with Susannah seems much less sexual than those with Cannon's other partners. And while John and Susannah certainly partook of the kind of sexual play in which long hours were spent in mutual caressing and kissing, Cannon is less than entirely forthcoming in his descriptions of these encounters and, instead, spends much time discussing Susannah's virginal chastity. This is certainly a result of the fact that John and Susannah were still married when the memoirs were written and is less likely to reflect reality than his other descriptions, but it is nevertheless relatively certain that John and Susannah had yet to have penetrative sex when they married.

John Gillis has described a fundamental transition in the nature of English marriage in the late seventeenth and early eighteenth centuries. While highly conscious of regional variation and exceptions, Gillis has argued that the early eighteenth century witnessed a move away from the 'great wedding', in which the whole community participated, to small and at times clandestine, though still public, weddings in which only the principals and witnesses were involved, and in which secrecy seems to have been an important element. Cannon's memoirs describe two weddings, each of which is of this latter type. The first was explicitly clandestine, and reflects some of the reasons why a marriage might be kept secret.

The marriage was between a rich widow and a younger, poorer man, and was deliberately held while a play was being performed on the far side of town. All the principals took different routes to the church, and the ceremony took place by candlelight at 11.00 at night. The couple then managed to keep the marriage hidden for over a month. While this may not have been an entirely suitable match in the eyes of community, and while the widow's 'children & grandchildren . . . was much displeased wth their mother's marriage', the element which seems odd to modern perceptions is the couple's desire to keep it a secret long after the ceremony. As with Cannon's attitudes towards penetrative sex, this reflects the extent to which marriage was a process rather than a ritual. After a month of marriage there could be little doubt of consummation, and it would be entirely possible that a pregnancy would already be established (although in this case it is unclear whether the widow was past childbearing). And as a result the ability of the relatives to challenge the marriage would be vastly circumscribed.[38]

Almost equally clandestine, although not technically so, was Cannon's own marriage. It took place by licence in the City of London, where Susannah was staying with relatives, and is minutely described. The ceremony itself is of only marginal interest. More striking are the attitudes which surround it. Although they had been courting for over a year the events leading up to the marriage seem extraordinarily abrupt. Having written to inform Susannah of the marriage, Cannon rode to London, arriving late one night, asked the approval of Susannah's relatives, procured a licence the following morning and married Susannah at St Katherine Coleman's in the afternoon. From here they went home, ate and were put to bed. The next day, 20 September 1714, George I triumphantly entered London, and the whole party toured the town and helped celebrate, admiring various aspects of the procession. The couple spent one more night together and then John Cannon left for his excise round and did not see Susannah again for several months.[39]

The reason for the secrecy in this case was the fact that at least three people had possible prior claims on Cannon. In order to prevent Mary Rose disrupting the ceremony, Cannon did not even inform his parents of his decision, in whose house Mary was still a servant, and likewise made every effort to ensure that no news reached Wycombe, where he was then based, until well after the ceremony.

* * *

The whole of John Cannon's sex life is important. Each element casts a strong light on the nature of sexual activity among plebeians and the middling sort, and what they emphasise is the diversity of practice which was commonplace during this period. There is, even for John Cannon, no single way of wooing, and while it is obvious that non-penetrative sex and mutual masturbation were the norm, it is likewise certain that a proportion of the members of this society were willing to step beyond this to the much more dangerous activity of vaginal sex. Cannon's experience also reinforces John Gillis' conclusions on marriage. They remind us that any undue emphasis on the historical development of marriage law and the ceremony itself is likely to draw our attention away from the all-important role of courtship and sex in the process of family formation.

In relation to the demographic transition which characterised the eighteenth century this evidence suggests two things. First, there was a significant change in the balance of sexual activity, and penetrative sex must have become relatively more common later in the century; but what it replaced was highly rewarding non-penetrative sex. And second, we are unlikely to find a simple, economic transition to explain changing patterns of courtship and hence fertility. If a single individual like Cannon is involved in a variety of courting practices, it is doubtful that we will be able to link economic divisions such as pastoral vs. arable, or even rural vs. urban, to specific courting behaviours.

By looking at slightly later evidence for the nature of sexual behaviour within courtship, changing patterns of wooing become apparent, as does the extent to which Cannon was active during a period of transition in courting practice.

Adrian Wilson has recently analysed the records of the Foundling Hospital in London, established in 1743. By looking at the age distribution of infants, the seasonality of demand, and the relationship between prices and the abandonment of infants, he has concluded that: first, the infants involved were bastards; second, London produced a remarkably high number of bastard children; and third, this was a result of a courting practice in which penetrative sex was a frequent part of premarital London life.[40] Combining these findings with E.A. Wrigley's evidence for rural changes in illegitimacy rates,[41] Wilson has suggested that a London pattern of courting in which penetrative sex came before betrothal was gradually spreading to the rest of the country during the middle of the eighteenth century.

In some ways this idea of a metropolitan fashion for penetrative sex fits rather well with the evidence of diaries and autobiography. Certainly, Francis Place was adamant in his condemnation of the lax attitude towards premarital penetrative sex that he ascribes to the London poor of the late eighteenth century. And James Boswell, while a poor witness for the sexual behaviour of non-elite English people, certainly appears to have believed that penetration was synonymous with sex.[42] Even Thérèse Le Vasseur, Rousseau's mistress, and a woman of many talents and polite opinions, was frustrated in her attempt to instruct him in the joys of sexual activity more complex than simply putting his penis in her vagina.[43]

The idea of a London fashion in courtship also has the advantage of suggesting some mechanisms for the transmission of these ideas. Besides being the focus for migration for a large percentage of the population, and the testing ground for much of eighteenth-century social policy, both factors in the spread of fashions and ideas, London's role as publishing capital of England and the broader English-speaking world is well established. Indeed, it has been argued that the very creation of the idea of fashion, and the invention of the whole gamut of techniques for its purveyance, are the product of eighteenth-century London entrepreneurs.[44] If we look at the material being produced by these same publishers relating to sex, their ability to popularize a range of attitudes which could impinge on courting practices is apparent. Roy Porter, for example, has recently analysed the content of *Aristotle's Master-piece*, demonstrating, first, that it was one of the most easily available and widely distributed pieces of literature in the eighteenth century and, second, that it was a guide to *penetrative* sex leading to procreation. In other words, young people reading *Aristotle's Master-piece* and other, similar works, in order to discover the secrets of sexual propriety would be strongly directed towards penetration at the expense of other forms of sexual behaviour.[45]

One can make the same point about the pornography, which, while derived from and directed at a narrow libertine audience, must have gained some readership beyond its bounds. Lawrence Stone, for instance, has recently analysed a court case in Norwich which includes detailed accounts of the activities of a group of apparent libertines. What he concludes is that these provincial, lower-middling-sort men and women were acting out the scenes and conventions common to contemporary pornography. To the extent that eighteenth-century pornography emphasised vaginal sex and flagellation, its readers and imitators naturally favoured penetration over manipulation.[46]

Of course these types of evidence are problematic. It is impossible to know how people actually read these kinds of works, or how they acted on them once read. Indeed, our ability to understand the assumptions behind and influences upon the actions of eighteenth-century middling-sort and plebeian peoples in general is remarkably limited – all the more so when looking at the very private world of sexuality. But, to the extent that the demography of the period demonstrates a change in behaviour in favour of penetrative sex during and before courtship resulting in a rising population, and the qualitative material supports this conclusion, we can confidently conclude that there was indeed a 'sexual revolution' in the eighteenth century. As with more recent sexual revolutions, however, the results of this one were not uniformly positive. In as much as the overall amount of sexual activity is unlikely to have changed, it is difficult to see how the eighteenth-century 'revolution' made for a more enjoyable sex life for those involved, while

at the same time it certainly did contribute to the denigration of the
economic position of women. By equating sex more firmly with activities that could lead to pregnancy, a larger proportion of women found
themselves responsible for bastard children without even the meagre
supports offered by the nuclear family.

4   The Body, Medicine and Sexual Difference

In 1677 a young apprentice iron-smith from Staffordshire found that gangrene had attacked his extremities. His arms, legs and penis began to rot away, and to be eaten slowly by maggots. The author of the published account of these events saw the young man's fate as a result of a rash curse he had made some time earlier. After having stolen a Bible, the apprentice swore his innocence, praying that his arms and legs should fall off if he was lying. But many of his fellow villagers saw his case in a rather different light. They believed that the young man's fate was the result of his past sexual behaviour. Whoring, buggery and bestiality were all adduced as possible causes for his condition.[1] In either case, an ill-considered word or action resulted in a horrific change in his body, a change which physically and naturally punished his sin in *this* world.

This chapter will look first at the assumptions about biology, reproduction and sex which underlay the explanations for this young man's gruesome death. It will then go on to examine how these understandings, as expressed in both elite medical texts and popular beliefs, changed over the course of the eighteenth century, and how they in turn reflected and created different attitudes towards sex and reproduction.

Eighteenth-century people did not see their bodies in the same way as we do. There existed a fundamentally different understanding of how one's body worked and what was important in regulating that working. While medical knowledge was far from uncontested, most people, both elite and plebeian, believed in a fundamentally humoral or Galenic model of the body in which the various humours controlled both health and development. That is, they followed the teachings of Galen of Pergamum (c.130–200 AD), who argued that the humours – blood, phlegm, yellow bile and black bile – created a balance in the individual between hot, dry, wet and cold characteristics. People conceptualised their own bodies as a balanced system in which the flow of these fluids, and their transition through various forms of heating or cooling, regulated both health and outward appearance.[2] The emphasis was much less on structures and organs than it would be a hundred years later and much more on fluids and processes. Indeed, the whole course of sex and generation was conceptualised as a problem of fluid dynamics in which the mixture and creation of specific fluids, in combination with the nature of the environment in which those fluids were located, determined the course of conception and the development of the foetus.

The significance of these views for both gender and sexuality are quite profound. Within this context women were deemed to be characterised by cold and wet humours, while men were dominated by hot and dry humours, and the process which differentiated them was seen as developmental. All people were believed to be on a gradient from male to female characteristics, depending on the quantity and quality of humoral life essence possessed by each individual. There were, of course, strong value judgements placed on the various poles of these gradients. Men were perceived to be naturally more rational, strong and intellectual than women, who were frequently thought to be lacking in the qualities endowed upon the individual by possession of a strong humoral essence. Women were hence likely to be irrational, physically weak and shorter lived. At the same time, however, women were revered for their greater spirituality, and men denigrated for their lack of this all-important characteristic.[3]

The process that created the individual as either male or female illustrates the basic biological assumptions underlying gender difference and begins to illustrate the importance of these views for sexuality itself.

Men's and women's genitals were seen as being essentially the same. Both were possessed of testes and a penis, and both 'concocted' or purified blood in order to create the semen which would go to make a child. The main difference, in anatomical terms, was that men's sexual organs were outside the body, or distended, and women's were inside. The vagina and possibly the uterus and womb were thought to be an inverted penis and scrotum (although some associated the clitoris with the penis), while the ovaries were thought to be female testes.[4] It was only the greater heat of the male body which drove these internal organs outwards to form the penis, scrotum and testicles.

During sex both the man and the woman ejaculated at orgasm, producing the humoral essence which then found a seat in the womb. Both men and women contributed to this process, but it was thought that the greater volume, heat and purity of male semen was a determining factor in the eventual qualities of the child. Once implanted in the womb, the site on which the foetus developed and the imagination and humoral balance of the mother were important in determining the nature of the child produced. While there were a number of different anatomical models of the structure and precise workings of the womb, the position of the foetus – whether on the right hand (male) or the left hand (female) side – was all-important in determining its sex.[5]

No unique material was deposited in order to make the foetus. Instead, its characteristics were determined by a combination of the qualities, or mix, of the man's semen, the nature of the woman's ejaculate, and the qualities of the womb in which it matured. What the mother ate, thought and did could all affect the course of the pregnancy. So, if she had the misfortune to imagine a particular scene or animal, it could easily be imprinted on the child within. This is what was supposed to have happened to Sarah Haynes of Chelsea in 1746, when she went to see the lions at the Tower of London only to find that she later gave birth to a dead foetus with 'the nose and eyes like a lion, no palate to the mouth, hair on the shoulders, claws like a lion instead of fingers . . .'.[6] The influence of the mother's imagination was also evinced to help explain the monster births of Mary Toft, popularly known as the Rabbit Woman of Godalming, who pretended to give birth to a series of rabbits in 1726.[7] Likewise, more strictly physical factors could also affect the child. Being conceived during a woman's menses would result in a child having either a birth mark or, at the least, red hair.[8]

Whether the foetus was high or low in the womb reflected its sex, but the process of its growth was far from straightforward. A child born in the eighth month of a pregnancy was thought less likely to survive than one born in the seventh, and the all-important ensoulment of the foetus, which in a very real way marked it out as actually becoming a human being, occurred at forty-three days, while the 'quickening' could be expected at ninety days.[9] In order for a pregnancy to result, both the man and the woman had to reach orgasm, preferably at the same time. It was believed that prostitutes were infertile, and that women in general were possessed of an aggressive sexuality, which in physical terms reflected the desire of the colder, wetter female body for the dry heat of male semen.[10]

Sex was seen as largely debilitating for men and positive for women. Whereas excessive sex for men would result in the loss of their heat, and hence such conditions as curvature of the spine, a sallow complexion and general poor health, for women the main difficulties arose from not enough sex. The green sickness, hysteria and a range of debilitating conditions could be cured by heterosexual sex or in some cases masturbation.

Overall, at the beginning of the century, most people believed that a moderate sex life in marriage was important to good health, and that any deviation from this was likely to result in both ill-health and physical changes. The cessation of sexual activity associated with widowhood was thought to put young widows in a particularly difficult position – making them much more likely to seek out sexual activity outside legitimate marriage. Likewise, women who masturbated excessively, or who were particularly libertine, were thought likely to grow a small penis. Their clitoris was thought to grow to the point where it could be used for penetrative sex. This belief was used to explain various cases of lesbianism.[11]

* * *

All of these beliefs and processes were, to begin with, part of a broadly shared culture. While the nuance and detail of the model varied depending on class, region and education, the fundamentals remained largely the same. But over the course of the eighteenth century, elite understandings of reproductive biology began to change. This process of intellectual transformation has been most fully charted by Thomas Laqueur. He has argued that the early Galenic understanding amounts to a 'one body' model of sexual difference, pointing out that in this schema biological sex was a matter of degree, rather than of type, and that the major transitions to which the body was subject were matters of experience and process rather than biological givens. He then suggests that between 1780 and 1820 elite and professional understandings created a 'two body' model of sexual differentiation. Laqueur's work, particularly his *Making Sex: Body and Gender from the Greeks to Freud*, has formed the intellectual basis for a series of debates around both the meaning for gender and sexuality of the existence of a Galenic understanding of the body, and how this understanding evolved during the course of the eighteenth century.[12]

Laqueur suggests that this transition from a 'one body' to a 'two body' model at the end of the eighteenth century resulted, not from greater observational accuracy or the discovery of anatomical fact, but from a broad social need to redefine women as fundamentally different from men. The increasing significance of the vagina, the association of different skeletal formations with men and women, the growing belief that women could become pregnant without an orgasm, and new forms of medical understanding of the roles of egg and sperm all contributed to this change.[13] Laqueur's argument is that this amounted to the creation of the two sexes as essentially different, rather than as slightly different versions of the same model, and that this new formulation was not necessary in order to explain new discoveries about the biology of reproduction. This is a powerful and illuminating suggestion which has received a great deal of, if not universal, support from a variety of early-modern historians. And while some writers reject Laqueur's whole approach, what is gradually emerging from the growing literature is a rather more nuanced version of this transition, which sites the overall process in the full century and a half between the 1670s and 1820s.[14]

Perhaps the most coherent critic of Laqueur's views is Lyndal Roper, who argues that he ignores the experienced nature of sexual difference, and who further suggests that while culture is immensely significant in how we think about our bodies, those bodies are not entirely plastic. Instead, the construction of gender, in Roper's estimation, must be based on the individual's experience of a biologically sexed body – the universality of a mother's experience of pregnancy and giving birth, for instance, must be seen as a biological constant which culture cannot entirely change. Roper continually comes back to the corporeality of existence, and forms a useful counterweight to Laqueur's argument, which if taken to the extreme might suggest that no thing or relationship can exist outside the languages used to describe them.[15]

Other historians have attempted to modify rather than refute Laqueur's views. Robert Martensen, for instance, has suggested that the rise in emphasis within the medical profession on the nervous system, and in particular the work of Robert Willis in the late seventeenth century, resulted in a new understanding of gender difference which at the least prefigures Laqueur's late eighteenth-century transition.[16] Likewise, the work of Mary Fissell has suggested a shift in the emphasis midwives and anatomists put on the vagina in the 1670s and 1680s. She believes that the vagina became an organ in its own right at about this time, and that this reflects a longer-term process of sexual differentiation than Laqueur allows.[17]

In sum, Laqueur has provided the framework for the debate, and perhaps more than any other historian, with the possible exception of Michel Foucault, has created a history of the body. But his precise chronology is open to revision, and both his starting point, the 'one body' model, and his mechanism for change are being slowly modified.

What has gradually emerged is a model of historical change which, in the first instance, suggests that the meaning, or indeed the acceptance, of a Galenic or 'one body' model was not as straightforward as has sometimes been argued. In his *Renaissance Notion of Woman*, Ian Maclean suggested over fifteen years ago that Aristotelian thought, with its highly misogynistic elements and denial of the significance of the female orgasm, had a greater purchase than is sometimes allowed. He likewise charts the existence throughout the seventeenth century of bodies of thought which conceived of women as 'perfect in themselves' and hence not as under-heated men, as a strict Galenic model might suggest.[18] So while all historians of the period agree that Galenic understandings of sexual difference were the dominant ones at the end of the seventeenth century, they were never universal.

From this starting point, a chronology has developed which gives greater significance to the late seventeenth century, suggesting that both the new emphasis on the nervous system and the redefinition of women's genitalia (stressing the clitoris and vagina over the uterus and womb) marked the beginnings of a gradual process of change.

The anatomical evidence which Laqueur adduces for the last two decades of the eighteenth century and the first two of the nineteenth then becomes the result of the working out of a process of change sited within both the elite medical discourse and society at large, which began much earlier. So, while, as Londa Shiebinger has demonstrated, it was only at the end of the eighteenth century that a differentiation between male and female skeletons was made, the discovery by Leeuwenhoek in 1677 of sperm in men's semen, and William Harvey's less certain proposal of 1653 that women's ovaries contained eggs, contributed to a reformulation of sexual difference.[19]

In the broadest terms this 150-year shift can be seen as part of the re-creation of medical understandings in general. Professionalisation, the rise of anatomy, the denigration of the female midwife and the rise of the man-midwife, as well as the development of surgery and a more structured form of chemical medicine, all contributed to the creation of an understanding of the body which was increasingly distant from the experience of most people. By the end of the eighteenth century a tradition of personal control by the patient over the course of an illness and its treatment was being substantially replaced by a system in which the professional, and now male, doctor was in control. In part, this was a result of the increasing distance between popular and elite culture. Gradually and over a longer period than is covered by this book, and at different times for different classes within society, it began to seem that the patient's understanding was grounded in popular culture and the doctor's in the elite variety. But this shift can also be seen as a subtler transition in the relationship between doctor and patient, in which the patient's body becomes an observed mechanism, whose illness is inscribed in an increasingly arcane language on that body's surface. The internal and conscious experience of the patient is denigrated, in favour of an external understanding. And hence, many of the opportunities for patients to participate in and retain control of his or her own treatment at the hands of doctors are limited.[20]

In terms of gender and sexuality, the new medical understanding of biology and reproduction substantially shifts definitions and descriptions of the female role into the hands of male doctors. At the beginning of the century, both through the existence of respected female midwives such as Jane Sharp, and through the greater power possessed by the patient, women had more opportunities to express their own experience of their bodies.[21] By its end, as a result of both the rise of the man-midwife to a position of leadership within the profession and the increasingly distant professional doctor, women were largely excluded.[22] In the process their bodies were quite dramatically redefined. They no longer needed to have an orgasm in order to conceive. Women became inherently and 'naturally' the weaker sex – even their skeletons conspiring to ensure they took a less assertive role. From being sexually aggressive, women were increasingly seen as sexually passive. What had been a set of (frequently misogynistic) definitions, which were open to the possibility of the existence of strong and assertive women, gradually became an understanding in which inequality and 'separate spheres' were writ in an inescapable biology. And while the model of causality which resulted in this transformation and its effects on individual lives is subject to fierce debate, the shape and direction of these changes is now beyond doubt.[23]

Of course, just as women's bodies were redefined, so were men's. Much less work has been done on transitions in male anatomy, and as a result men's bodies have tended to be seen as the norm against which women's bodies might be measured. But, just as the female orgasm was seen as less necessary, so the male orgasm became more important. The existence, quality and role of male sperm and semen were increasingly significant. And while women were redefined as sexually passive, men were likewise redefined as 'naturally' sexually aggressive. In a previous chapter we saw the ambiguity towards sex felt by a man like John Cannon. He was, in a very real sense, both in control of his own sexual behaviour and intimidated by women's powerful sexuality. By the end of the eighteenth century, this ambiguity was much less apparent. Men were increasingly defined by their sexual role. They were expected to

find women attractive and to define their masculinity through their
roles as sexual partner and biological father.[24]

These aspects of the story of gender redefinition may be seen clearly
reflected in economic and social history, and have been immensely
significant to feminist and women's historians. The story of the maternalisation of women's bodies, with its new emphasis on the role of
'mother', as well as the rise of a 'separate spheres' ideology at the end
of the eighteenth century, which increasingly restricted women to the
private sphere of the household, both strongly reinforce the impression
of an intimate relationship between the history of medicine and the
broad course of social change. They likewise reinforce the chronological
parameters outlined above.[25] But it is important to remember that the
changes described above were largely articulated within a narrow and
elite medical discourse. It is unclear, for instance, how much significance we can ascribe to changes in the ways of thinking characteristic of
a few highly specialised, university-trained doctors. It is certain that few
people read the works used as evidence for much of Thomas Laqueur's
analysis. And it is likewise clear that very few people, besides the very
rich and professional doctors, were able to examine the new depictions
of male and female anatomy created at the end of the century. So, while
this transition in medical understanding was of immense importance,
and forms a central element of our knowledge of eighteenth-century
gender and sexuality, it should not be taken as a direct reflection of
popular beliefs about sex and reproduction.

* * *

There are, however, other bodies of literature through which we can
approach the concerns and beliefs of non-elite people. In particular,
historians have made great use of the popular sex manuals which were
a characteristic production of the eighteenth-century press. By looking
at these and associated publications, a slightly different and more
balanced and representative view of popular beliefs about the body
begins to emerge.

The most common sex manual of the eighteenth century was *Aristotle's
Master-piece: or, the Secrets of Generation Displayed in all the Parts Thereof.* First
published in 1684, the anonymous *Master-piece*[26] went through at least
forty-three editions by 1800, and became, if anything, more popular
during the nineteenth century.[27] Its popularity was only rivalled by Dr
Nicholas Venette's *Tableau de l'amour conjugal* (1696), which was first
published in an English translation as the *Mysteries of Conjugal Love
Revealed* in 1703. It too went through numerous editions, and was still

in print in the 1950s.[28] James Graham's *Lecture on Generation* (1783) also formed a possible source of popular medical knowledge about sex,[29] while the numerous works by medical popularisers, most notably William Buchan, provided yet another source of insight. One should also note that generic boundaries were not always clear and that popular guides to midwifery, such as those by Culpeper and Jane Sharp, were also available to a wider audience than the midwives they purported to address.[30]

We know, therefore, that information on sex and sexuality directed at a popular audience was widely published in the eighteenth century. What is much less clear is whether anyone took this information seriously or, indeed, bothered to read it. Certainly, John Cannon used his copy of the Culpeper's *Midwifery* as a masturbatory aid (see Chapter 3) and Francis Place read *Aristotle's Master-piece* while still at school.[31] The most popular novel of the eighteenth century, Lawrence Sterne's *Tristram Shandy*, draws on the *Master-piece* extensively.[32] But whether it and the other contributions to popular sexual knowledge were the detailed stuff of popular belief is much less clear, as is the overall shape of the body of knowledge contained within these works.

Indeed, the content of several of these manuals changed from edition to edition, apparently depending on the energy, or lack of it, of the particular compiler or publisher. They mix, in what at first sight seems almost a random order, magical and Galenic understandings of sexual processes, juxtaposing apparently commonsensical advice with detailed directions on appropriate sexual positions and the course of foetal development. Roy Porter has described the content of the *Master-piece* as a 'codification of sexual folklore' directed at the readers of ballads and almanacs.[33] But, more significantly, what the analysis of these works has pointed out is their pro-natalist content.

Roy Porter, in a series of articles and books, has argued that these works were guides to having babies, rather than to having good sex. He argues that they were predicated on the assumption that having babies was a good thing and that the boundaries around sexual behaviour were precisely those between reproductive and sterile forms of sex. Hence, the sexual positions recommended by both the *Master-piece* and Nicholas Venette were those thought to produce conception, with what would later be dubbed the missionary position being the most highly recommended. Variations from this recommendation were only allowed where factors such as obesity made them imperative. Likewise, while female sexual pleasure was strongly emphasised, and the necessity of the female orgasm to conception insisted upon in all these works, emphasis was also placed on the need to lie still after sex in order to encourage conception. The time of the month during which sex was most appropriate, and the diet of both couples seeking to conceive and pregnant women were matters these works felt it reasonable to comment upon, as was the frequency of sexual activity in marriage.[34]

At the same time they were concerned with sexual dysfunction. Diets to encourage greater sexual appetite in men and to discourage the overwhelming appetites of women were included, as were discussions of love sickness and infertility. In *Aristotle's Master-piece* in particular, it was generation rather than sexual technique which formed the fundamental focus of the work. And while Venette and James Graham were perhaps more interested in technique – Graham, for instance, believed boredom might set in if people did not celebrate 'the rites of Venus in a variety of ways' – they too were most concerned to ensure that people had healthy babies.[35]

On the basis of Porter's work in particular, we can reliably conclude that these publications were overwhelmingly concerned with the creation of babies. But both Angus McLaren and latterly Roy Porter have pointed out that the content could be read in a slightly different way. Although the superficial intent was certainly pro-natal, the text could as easily give instructions on how to limit fertility. If one knew that some positions were more likely than others to produce a conception, those positions could as easily be avoided as practised. Similarly, injunctions against movement after sex, and against certain types of food, were grist to the mill of anyone wanting to avoid pregnancy. In McLaren's view, popular eighteenth-century sex manuals are certainly concerned with conception, but not necessarily with its encouragement, and their overwhelming popularity and longevity should perhaps be put down to the very ambiguity which he and Porter identify. These manuals, in a very real sense, empowered the individual couple to take control of their reproductive activity and seem to have been valued as a result.[36]

* * *

What the existence of these sex manuals and the elite medical discourses discussed earlier in this chapter created were two apparently divergent traditions in medical thought. On the one hand we have the popular medical literature specifically directed at sex and sexuality whose effect was to give control over reproduction to the individuals involved, and whose advice was drawn from an eclectic mix of popular culture, magic and Galenic medicine. On the other hand we have seen an increasingly elite and professional body of medical knowledge which changed over the course of the eighteenth century, and which, by the early nineteenth century, had effectively redefined both men and women as fundamentally and 'naturally' different. The apparently contemporaneous existence of these traditions leaves us with at least two questions. First, how much control did people have over their reproductive lives? Second, how significant was the elite medical discourse, and how was that significance translated into individual experience?

A great deal of work has been done on contraception in past societies, most of which asks whether or not people employed any. And in relation to eighteenth-century England and Wales the answer has to be a qualified yes. Angus McLaren has demonstrated that a wide range of techniques for the control of fertility were practised.[37] And although it is impossible to come to a precise conclusion about which were most common, or how effective they were, the list is a relatively comprehensive one, including coitus interruptus, barrier methods and, perhaps most importantly, abortion.

Abortion of one sort or another was certainly the form of birth control spoken of most frequently. Throughout the early-modern period recipes for medicines to 'bring down the flowers', or to regulate menstruation, were a common component of any herbal or recipe book, and could certainly be obtained from the local apothecary. The fact that an early abortion could likewise be induced is seldom mentioned in contemporary literature but was certainly widely known. Sometime around mid-century an advertisement appeared in the *Morning Post* which clearly suggests an awareness of what these medicines were used for:

> To the Ladies.
> The female mixture, which removes all sorts of obstructions or irregularities, in certain cases of ever so old a date, with sore and swell'd legs, shortness of breadth, giddiness, and all the symptoms which attends when change of life, with ease, safety and certainty.
>
> A caution to pregnant women. – As pregnancy is often mistaken for obstructions, whoever has reason to believe herself with child, must not use this powerful mixture, as it will certainly bring on a miscarriage.
>
> It is sold at the . . . Warehouse, in Church-street, St. Anne's Soho, the second house from Greek Street, next door to the Coach and Horses ale house, and no where else; at half a Guinea, and a Guinea a bottle, with proper directions how to use it.[38]

It should be noted that abortion was only made illegal in statute law in 1803. After that time procuring an abortion after the 'quickening' became punishable by death, while an abortion prior to the 'quickening' became a lesser felony.[39] The story of the criminalisation of abortion is intimately tied up with the rise of the man mid-wife, and the state of the then current infanticide laws, which essentially assumed that any woman concealing the birth of a child who then died was responsible for its murder.[40] But the range of eighteenth-century commentary on abortion, the existence of widely known recipes for abortifacients and the new laws at the beginning of the nineteenth century, which essentially assumed the widespread existence of abortion, all suggest the pervasive character of abortion as a solution to the problem of unwanted pregnancies.

Other forms of birth control, contraception in particular, were less certain. Coitus interruptus was certainly condemned in popular medical literature, suggesting that it was both known and probably practised, while particular sexual positions were thought to discourage conception. One popular poem suggested the following:

> Thus in a Chair the Cautious Dame,
> Who loves a little of the Same,
> Will take it on her Lovers Lap,
> Sure to prevent, this way, Mishap:
> Subtle Lechers! Knowing that,
> They cannot so be got with Brat.[41]

Magical amulets were still available and believed effective by some people, and the eighteenth century was also the period during which the condom first reached a wider public.

Condoms were widely available in London throughout the century, although they were generally associated with libertinism and prostitution. The sort of sheath then sold would have been made from the pickled duodenums of sheep and furnished with a small bow to keep them in place during sex. Their role in contraception is, however, problematic. Most people seem to have used them as a prophylactic against venereal disease rather than as a contraceptive device. Although most of our knowledge of them comes from a male (and frequently libertine) perspective, their use as a form of birth control by some portion of the population cannot be ruled out.[42]

In combination with the markedly pro-natal stance evinced by popular sex manuals like *Aristotle's Master-piece*, the range and availability of birth control and contraception suggests a perhaps unexpected attitude towards sex and reproduction. The apparent contradiction between the published directions for the best way of conceiving children and the apparently widespread use of abortifacients and other forms of birth control suggests not hypocrisy, but rather a more positive and complex attitude towards procreation than we are perhaps familiar with. Indeed, Angus McLaren has convincingly argued that eighteenth-century sexual practice can be best understood in the context of a desire to control when conception occurred, rather than with an overriding desire to prevent it completely. His point, drawn largely from anthropological analysis of contemporary societies, is that early-modern people would be more likely to seek out sexual knowledge and techniques that gave them positive power over their reproductive lives – information about how to space one's children – rather than the negative power associated with modern contraception. In this context, abortion as birth control would seem to have suited early-modern people tremendously well.[43]

* * *

Neither attitudes towards abortion nor the content of popular sex manuals seem to have changed significantly over the course of the eighteenth century. And yet we have already seen that elite medical understandings of sex and reproduction certainly did develop. One way of looking at the relationship, and indeed the apparent non-relationship, between these two literatures is through one of the great sexual crises of the eighteenth century – that associated with masturbation.

Until the beginning of the eighteenth century the sin of Onan was generally associated with coitus interruptus. Masturbation, while it was expected to have ill effects, was considered a relatively minor sin. Indeed, at least one commentator has rather implausibly suggested that the lack of comment on masturbation prior to 1700 suggests that the act itself was relatively rare before that date.[44]

Accepting the impossibility of demonstrating this point one way or another, what is apparent is that there was increasing concern about the masturbatory habits of both men and women, and that by the end of the eighteenth century male masturbation in particular had been transformed for both elite and popular audiences into a serious medical and social concern, on which many of the social problems of the day could be heaped.

The earliest condemnatory pamphlet was Josiah Woodward's *Rebuke of the Sin of Uncleanness* published by the Society for Promoting Christian Knowledge in 1704. The SPCK was associated with the Societies for the Reformation of Manners, and its pamphlets were widely distributed free of charge to the poor throughout the country. Its involvement with both this pamphlet and with Jean-Frédéric Osterwald's *The Nature of Uncleanness Consider'd* (1708) reflect one of the origins of much of the concern around masturbation at this time, and its relationship with other contemporary sexual purity movements, such as the persecution of prostitutes and homosexuals pursued by the Reformation Societies.[45] But the popular breakthrough for anti-masturbatory literature came with the publication of the enormously successful *Onania, or, The Heinous Sin of Self-Pollution, and All its Frightful Consequences in Both Sexes* in 1708.

Anonymously produced, but the work of a clergyman cum quack named Beckers or Bekkers, *Onania* was a pseudo-medical account of the horrible consequences of masturbation.[46] Within an essentially Galenic framework, *Onania* warned of the debilitating effects of loss of vigour for both men and women. Simply to list some of the consequences adduced by the author gives a flavour of the whole volume. For male masturbaters growth could well be hindered, they could suffer from priapisms, gonorrhoeas and stranguries, their seed could become waterish, and they could suffer from fainting fits. Women might expect hysteria, barrenness and imbecility, and a 'total ineptitude to the Act of Generation itself'.[47] The dangers for both the individual and the society were continually stressed, and a cure, available from a London publisher by mail order, was recommended as the surest remedy.

What assured the volume's success, however, was the inclusion in later editions of readers' letters, and the advice of the author in response. This book went through some nineteen editions and sold almost forty thousand copies, and in the process helped to create what has been described as a 'general neurosis'.[48] What started as a pamphlet of some sixty pages, rapidly grew to 194 pages and later received a 142-page supplement – most of the additional material being composed of lurid accounts of the masturbatory habits of various men and women. The flavour of these letters can be gleaned from a single example:

Sir, Providence has been so kind as to direct me to your excellent book, call'd ONANIA . . . I sent three or four times for it, and at last I got one, and read many Cases in it, something like my own Case, but yet of none of my Sex that began the wicked practice of Self-Pollution so soon as my self, for I began with it at 11 Years old, by the Devil's leading me to it, I think, and follow'd it till I was quite 17, but was always pale and weakly when a Girl, and never had the Course of Nature but twice till I married; and I must own my farther wickedness, which was, that I used that base and cruel practice after I was Married, and had a great deal more Pleasure of it than when my Husband lay with me, altho' he is a young brisk Man, and till I read your book, I followed it almost daily, and have been married four years, but never was with Child, nor been in Order as Women should be . . . but now by reading your wonderful good book I see what the cause is, and thank the Almighty I have left it off . . . Sir, Your most distressed unknown humble Servant, A.Q.[49]

A few months later this same correspondent wrote in to describe the good success of the cure, claiming that she now had 'a great deal of Pleasure in the Act, but cannot tell if I have so much as other Women have, and great Inclinations to it sometimes' and moreover, that she could now 'keep the Seed after Coition longer than I used to do'.[50] The provenance of the letters included in *Onania* is doubtful, and it is certainly possible that the compiler wrote them himself and included them as a source of pornographic titillation. But, in the process of selling anti-masturbatory accounts as pseudo-medical pornography, a largely new social problem was created, and a new medical concern popularised, which was then taken up by perhaps more serious commentators.

In 1758, the Swiss doctor Samuel Tissot first published his *L'Onanisme: ou Dissertation physique sur les maladies produites par la masturbation*, which was translated into English as *Onanism: or a Treatise upon the Disorders Produced by Masturbation*. It remained in print until 1905 and formed the basis for a respectable medical theory of the debilitating consequences of masturbation.[51]

Tissot's theories were based on the assumption of the importance of sperm, and in many ways were within a solidly Galenic tradition. What is significant, however, is, first, that he places so much greater emphasis on a spermatic economy of health than previous writers and, second, that his work was and remained so popular. From the publication of *Onanism* onward, it became almost impossible to write a popular health text without roundly condemning the likely consequences of masturbation for both men and women. By the nineteenth century, the process of medicalisation had progressed so far that hospital deaths were regularly being ascribed to excessive masturbation. In women it was believed to lead to nymphomania, in men to debilitating illnesses of all sorts.[52]

Historians have treated the popularity of *Onania* and Tissot's *Onanism* in a number of different ways. *Onania* has been seen largely in the context of the development of eighteenth-century pornography, while Tissot's emphasis on the spermatic economy has been associated with mercantilism. The eighteenth-century emphasis on masturbation in general has been associated with the redefinition of childhood identified by Phillippe Aries, and the search for new 'scientific' explanations for madness during an age of growing rationality.[53]

All of these analyses provide useful perspectives on the rise of a literature of masturbation. But this material is most significant as a reflection of the mutability of social understanding of sexual difference, and at the same time the increasing emphasis on heterosexual, penetrative sex (as described in the previous chapter).

Despite the redefinition of men and women's bodies at the end of the eighteenth century, popular medical literature continued to see both as suffering from masturbation, even after the idea of female ejaculation had been abandoned. In other words, the social importance of controlling personal behaviour seems to have been more important than the logic of anatomical and medical understanding. Indeed, it was professional medicine which reorganised itself in line with popular writing (and possibly beliefs), rather than the other way around. At one level this conclusion admirably supports Thomas Laqueur's analysis of the direction of influence in the reconstruction of gender difference, but at the same time it suggests again that the chronology must be seen to have been much longer than he allows and that, hence, medical discourses, while certainly reflective, were not necessarily effective agents of social change in themselves.

Beyond these conclusions, the literature on masturbation must be seen in the context of growing emphasis on penetrative sex. Fear of masturbation must not simply be equated with the lonely activities of men and women, but must also be seen as an attempt to influence plebeian and middling-sort beliefs surrounding courtship and mutual masturbation. Like the ubiquitous popular sex manuals of the period, the literature on masturbation contained a strong pro-natalist message. One way in which to view this material is to see it as a policing literature concerned to ensure that penetrative, heterosexual sex leading to pregnancy and birth became increasingly the only form of sexual activity which could be countenanced.

5 Subcultures and Sodomites: the Development of Homosexuality

The literature on eighteenth-century male homosexuality has grown tremendously in the last twenty-five years. Through the work of historians such as Randolph Trumbach, Alan Bray and Antony Simpson the creation of an identifiable homosexual subculture in the eighteenth century has become central to our understanding of the development of modern sexualities in general. The initial impetus for the expansion of this field was the increasing self-confidence and political activism of the modern gay community, but the influence of the ideas developed here have had a significant impact on the broader history of the eighteenth century.

This literature has addressed two fundamental concerns: first, how people who engaged in homosexual sex both perceived their own actions and presented themselves to the rest of society and, second, how society, primarily through the courts but also through literature and the theatre, presented and treated people engaged in male-on-male sex.

In the process two significantly different historiographies of eighteenth-century English homosexualities have developed. One concentrates almost exclusively on the development of a 'molly' subculture in London during the late seventeenth and early eighteenth centuries. The culture of the 'molly houses', that is clubs and ale houses where men met, socialised and had sex together, has been the primary object of study for historians who have argued that the eighteenth century witnessed the creation of the first recognisable homosexual identity. The other historiographic tradition looks primarily at the punishment of sodomites either in homosocial institutions like the British Navy, or in rural settings where the possibility of the existence of a subculture was limited.

The first of these traditions was begun by Mary McIntosh in the mid 1960s, and has since been furthered by the detailed research and analysis of Alan Bray, Randolph Trumbach and Antony Simpson.[1] We now know a great deal about the circumspect world of London homosexuality. Forms of address and dress, means of self-identification, rituals and distinctive argots have all been discovered among the

58

habitués of the molly houses. On the basis of these factors it has been argued that eighteenth-century London witnessed the creation of a distinctive self-identity. Randolph Trumbach has even gone so far as to suggest that aspects of molly house culture bear a remarkable resemblance to their twentieth-century equivalents.[2] But not everyone has accepted the importance of this phenomenon or his analysis of it. In particular, Michel Foucault and Jeffrey Weeks have argued that it was only with the creation of a 'scientific/medical' label of 'homosexual' that men who engaged in sodomitical sex could begin to think of themselves as an entirely separate group. In other words, it was the creation of a label by the sexologists, psychiatrists and theorists of the social purity movements at the end of the nineteenth century which created the category 'homosexual', and this in turn was adopted by men seeking their own identity. Weeks sees the eighteenth-century molly culture as merely evidence of a nascent identity rather than a fully created one.[3]

From the point of view of the historian of the eighteenth century this is a rather arid debate, and from whichever side it is viewed, there remains no doubt that eighteenth-century London witnessed a new phenomenon which needs to be both described and explained. Also, the emergence of a molly culture based on persecution and new forms of sociability does not preclude the development of a separate category of 'homosexual' at the end of the nineteenth century. And even if, as Weeks argues, molly culture represents a nascent, rather than fully fledged, identity, this does not negate its importance.

The alternative, but related, historiography was begun in earnest by Louis Crompton, and for eighteenth-century Britain has been most actively pursued by A.N. Gilbert.[4] This literature is less concerned to describe a uniquely 'homosexual' culture and more interested in charting the treatment of homosexuals by the courts and the state, i.e. the regulation of homosexuality. In detailed articles on the development of anti-sodomitical laws and attitudes, and on the treatment of convicted sodomites in the British Navy and similar institutions, historians working on Britain, Europe and colonial North America have both described the legal framework within which homosexuals were persecuted, and given us an insight into the types of sodomitical acts which characterised the behaviour of at least those taken up by the legal system. In part, this literature has been concerned to demonstrate the existence of a continuing anti-homosexual strand within Western culture, which in its more extreme formulations has been characterised as a type of genocide.[5]

This literature has created its own martyrs and villains, and has played a significant role in the contemporary politics of gay liberation. But, more significantly in this context, it has provided the basis for a clear understanding of the development of the legal practices of a whole range of Western societies during the last millennium, as well as giving us a good idea of the extent to which these laws and procedures were actually implemented.

Before going on to examine the unique and new culture which developed in the molly houses of London, it is first necessary to review the legal framework within which sodomy was prosecuted in the eighteenth century, and to examine the background of sodomitical behaviour out of which molly culture arose.

* * *

Throughout the period covered by this book sodomy was a capital crime, and tens, if not hundreds, of people died on the scaffold in England as a result. Sodomy first became a civil crime in 1533, and became a criminal offence in 1562, although it had been a capital crime under ecclesiastical law long before this.[6] From the sixteenth century onward sodomy was defined as a felony without benefit of clergy, i.e. the most serious sort of capital crime. Cases could be tried through either the Assize Courts or the Quarter Sessions and, if convicted, the accused was hanged. In order to prove sodomy, however, several elements had to be demonstrated. In the early seventeenth century Sir Edward Coke explained that in order for an act to be sodomy there had to be both penetration and ejaculation – one by itself was insufficient.[7] There also normally needed to be two witnesses who could attest to both factors being present.[8] In the case of homosexual rape these criteria could occasionally be met, but in cases of consensual sex it was extremely difficult to obtain both the proofs and the witnesses, especially since English law made no distinction between the active and passive partner. Both participants were subject to the death penalty, and hence neither was likely to want to give testimony against the other. By the eighteenth century, medical evidence was becoming an increasingly important element in these trials but, even so, it remained very difficult to obtain a conviction under the aegis of the capital statute. As a result the vast majority of cases involving sodomy were brought under the rubric for assault, which required less stringent proofs and which would lead, in most cases, to a period of imprisonment, public humiliation in the pillory (with the possibility of physical injury or death) and possibly a fine. In his analysis of the *Old Bailey Sessions Papers* for the period

1730–1830, Antony Simpson has found seventy-one sodomy cases dealt with as felonies compared with 172 treated as 'assault with intent'.[9]

There remained, however, a profound difficulty over definition. Sodomy could include anal penetration of either a man or a woman, bestiality, child molestation and possibly even fellatio. Legally, in England and Wales at least, it seems to have excluded non-penetrative lesbian sex, although female-on-female sex which included the use of a dildo might be considered sodomitical (as in the case of Catherina Margaretha Muhlhahn, in Prussia, who insisted her female lover perform oral sex on her leather dildo).[10] 'Sodomy' was a catch-all expression for a number of sins against God and the commonweal, and the legal antipathy to it was extreme. In part this antipathy was a result of biblical injunction. It was the sin of Sodom, and if practised would bring down upon the nation the punishment meted out to Sodom and Gomorrah by a rather judgemental Old Testament God. Sodomy was also strongly associated with witchcraft and heresy and, in Europe at least, the prosecution of the sexual crime was frequently associated with anxiety about religious deviance.[11] Similarly, in an English context sodomy was frequently linked with popery, and condemnations of it became a standard element of the highly colourful anti-Catholic rhetoric and beliefs associated with English Protestantism.[12] But at the same time there was a large amount of clear water between the legal framework within which sodomy was defined, and the practice of the courts throughout the early-modern period.

B.R. Burg has argued that during the sixteenth and seventeenth centuries there was little active interest in pursuing prosecutions for sodomy, and that what little effort there was centred around bestiality. He quotes the case of George Dowdeny, who was accused of sodomy at the Somerset Quarter Sessions in 1622. What emerged at the trial was that Dowdeny had been a practising sodomite for at least the previous fourteen years, and had aggressively importuned a number of people. He had raped one witness over a decade before his trial, and had become increasingly conspicuous in the months leading up to his prosecution. The point is that Dowdeny's insistent and obvious behaviour was the primary trigger which set in train the complaint made against him.[13]

This is a pattern which seems common in the sixteenth and seventeenth centuries and, to a lesser extent, the eighteenth. The vast majority of cases involved sodomical acts which are startling for their public character. People are frequently accused of sodomy by others sleeping in the same room, or the adjoining hammock, or by people who were offended by an engrossed pair in a public park or a side alley. Lawrence Stone has argued that the early-modern period, and the eighteenth century in particular, comprised a 'voyeuristic' society in which privacy of any kind was extremely uncommon. But the fact that so many sodomy trials involved individuals who felt willing to commit a capital crime while their fellow workers slept in the next bed must also be a reflection of popular attitudes towards the crime itself.

Another important element in the response to sodomy in the early-modern period is that it was not treated as seriously in all circumstances. Bestiality and homosexual rape, particularly of children, was deemed much more serious than consensual sex between men and boys above the age of consent. This is particularly true in the seventeenth century, and according to Antony Simpson, less true as the eighteenth century progressed. The emphasis on bestiality can be explained as a reflection of the perception that the act was a sin against the natural order, an order in which a deeply perceived boundary between people possessing souls and the brutes of the fields was being transgressed. Also, the Galenic or humoral belief that monster births could result from the liaison would have increased concern.[14] In the case of assault on children, the reasons for it being taken as seriously as it was are more difficult to assess, but it is clear from a number of eighteenth-century cases that the likelihood of being executed as a result of the rape of a child, in either a heterosexual or homosexual context, was very high indeed.[15]

This is not to suggest that there was general tolerance of sodomitical acts amongst consenting adults, but rather that there was both a disparity between the legal definition of sodomy and the popular perception of what known individuals did, and serious deficiencies in the mechanism for policing sexual offences.

Throughout the early-modern period, and until the second quarter of the nineteenth century, there were few effective agencies for the prosecution of offenders. If a prosecution was to be brought, it generally had to be pursued by the injured party and would necessarily incur a deal of expense and trouble. In the case of an essentially victimless crime it is perhaps not surprising that few people were willing to go to the trouble unless the activities involved were blatant enough to seriously impinge on the individual's sense of good order. Of course, in the eighteenth century, organised campaigns to prosecute blasphemers, prostitutes and sodomites ensured that a larger number of people were caught up in the legal system, but for most people in most places throughout the early-modern period, the likelihood of being prosecuted for consensual sodomitical behaviour was limited.

It is, of course, impossible to know whether a large proportion of the English population were sodomising each other while the law simply turned a blind eye. But it is likewise obvious that the level of tolerance of deviant sexual behaviour was much higher than the draconian punishments laid down by statute would suggest. Alan Bray has argued that this was a result of a kind of intellectual double-think: i.e. while the sodomite existed as a figure of deep opprobrium within the profoundly religious world view of the sixteenth and seventeenth centuries, it was very difficult to associate that image with one's work mates, friends and neighbours. Once the process of identifying an individual as a 'sodomite' had begun through the bringing of charges, the full force of popular fear and loathing would be brought to bear through the courts, but until that time it was difficult to associate anal sex with biblical retribution.[16]

It has also been pointed out that in the period until 1660 the Puritan conception of all types of sin was such that anyone could be subject to any sin. It was not that sodomy was anything other than the most deeply reviled of sins, and indeed Peter Lake has argued that it formed one element of a coherent image of the world in which popery, with its attendant sodomy and tyranny, formed the counterpoint to a Protestant ideal of a godly commonwealth. At the same time, however, it was a sin which might ensnare any unwary Christian. Like marijuana leading to heroin, the apparently harmless but sinfully enticing luxuries encountered every day by most Protestants could lead to the devasting infamy of sodomy and Catholicism. There was, however, little of the nineteenth- and twentieth-century attitude that sodomy was an activity which was performed by an 'other', a separate group within society. As a result there was greater emphasis on the redemption of the individual sinner than on the persecution of the identified 'homosexual'.[17]

All of this begs a series of questions. What did traditional, non-molly house, sodomitical behaviour look like? Who was sodomising whom? In what circumstances? And what were their feelings about it? There is a reasonably large literature which attempts to answer these questions for the seventeenth and eighteenth centuries.

* * *

The vast majority of eighteenth-century men who committed sodomy did not think of themselves other than as ordinary, everyday members of their society. They did not belong to a subculture, nor did they have a distinctive self-identity. They would have seen sex with another man simply as an extension of the forms of sexual behaviour common in courting and marriage. Certainly, they would have considered sodomy a transgression against the mores of their own society, but not as something which fundamentally changed their self-perception. Indeed, it is probable that many people, particularly those living in homosocial organisations, saw sodomy, and likewise bestiality and masturbation, as available alternatives to heterosexual/vaginal intercourse.

Throughout the early-modern period, until the middle of the eighteenth century, most men did not marry until their mid-to-late twenties, and while we have seen that mutual masturbation was an integral part of the courting process among plebeian and middling-sort groups, there were still likely to be long periods of one's life when almost any form of penetrative sexual activity would have been deemed a severe transgression. Particularly for men in the Navy and to a lesser extent the Army, for youths and tutors in the universities, and for school children, normal social experience would bring them into contact with other men and boys, to the exclusion of women and girls. Sleeping arrangements were at best crowded, and it was considered normal for men to share a bed on an almost casual basis.

Many of the cases tried in the courts suggest that these circumstances led on occasion to sodomitical encounters of one sort or another. The Guards were famous, or notorious, 'from the eighteenth century and throughout Europe for their easy prostitution'.[18] Likewise, A.N. Gilbert has demonstrated that sodomy was common in the British Navy. His work on the early-nineteenth-century *Africane* court martial suggests that it was widely practised, and that some crew members considered it entirely acceptable.[19] The situation at Oxford and Cambridge is slightly more difficult to assess, but the attempted rape of the commoner William French by the warden of Wadham, Robert Thistlewayte, in the early eighteenth century at least suggests that sodomy was not unknown.[20] And Dudley Ryder's 1715 diary entry suggesting that 'among the chief men in some of the colleges sodomy is very usual and . . . that it is dangerous sending a young man that is beautiful to Oxford' is equally suggestive.[21]

The point about these examples is that there is no suggestion that any of the people involved in sodomy in these homosocial circumstances, with the possible exception of some of the soldiers stationed in the London area, were in any way involved with the developing homosexual subculture of the capital. Among the literate and educated elite it is possible that there would be an awareness of the existence of molly houses, possibly through the libertine culture with which they were sometimes associated, but for most non-metropolitan, plebeian and middling-sort sodomites, their behaviour was part and parcel of 'normal' sexual behaviour – a grievous and mortal sin, certainly, but not an identity.

* * *

As an account of the vast majority of male-on-male sex in the eighteenth century the description given above is accurate, but it does not provide a full picture of the history of eighteenth-century sodomy. There are two elements missing: first, a kind of elite libertinism particularly associated with the court, the literature on which includes frequent reference to sodomy, and also, of course, the molly houses themselves.

While most acts of sodomy probably occurred between consenting plebeian and middling-sort men, sodomy itself was inextricably bound up in the minds of early-modern people with the luxury and dissipation of the court and, to a lesser extent, the theatre.

One popular activity of historians of homosexuality has been a kind of retrospective 'outing', wherein lists of the great, the good and the artistic who were also sodomites is constructed as a kind of talisman of self-identity.[22] But beyond the rather voyeuristic glee that this might give, or the even more dubious attempt to associate artistic genius and creativity with homosexuality, there is a serious point to be made about early-modern attitudes towards sodomy. First, in the context of court circles it was seen largely as an extension of a more pervasive libertinism. While James I, the Earl of Rochester and William III may all have been sodomites, it was generally part of a pattern of bisexual behaviour in which sex came to represent power relationships more strongly than gender. Indeed, the classic image of the seventeenth-century libertine as having a catamite on one arm and a whore on the other expresses clearly the extent to which bisexuality was the norm. Sodomy also, however, fitted rather well the hierarchical structures of court patronage, through which political power and social relations were expressed.

Elite sodomy was also a highly charged political weapon. During the course of the seventeenth century, in particular, any hint of court sodomy would impinge upon the legitimacy of the sovereign's power. In the case of someone like William III, such a charge could easily undermine his carefully constructed public image as the leader of the cause of Protestantism. In a period when providentialism was central to the perceptions of the political process, and in which each earthquake and military setback was constructed as a reflection of God's displeasure, the charge of sodomy directed against a monarch, with its implications of tyranny and popery, whether true or not, could, if popularly believed, have a corrosive effect on their grasp of political power.[23]

The two most famous sodomy trials of the early-modern period, those of the Earl of Castlehaven in 1631 and of Bishop Atherton in 1640, can both be analysed almost entirely in political and religious terms. The Earl of Castlehaven was charged both with committing sodomy with a number of servants, and with encouraging a servant to rape Castlehaven's wife. While there is little doubt that he did both these things, it is also obvious that his Catholicism played a major role in ensuring that he was tried, and that the rape and the participation of servants were more important than the charge of sodomy. He was executed in 1631 and two of his servants were hanged the following year.[24] The trial and execution of John Atherton, Bishop of Waterford, in 1640 is even more evocative of the political uses of a charge of sodomy. An appointee of Archbishop Laud, there is strong reason to believe that his trial was pursued because of his religious and political role rather than from a profound desire to root out sodomy.[25]

Court sodomy was associated with luxury and dissipation and frequently paired with rape, adultery and incest.[26] It was certainly common enough in seventeenth- and eighteenth-century court circles, but broader social attitudes towards it were largely a reflection of the ambivalent role of the court in a society which saw luxury as a sign of religious lassitude. More than this, the ambiguous role played by the monarch and court in the religious life of seventeenth-century England allowed the paired charges of sodomy and popery to be used against them. During the course of the eighteenth century, however, the new images of the homosexual as effeminate, or as an 'other', separated from the rest of society by 'nature' rather than culpability in sin, tended to undermine the ability of critics to use the charge effectively against the increasingly marginal court. Certainly, this transition to a 'naturalised' homosexuality had the effect of helping to eliminate the important religious dimension, which had encouraged the use of sodomy in seventeenth-century political rhetoric. And although the charge of sodomy continued to be levelled against many European courts and monarchs, the major discourses surrounding Georgian court life had more to do with the bumbling, mad or simply stupid nature of various Kings, than it did the sexual proclivities of these monarchs and their favourites. This was in part a reflection of the changing nature of the court but, more importantly, it reflected changing views of homosexuality. In the 1690s it had been entirely possible that William III's homosexuality could exist side by side with his rather macho image as a military hero; by the 1790s homosexuality had been thoroughly associated with the effeminate, cowardly and weak. The process which brought about this shift in attitudes is intimately bound up with the creation of a homosexual subculture, the molly house culture of London.

* * *

At a trial in 1726 an informer for a Reformation of Manners Society described his experiences in a molly house in the City of London:

> On Wednesday the 17th of November last I went to the prisoner's house in Beech Lane, and there I found a company of men fiddling and dancing and singing bawdy songs, kissing and using their hands in a very unseemly manner . . . In a large room there we found one a-fiddling and eight more a-dancing country dances . . . Then they sat in one another's lap, talked bawdy, and practised a great many indecencies. There was a door in the great room, which opened into a little room, where there was a bed, and into this little room several of the company went . . .[27]

The trial from which this deposition was taken was the result of a series of raids on molly houses throughout London conducted by a Society for the Reformation of Manners in 1726. There had been similar raids in 1698 and 1707, and there would be similar raids against molly houses and other places of public assignation in the mid 1760s, 1776 and 1798.[28]

The reasons for these persecutions will be dealt with below, but the trial evidence and printed accounts indicate that in London from the beginning of the eighteenth century there existed a well developed and sophisticated homosexual subculture. There were perhaps twenty molly houses in existence at any one time, and the descriptions of them suggest that many were quite large establishments, allowing certainly tens of people to congregate at one house.

What is also apparent from the prosecutions is that by 1700 there was a well established set of outdoor meeting places distributed throughout London, and that a separate culture of gesture, expression and dress allowed homosexual men to recognise each other and to contextualise their love-making within a sophisticated ritualised formula.

To list briefly some of the molly houses and places of open-air assignation gives a sense of their prevalence. There was Margaret Clap's house in Holborn, a house in Beech Lane at the heart of the city, another near the Old Bailey and a fourth next to Newgate prison. Soho also had a molly house, as did Charing Cross, Drury Lane and St James's Square in the West End. Outdoor meeting places were common too, and apparently well recognised by both the homosexual community and the agents of the Societies for the Reformation of Manners. The piazzas of Covent Garden, the latrines at Lincoln's Inn, Moorfields, Kensington Gardens, Hyde Park, Green Park, St James's Park and St Paul's Churchyard were all associated with outdoor sex.[29]

The existence of these houses and recognised sites of assignation certainly demonstrates the size and vitality of the London homosexual community. But what has struck historians most forcefully is the extent to which this community had developed its own culture and self-identity. A description of an evening in a molly house in the Old Bailey gives a flavour of the kinds of behaviour historians have cited as normal within molly-house society:

> . . . they had no sooner entered but the Marshal was complemented by the company with the titles of Madam and Ladyship. The man asking the occasion of these uncommon devoirs, the Marshal said it was a familiar language peculiar to the house. The man was not long there before he was more surprised than at first. The men calling one another 'my dear' and hugging, kissing, and tickling each other as if they were a mixture of wanton males and females, and assuming effeminate voices and airs; some telling others that they ought to be whipped for not coming to school more frequently . . . Some were completely rigged in gowns, petticoats, headcloths, fine laced shoes, furbelowed scarves, and masks; some had riding hoods; some were dressed like milkmaids, others like shepherdesses with green hats, waistcoats, and petticoats; and others had their faces patched and painted and wore very extensive hoop petticoats, which had been very lately introduced.[30]

This quote comes from a pamphlet using the accusation of association with molly houses in order to attack Charles Hitchins, a prominent thief-taker in London in the 1710s. But the effeminacy and transvestism which mark this description do seem to have been common characteristics of the culture. This is attested to in both second-hand accounts designed for public consumption, and by depositions given during the many trials which punctuate the history of the molly houses. Some reports suggest that the habitués of molly houses frequently participated in theatrical weddings and pretended to give birth, and that they acted out an extreme form of mocking effeminacy which suggests, in turn, that they were self-consciously separating themselves off from the world of eighteenth-century masculinity.[31]

There is also evidence to suggest that outdoor assignations had their own conventions and assumptions. In Moorfields and St James's Park men signalled their mutual interest in a number of ways:

> If one of them sits on a bench he pats the back of his hands; if you follow them, they put a white handkerchief through the skirts of their coat, and wave it to and fro; but if they are met by you, their thumbs are stuck in the armpits of their waistcoats, and they play their fingers upon their breasts.[32]

Once a partner had been identified the pair frequently made love in a secluded corner of the park or in a quiet alley.

The people who inhabited this subculture were men between the ages of eighteen and fifty. They tended to come from the lower social classes, and included a range of people from chairmen and servants to independent artisans and merchants – there is no evidence that any significant number of gentlemen frequented the houses, although it is possible that elite men were simply shielded from prosecution.[33] And while some devotees of the molly houses certainly lived within this culture – one defendant in 1726 claimed to have lodged at the Mother Clap for over two years – the vast majority stepped into and out of the culture at will, taking up and putting off a homosexual identity as they did so.[34] Many were married with children, and none could construct an entire life within the norms and assumptions of the subculture alone. In part this was true because of the dangers of persecution. Someone like John Ridgeway, who was taken up in 1703 while wearing women's clothes by a constable and charged as idle and disorderly, was not only committed to the house of correction, but then forcibly enlisted in a company of Fusiliers.[35] And two years later he was again 'taken in the streets abt. one of the clock in the morning in women's cloths having picked up a man and known to be a strolling vagrant'. Noting John Ridgeway's advanced venereal disease, this time the court sent him to St Thomas's Hospital for a cure before committing him to Bridewell.[36] It was largely unacceptable for men to wander the streets of London in women's clothing, or to draw too much attention to themselves through extravagant effeminate behaviour of any sort. But perhaps more importantly people continued to have to make a living and construct a life within the broader community. While John Ridgeway may have done so through prostitution this was not an option open to most people. And although London in this period did have its anonymous corners, and while it was possible to escape some forms of traditional society, the vast majority of the population, including homosexuals, continued to live in or head hierarchical households within a patriarchal social organisation. Although London was the largest city in Western Europe, it still retained many of the characteristics of a face-to-face village society. The first street signs and numbered addresses were only put up in the late 1740s, reflecting the extent to which knowing the city, and being known within it, remained important elements of urban life.[37]

Even if a homosexual identity was taken up and put off only occasionally, the existence of the molly houses did mean that the lives of the members of London's homosexual community were far different from their sixteenth- and seventeenth-century counterparts and rural brethren. The molly houses acted as places of safety, wherein homosexual men could develop a unique attitude to their society and to themselves.

Randolph Trumbach has argued that there have been homosexual subcultures and networks throughout urban Western Europe from the twelfth century, and that the peculiar characteristic of eighteenth-century London is that these subcultures become more apparent.[38] But whether or not this is true, there can be no doubt that molly-house culture had a greater effect on the broader social constructions of gender and perceptions of homosexuality than any of its possible forebears. The molly houses created, in symbiosis with the broader London community and a changing heterosexuality, a homosexual character and caricature, which has had a profound influence on Western attitudes towards homosexuality, and on the self-image of later homosexuals. The molly houses became synonymous with homosexuality, and gradually over the course of the eighteenth and nineteenth centuries contributed to the broader transition, both in perception and reality, from the sodomite to the effeminate homosexual.[39]

* * *

The process whereby molly-house culture was publicised to the wider population is intimately bound up with the persecution of homosexuals by the Societies for the Reformation of Manners. Between 1690 and 1738 a series of Reformation Societies were established, first in London and then in several provincial cities throughout the country. They were driven by a providential millenarianism, which saw England and the English as God's chosen land and people, and suggested that sin and vice would be specifically punished by God.

The Societies for the Reformation of Manners, along with a range of voluntary societies, like the Society for the Promotion of Christian Knowledge (1698) and the Society for the Propagation of the Gospel in Foreign Parts (1701), sought to implement an agenda of social reform which would eliminate religious ignorance, idleness and, of most importance to the Reformation Societies, blasphemy and lewdness. Each, through their own means, sought to revivify Protestant church-manship after the turmoil of the Restoration era. In the process the Societies for the Reformation of Manners attempted to use the legal system, in particular the Middlesex Quarter Sessions, to eliminate Sabbath-breaking, drunkenness, swearing and cursing, and, what is most important in this context, lewd and disorderly behaviour and the keeping of bawdy houses. As a result, the societies became a noticeable force within the social world of early eighteenth-century London. Robert Shoemaker has recently suggested that there were four societies operating in London during the first four decades of the eighteenth century, and that only one concentrated its efforts primarily on lewd-ness. This society was made up of artisans and small traders, and used informers and agents in order to gather evidence on lewd and disorderly behaviour. It also helped to finance the prosecution of both individual offenders and bawdy house keepers.[40]

The activities of the reforming societies were not popular. Their use of informers, in particular, was felt to be highly inappropriate by the majority of Londoners, but they did retain at least the tacit support of a large proportion of the hierarchy of the Anglican Church, as well as the support of some dissenters.

The most frequent victims of the societies were prostitutes. Over a thousand people a year were subject to prosecution for lewd and disorderly behaviour during the course of the 1710s and 1720s, but it was their attacks on specific molly houses in 1699, 1707 and 1726 which both provides much of the evidence for the existence of molly culture and had the greatest effect on the image of homosexuals.

The 1726 raid was the best organised and most comprehensive. Based on information collected over the previous months by Samuel Stevens and others, the raid on Margaret Clap's house, along with raids on at least three other houses, resulted in the prosecution and eventual execution of Gabriel Lawrence, William Griffin and Thomas Wright, and the conviction of a number of others on lesser charges.[41] In part, these raids and trials are significant because they appear to be the first organised attempt to persecute homosexuals in England en masse. They identified a group of men, rather than persecuting individual sodomites.

Just as important, the raids had the effect of identifying the homosexual as a type of person. They also must have strengthened the bonds of fear within the molly houses themselves.

The vast majority of the efforts of the Societies for the Reformation of Manners were taken up with the prosecution of heterosexual prostitution, swearing and Sabbath-breaking, but by also targeting the molly houses, if only intermittently, they had a profound influence on the history of homosexuality. One of the main tools of the societies was publicity. Trial reports, annual sermons, pamphlets and accounts of the societies' own activities were all used to raise money and proselytise for the cause. The molly-house raids provided just the kind of colourful copy which would appeal to the propagandists of the early eighteenth century. And from the late 1690s references to molly-house culture, and sodomy in general, appeared more and more frequently in the cheap pamphlets and newspapers which poured from the London presses. In 1699 the first published account of the trial of the Earl of Castlehaven was produced.[42] During the next three decades pamphlets such as *The Woman-Hater's Lamentation* (1707), and Ned Ward's *History of London Clubs* (1709) and *Hell upon Earth: or the Town in an Uproar* (1729), adumbrated a clear and consistent caricature of homosexuals to the broader public.

The Societies for the Reformation of Manners ceased operating in 1738, but this did not end the persecution of either homosexuals or molly houses. In the mid 1760s a coherent campaign to clean up Moorfields was initiated (probably by William Payne) which resulted in a number of arrests, and at the end of the century a series of prosecutions was begun which would culminate in a flurry of anti-homosexual activity in 1810.[43]

Antony Simpson has argued that the prosecution and persecution of consensual homosexual men can be dated from the 1780s. We can likewise see from the Reformation of Manners material that at least some primarily religiously inspired groups were anxious to prosecute all forms of homosexual behaviour long before the 1780s. Perhaps the most important conclusion to draw from the history of the persecution of homosexuality in London is that it was spasmodic and relatively uncommon at any time. Most of the members of the molly-house culture could feel relatively safe throughout the period, assured that to be prosecuted for felonious sodomy and executed, one would have to be horribly unlucky.

* * *

Of course, to be tolerated is not to be liked. The lack of a consistent or effective prosecution of London's homosexuals does not suggest that popular attitudes towards these men were any less vitriolic than they had been in the sixteenth and seventeenth centuries. There continued to be a kind of popular double-think in regard to homosexuality. While homosexuals sought to hide their activities, they could be conveniently ignored, and the desire to persecute individuals was minimal. There is, for instance, little doubt that the neighbours and friends of the keepers and frequenters of molly houses were aware of the activities pursued within them. Nevertheless, it was only the religious fanatics of the Reformation Societies who made any attempt to close down these institutions.

Once identified as a 'molly', however, as with seventeenth-century sodomites, the reaction of the London crowd could be extreme. Accounts of the experience of homosexuals sentenced to being publicly exposed on the pillory make grim reading. While for most offences a degree of control was maintained over the activities of the crowd, this does not seem to have been the case in relation to men exposed for sodomy. Many were severely injured, at least one was permanently blinded, and several died as a result of their experience.[44] Indeed, it has been argued by Antony Simpson that the antipathy towards homosexual men increased markedly over the course of the eighteenth century, and that both in the pillory and in life in general, known homosexuals began to receive harsher and harsher treatment.

A sense of popular attitudes towards homosexual men can be gleaned from the experience of John Cooper, an unemployed gentleman's servant, who was described as an effeminate 'molly' in court in 1732. He had been robbed by one Thomas Gordon, a leather breeches-maker, who was later put on trial for the crime. But rather than discussing the merits of the case, much of the court record is taken up in describing Cooper's effeminate ways. Cooper testified that while he was attempting to arrest Gordon, he sought the aid of a passer-by: 'I desir'd his assistance; but [Gordon] telling him I was a Molly, he said I ought to be hang'd, and he'd have nothing to do with me.'[45] Cooper eventually did arrest Gordon and bring him to trial, but this resulted only in an acquittal. Given the seriousness with which all crimes against property were taken in the eighteenth century, the response of the passer-by reflects the popular spleen which identified homosexuals could quickly generate.

The image one is left with is of a developing, and increasingly self-confident, homosexual subculture, which had a growing influence on the lives and self-images of its devotees. It was relatively small, and almost entirely restricted to London (there is some evidence of the existence of a molly house in Exeter in the 1790s), but at the same time it was a culture which came to epitomise the 'homosexual' in the minds of the broader population. The vast majority of love-making between men continued to occur in homosocial organisations, or among friends and neighbours in the countryside, but increasingly it was the effemin-ate 'molly' who was perceived to practise sodomy, while all other men were assumed to desire women to the exclusion of men.

A number of theories have been put forward to explain these developments, none of which is entirely satisfactory. Antony Simpson has suggested that the development of molly culture is a reflection of a crisis in working men's masculinity, particularly in London. He argues that the rise of enclosure, and consequent urbanisation and wage dependency experienced by working men, left them feeling increasingly powerless, and that this in turn resulted in a sharper definition of gender roles as a way of replacing lost economic power with domestic authority. The molly was created, or identified, as an 'other' in order to give heterosexual men a measure against which to judge their own masculinity.[46]

Randolph Trumbach has also identified changes in broader gender relations as the root cause of the development of molly culture. He suggests that it was the creation of a new companionate marriage in the late seventeenth century, with its greater emphasis on the domestic, which effectively excluded alternative forms of sex, and created the conditions in which a subculture could thrive.[47] And finally, Alan Bray draws attention to much broader transitions in European culture to explain the existence of the molly houses. He sees the creation of possessive individualism, scientific rationalism and the new philosophies of Locke and his contemporaries as triggers for the growth of the effeminate homosexual. While not really saying how these new world views affected the self-images of individuals, he suggests that the assumption of natural plurality which these philosophies contained encouraged conditions of tolerance which allowed the culture to flour-ish.[48]

None of these explanations are of themselves entirely satisfactory, but they do each contain valuable insights into the nature of the historical processes at work. Inevitably, broader philosophical, economic and institutional developments must have impacted on the individuals who participated in the creation of molly culture. And while none of these explanations really provides a mechanism through which the influences are written upon the lives of participants, each of these historians has identified an important element in the process.

One possible mechanism which has been largely ignored by the historians of homosexuality, but which likewise must have played a role in the creation of molly culture, is the phenomenal growth in new forms of public culture which characterised the eighteenth century, and eighteenth-century London in particular. Is it surprising, after all, that the century which gave us the debating society and the chapel, in which clubs and societies of all sorts were created, should also give us a homosexual subculture? One need only look very briefly at the literature on clubs and societies in the eighteenth century to see that many developed the characteristics which go to define a subculture. If unique handshakes, jargon, dress and ritual are the hallmarks of such a culture, then the Masonic order fits as well as the molly houses, and no artificial intellectual barrier should necessarily suggest that we need understand the two phenomena in different ways.

6 Tribades, Cross-Dressers and Romantic Friendship

In 1722, at the age of thirty, Ann Carrack, a spinster, set up a milliner's shop with Mary Erick in the parish of Christ Church, London. They rented a shop worth thirty pounds a year and went into partnership – 'share & share alike' – working together and living together in and above the shop. In 1725 they rented cheaper premises in Bull's Head Court, just off Newgate Street, where they lived until 1729. At this point the partnership broke up and the two women went their separate ways – Ann Carrack making her living as an independent needle-woman, while Mary Erick went on to set up a small shop in the parish of Chelsea.

Some ten years later they once again moved in together, sharing Mary Erick's shop in Chelsea and its accommodation for the next twenty years. It was only at the age of sixty-nine, forced onto the parish by old age, that this thirty-nine-year relationship was finally broken asunder when Ann was removed to the parish of Christ Church, where the original partnership gave her a legal claim to poor relief.[1]

In a society in which perhaps a fifth of the population never married, and in which the boundaries between men and women were strictly policed, the experience of these two women was far from unique. A substantial proportion of the population lived in the kinds of circumstances exemplified by their experience. And yet we have no single framework in which to understand their relationship. Economic historians would see their partnership as one of necessity, deploying the low wages available to women and the economic insecurity they suffered as evidence for why two women should choose to live together. The continental phenomenon of 'spinster clustering', wherein groups of unmarried or widowed women seem to have congregated in particular locations, would in all likelihood be used as an analogy for the experience of Mary Erick and Ann Carrack.[2] Alternatively, writers on lesbian history might see them in one of two ways. On the one hand they might be classified as 'romantic friends', suggesting, in line with the conclusions of historians such as Lillian Faderman, that theirs was an entirely platonic relationship, innocent of lust or genital contact, and based on an intellectualised tradition of homosocial love.[3] On the other hand, they might be seen, in line with the work of writers such as Emma Donaghue and Terry Castle, as likely to have been fully active lesbians, the inner life of whose relationship has been lost, but who were able to pursue their love as an independent, if poverty-stricken, couple.[4] In this context they might be seen as part of a tradition, a lesbian continuum, to use Adrienne Rich's expression, hidden from history by an apparent lack of legal persecution and surviving records.[5] The difficulty is that the evidence may be used to support any one or more of these conclusions.

This chapter will first look at the legal and medical discourses surrounding lesbianism, and then assess the various historiographical trends in light of the available evidence. Finally, it will look at the phenomenon of female cross-dressing, as a way of gaining an alternative perspective on the culture of women's sexuality.

* * *

Unlike sodomy, lesbian sex has never been illegal in England. While it has been demonstrated that continental lesbians occasionally suffered legal persecution during the early-modern period, and at least one German lesbian was executed in 1721, no single case can be cited in an English context.[6] Moreover, because sodomy was defined in terms of penetrative sex, the laws against it were not generally available for the persecution of lesbians. In other words, the highly phallocentric nature of the laws on sexual misconduct ensured that lesbians escaped prosecution (see Chapter 5). Indeed, the one European lesbian executed during the eighteenth century was found guilty because she used a dildo to sodomise (in this instance to be fellated by) her partner, indicating that it was impossible to have illegal sex without at the very least an artificial penis being involved.[7]

Occasionally, one does find lesbian activity arising in the context of the law, but only very rarely, and generally in circumstances in which it is unclear if the nature of the sexual behaviour is of fundamental concern. Ann Marrow, for example, was prosecuted for fraud in 1777, on the grounds that she had married several women while dressed as a man in order to steal their savings. She was convicted and sentenced to the pillory. The crowd treated her brutally, and she was either killed or permanently blinded, a reaction completely out of proportion with the crime for which she was convicted. Antony Simpson has suggested that the sexual aspects of the case were at the forefront of the minds of the participants of the crowd, and that their brutal treatment of her reflects an underlying and very knowing hostility to lesbians. But nevertheless, it was fraud rather than lesbianism which put her in the pillory in the first place.[8]

Another legal context in which lesbian behaviour occasionally surfaces is in the Church Courts. Typical of the kind of report found in these records is the following rather opaque reference. In 1693 Ralph Hollingsworth tried to explain why he had failed to mention the existence of his five previous wives to his current partner, Mary Sealy. He suggested that one of these previous wives, Susannah Belling, was no true wife: 'she knowing her infirmity ought not have marryed; her infirmity is such that no man Can Lye with her, & because it is so she has wayes with women . . . wch is not fit to be named but most Ranke whoreish they are . . .'.[9]

Several historians, most notably Terry Castle and Emma Donaghue, have argued that this apparent dearth of legal persecution reflects not so much a lack of desire to punish lesbians, but a 'morbid paranoia' on the part of the legal system. Both Castle and Donaghue have suggested that beneath the apparent tolerance of lesbians was an attempt to erase lesbian love from the social imagination. In other words, the judges and legislators were subtly suppressing the knowledge of lesbianism by ignoring it, and in the process oppressing women who would otherwise choose lesbianism over heterosexuality.[10] The profoundly unsubtle nature of the eighteenth-century legal system makes it difficult to accept this argument. In a century that saw the passage of such blunt instruments for maintaining social order as the 'Black Act' of 1723, and which made over fifty apparently minor offences, such as appearing abroad in disguise, subject to capital punishment, it is difficult to credit the system involved with sufficient sophistication to choose subtle censorship over brutal suppression.[11] Likewise, there are other areas in which lesbians take a much higher profile – perhaps most notably in the literature on medicine and anatomy.

* * *

At least during the early part of the eighteenth century there were relatively clear categories through which to think about and discuss lesbian behaviour. We have already seen in Chapter 4 that the century witnessed a gradual transition from a 'one body' to a 'two body' model of human reproduction and sexual difference. The 'one body' model, with its continuum of sexual types between extreme female and male characteristics, and the mutable physical form it assumed, provided a range of categories, including the hermaphrodite and tribade, within which lesbians might be placed.

At the very heart of Galenic understanding of sexual difference lay the idea that men and women were essentially two sides of the same coin, that both were possessed of the same genitalia – women's being contained within their bodies and men's outside. In the case of lesbian behaviour this meant that there was always a degree of ambiguity about the sex of the people actually involved. Eighteenth-century medical writers also used the category of hermaphrodite much more widely than would be the case in later centuries, again making it possible to see lesbian behaviour as a reflection of a physical state. Even if both of the individuals involved were apparently female, there was always the possibility that one of them possessed partially male genitalia, or else that her genitalia had 'fallen', and hence become male.

Perhaps more typical of early-eighteenth-century medical discourse even than the use of the category of hermaphrodite, is that of tribade – literally, a woman who rubs, or who could enjoy sex through rubbing rather than penetration. It has been mentioned before (see Chapter 4) that eighteenth-century commentators believed that when women masturbated, either by themselves or with someone else, their clitoris could grow and become rigid – would, in fact, come to take on the appearance and biological function of a penis. This condition is normally associated with tribades, and the presence or absence of a distended clitoris was occasionally appealed to in medical examinations where sex was indeterminate. It is to this belief that the anonymous author of *Onania* appealed when he published the following letter purporting to be from a young woman worried about the consequences of masturbating:

I began, Sir, the folly at eleven years of age; was taught it by my mother's chamber-maid, who lay with me from that time all along till now, which is full seven years, and so intimate were we in the sin, that we took all opportunities of committing it, and invented all the ways we were capable of to heighten the titilation, and gratify our sinful lusts the more ... We, in short, shamefully pleasured one another, as well as each ourselves ... but for above half a year past I have had a swelling that thrust out from my body, as big and almost as hard and as long or longer than my thumb, which inclines me to excessive lustful desires, and from it there issues a moisture or slipperiness ...[12]

What is significant in this context is that the existence of the possibility of the 'clitoris as penis', or tribady, allowed for a further biological explanation of how two women could have sex, and how women could come to find other women attractive.[13]

For early eighteenth-century commentators the pleasure and point of sex was to do with the secretion of seminal fluid, by both men and women, and its subsequent absorption by women. And while this view seems, at least superficially, to have been at odds with the practice of mutual masturbation so commonly adopted by courting couples, it ensured that the public discourse associated with sexual practice was one of penetration and ejaculation. For men this amounted to a release of a humoral build-up, while for women it represented the gain of a powerful and heat-producing substance. This meant that the idea of two women having non-penetrative sex in which no semen was deposited made little sense. It was only by conceptualising the mechanics of lesbian sex within a heterosexual or at least wholly penetrative context, that it could be explained within a Galenic world view. In turn, this meant that any woman could become a tribade, but would be unlikely ever to develop to the extent that lesbian sex could be as fulfilling as the penetrative varieties.[14]

The presumption that lesbian sex could never be fully satisfying must provide one explanation for why the law apparently tolerated lesbian behaviour. If it could never be entirely satisfactory, it likewise could not represent a true threat to heterosexuality and hence patriarchy. This also helps to explain why the history of the treatment of male homosexuality and lesbianism are so different. Because male sodomy satisfied the requirements of penetrative sex – i.e. included penetration and ejaculation – it could be viewed as a positive alternative to heterosexual penetration. Indeed, because the passive partner absorbed male semen, it might be considered more satisfying than, and hence uniquely dangerous to, heterosexual sex. Lesbian sex could not be conceptualised in these terms. Even if penetration occurred a tribade could not produce fully active or concocted, and hence male, semen (see Chapter 5).

The other facet of both popular cultural and medical understandings of early eighteenth-century conceptions of both lesbianism and female sexuality of which we must be aware is the sexual aggression generally attributed to women. It was believed that once a woman had discovered the joys of sex, she would rapidly become insatiable. It is to this belief that we must attribute the characterisation of widows as particularly lascivious.[15] In the case of lesbians, it was generally believed that once the process of sexual discovery had commenced, once a woman had

begun to masturbate, the strong libido which was believed to characterise female sexuality would ensure that she would eventually choose
heterosexual penetrative sex over either lesbian love or lonely masturbation. It is to this logic that one must attribute the actions ascribed to
Fanny in Cleland's *Memoirs of a Woman of Pleasure*. The role of lesbian
sex in this novel is as a foretaste of and precursor to penetrative
heterosexual activity. In this context lesbian love is neither dangerous
nor offensive because it is made clear that fingers and tongues cannot
replace the penis.[16]

Of course these characteristics and forms of understanding were in
the process of change and, while both plebeian and elite women had
recourse to these assumptions throughout the century, they were being
gradually replaced by a very different world view which would have
extreme consequences for the presentation of and contemporary understandings of lesbians and lesbianism. The eighteenth century saw both
the decline of the idea of women as aggressively lascivious, and the rise
of the belief that they were likely to be sexually passive. It was in the
eighteenth century that the medical profession concluded that women
did not need to have an orgasm in order to conceive, and in which male
and female genitalia became irrevocably separated into naturally different types of organs. In the process, and by the end of the century, at
least elite medical belief had confirmed the illusory nature of tribady
and the rare peculiarity of hermaphroditism. Over the course of the
century, therefore, two categories used to characterise lesbian women
had been largely eliminated, and the 'nature' of women redefined to
ensure that they would be conceptualised as the passive objects of male
sexual desire.[17] It is against this background that our understanding of
the main historiographical traditions which characterise lesbian history
must be placed.

* * *

Perhaps more than any other form of sexuality, the lack of evidence,
either in terms of pregnancy or legal persecution, has allowed historians
to deny the existence of lesbian love in past generations. In consequence
the familiar creation myth for sexual behaviour, in which late nineteenth-century sexologists named and then defined forms of sexual
'inversions' which then somehow brought into being people willing to
identify themselves with these terms, has survived more fully in relation
to lesbianism than to any other equivalent category of individuals. As a
result, one is left with a historiography which until recently has looked
to homosocial relationships among women as a pre-history to lesbian

activity, but which has tended to deny the physicality of past female friendships.

The starting point for much of this literature, and still the only comprehensive history of Anglo-American lesbianism in the early-modern and modern periods, is Lillian Faderman's *Surpassing the Love of Men*.[18] In this volume Faderman places great emphasis on the rise of the idea of 'romantic friendship', spending much of the book charting the development of a cult of female friendship between the late seventeenth and mid nineteenth centuries. Against this tradition she juxtaposes female libertinism, which she identifies as a seventeenth-century phenomenon which is only incidentally lesbian in character, and the gradual development in the nineteenth century of a medical/scientific belief in the possibility of sexual 'inversion'.

For Faderman, the eighteenth century witnessed a flowering in 'romantic friendship'. A positive fashion was created in which a high-flown emotional language was deployed for the expression of women's feelings for other women. The exemplars for this type of friendship were the 'Ladies of Llangollen'. These were two well-educated and wealthy women who eloped with the help of friends and relatives in 1778. Sarah Ponsonby and Eleanor Butler lived most of their lives in highly publicised retirement, dressed at least partially in male attire, and entertained a constant string of the great and the good of late-eighteenth- and early-nineteenth-century literary society.

Eleanor Butler and Sarah Ponsonby worked very hard to create around themselves an image of Edenic splendour, and of high-brow other-worldliness, far removed from the demands of the flesh. And for the most part they succeeded. Certainly their example was lauded by commentators as rigidly correct as Edmund Burke. Although attacked for their same-sex relationship in 1791, they nevertheless became the acceptable face of female friendship, and in turn created a model for romantic friendship in general. Elizabeth Mavor, in her biography of the Ladies of Llangollen, goes so far as to define romantic friendship in terms which epitomise the experience of these two women, suggesting it was characterised by '"retirement", good works, cottages, gardening, impecuniosity, the intellectual pursuits of reading aloud and the study of languages, enthusiasm for the Gothick, journals, migraines, sensibility and often, but not always the single state'.[19]

While even Faderman admits the suspicion that lesbian sex was available to late-eighteenth-century people, citing the homophobic and generally vicious comments of Hester Thrale Piozzi, the mainstream of powerful female friendships is thoroughly cleansed of any possibility of genital contact and left to the charms of sighs and love letters.[20]

While the accuracy of the emphasis placed on non-genital love within this literature is open to question, it is important to note the chronology generally associated with the rise of romantic friendship. Both in an English and American context the 1760s and 1770s are seen as central to the process of creating these relationships. The rise of 'sensibility', of early romanticism and the Gothic are each associated with this trend, which is then seen to strengthen and deepen over the course of the next century – only late in the nineteenth century merging with phenomena such as the Boston marriage. It is also associated with the rise of the 'passionless' woman of late-eighteenth- and early-nineteenth-century ideology.[21]

* * *

More recently there has been a reaction to this historiographical tradition. In the works of Emma Donaghue and Terry Castle, among others, can be found a much more robust analysis of the activities of eighteenth-century women. Emma Donaghue, in particular, has brought together a rich collection of sources which paint a very different picture from that described by writers on romantic friendship. Using primarily literary and theatrical sources, Emma Donaghue has begun to sketch out a model of eighteenth-century lesbianism that contains a number of different strands. The tradition of cross-dressing and female marriage, both in a theatrical and more day-to-day context, is explored, as is libertinism, and the existence of a large number of homosocial communities, particularly of an elite variety. What Donaghue postulates, drawing on a number of earlier theorists, is the existence of a lesbian continuum, stretching from non-sexual female friendship through explicit sexual relationships, including a variety of both types of couples and groups of women, whose sexual preferences range from bisexuality to non-penetrative lesbian sex, to individuals who regularly took on more explicitly masculine roles by adopting strap-on dildos and extreme gendered behaviour.[22]

What Donaghue has done is create a celebration of the variety of lesbian love possible in an eighteenth-century context. She demonstrates this continuum by pointing to people like Charlotte Charke, the daughter of Colley Cibber, who cross-dressed throughout most of her adult life and who shared her life with a much-loved female companion for many years, and Anne Damer, Horace Walpole's niece and heir.[23]

Damer was notoriously linked with the comic actress Elizabeth Farren in the 1780s and '90s, and became the object of widespread gossip. In 1794 a pamphlet appeared which commented on Elizabeth Farren's attitude to a prospective marriage:

> her amorous passions are far from being awakened by the idea. Superior to the influence of MEN, she is supposed to feel more exquisite delight from the touch of the cheek of Mrs. D—r, than from the fancy of any *novelties* which the wedding night can promise.[24]

The existence of these types of characters, and gossip, along with the outraged comments of contemporary prudes such as Hester Thrale Piozzi, create an image of sexual possibility which is a great distance from the world of platonic friendship preferred by Lillian Faderman.

There is also the suggestion of the beginning of a lesbian subculture in London. The use of the slang term 'tommy' to describe lesbians is well attested from the mid-to-late eighteenth century, while the comment contained in the 1749 pamphlet, *Satan's Harvest Home*, that the 'Game of Flats' was commonly played at Twickenham has been taken to suggest the beginnings of a public awareness of a lesbian subculture.[25]

But the body of evidence and the scholarly work which has most thoroughly defined the difference between these two traditions is that associated with the journals of Anne Lister. In both the volumes edited by Helena Whitbread, and in the work of historians such as Terry Castle, a whole new perspective on lesbian sexuality as it existed at least at the end of our period can be found.[26]

Anne Lister was born to a slightly down-at-heel Yorkshire gentry family in 1791. She was well educated, active, assertive, well travelled and sophisticated. She did not become sexually active until just after the precise end of our period, but her experience is the best, indeed the only, documented and detailed English lesbian life history we have for any period before 1900. And what is revealed in her journals is a remarkable picture of a homosocial world, a world filled with upper-class women, with money and energy, who flirt and seduce each other, and who at least occasionally dedicate themselves to the exclusive love of women.

Anne Lister had numerous lovers over the course of her life, most of whom were of her own social class. She contracted venereal disease in the process, but continued to seduce women both within her group of intimates in Yorkshire and among her broader circle of friends in Paris. What is remarkable about Lister's story is that it all seems so normal.

Her advances are accepted, even anticipated, by her many friends and, while she is occasionally rejected, she is never denounced as unnatural or perverted. To quote just briefly from her voluminous journals gives a flavour of the kind of world she inhabited and the extent to which lesbian behaviour was at least tolerated by upper-class and middling-sort English women at the end of our period. Recording her experience of seducing a young English widow, a Mrs Barlow, at her pension in Paris, Lister wrote:

> I begin to rather flirt with her but I think she has no consciousness of it, or why she begins to like [me]. I spoke against a classical education for ladies in general. It did no good if not pursued & if [it was], undrew a curtain better for them not to peep behind. Having all along told her I should not marry.[27]

While Lister's lack of subtlety is striking, her success is even more so. Within a matter of weeks Anne's relationship with Mrs Barlow had changed, and she was describing interviews a of very different sort:

> Very soon after she came, she lay on the bed. . . . She got in and I had my arms round her, she lying [with] her back to me, my right leg under and left leg over, her. I got a hand towards her queer by degrees. She so turned round, that my left hand got to her very comfortably and by degrees I got to feel and handle her.[28]

In combination with Lister's use of an evocative slang in which 'gone to Italy' meant full sex, and 'grubbling' meant masturbating her partner, an image of sexually aware and alive women is created which is at wide variance with the platonic content of romantic friendship.

There is, however, one major difficulty with this historiography of a 'lesbian continuum'. It presents no model of change. One of Donaghue's most fervently argued points is that she can identify no substantive developmental process during the course of the eighteenth century, and instead argues that all of the categories and possibilities she describes were available to most women throughout the century.[29]

Nor does the literature based on Anne Lister's journals help in this regard. The unique nature of the source, and its very private form, allows historians either to argue for the singular nature of Lister's experience or to suggest that she is in fact reasonably typical of a large number of women.

A further difficulty with this literature, as well as that on romantic friendship, is the overwhelmingly upper- and middle-class bias of the evidence adduced. While the restrictions associated with researching a topic which seems to have left little trace on the historical record can account for some of this bias, there has been a marked lack of work on the attitudes towards lesbianism in popular culture and amongst the labouring poor. We know a reasonable amount about the behaviour of a few London actresses, and a collection of well-researched cross-dressers, but of the vast majority of women who participated in homosocial friendships we know nothing.

In part this is a reflection of the politics of lesbian history. The need to present positive models has discouraged historians from looking for their foremothers amongst the illiterate, ill educated and criminal.[30] But continental scholarship is beginning to demonstrate the existence of lesbian communities among the very poor, and to identify clusters of spinsters living together. Indeed, with the exception of Anne Lister's love affairs, perhaps the best-documented set of lesbian relationships in eighteenth-century Europe is found amongst a group of poverty stricken and pauperised women in 1790s Amsterdam. A vicious murder motivated by jealousy ensured that an account of this group of women would survive, but there is no reason to suppose that its inhabitants are less typical than the educated women known to Anne Lister.[31] And in the English context it is important to remember that just as male homosexuality was likely to flourish in the homosocial worlds of the Navy and Army, lesbian relationships might likewise flourish amongst the huge number of women who were regularly forced into the equally homosocial world of the workhouse and house of correction. Approximately 50 per cent of the population of English workhouses in the eighteenth century was made up of adult women, compared to 20 per cent adult men. By the end of the third quarter of the eighteenth century upwards of forty-five thousand adult women were sharing beds and huddling to keep warm in these institutions. Amongst this variegated population it is difficult accept that no 'grubbling' took place late at night.[32]

Even outside the workhouse, both servants and independent women were likely to share accommodation and sleeping quarters. And while it is perhaps fanciful to assume that just because people slept together they had sex together, it is likewise difficult to believe that a proportion of the female population didn't progress from the almost mandatory hug and kiss at night to more profound forms of sexual satisfaction.[33]

Equally problematic from the point of view of the historian of lesbianism is the extent to which this literature depicts sexuality as being innate rather than constructed. Much of the most recent literature concentrates on describing the range of identities available to lesbians, while refusing to suggest a chronological framework for their development. This has proved possible, in part, as a result of the apparent non-existence of a well-developed subculture, the history of which would force historians of the lesbian experience to address the issue of chronological development. But in the process it has meant that there remains no accepted historical time frame for the evolution of lesbianism.

There is not, however, any lack of recognised developments in the language and categories deployed to describe lesbian and more generally female sexuality, the chronology of which at least hints at a process of historical change. Women at the beginning of the eighteenth century for instance (and women of the labouring poor throughout our period) were regularly informed that they possessed a dangerous and lascivious sexuality which was likely to overcome their better judgement at any moment. The existence and subsequent decline of this belief provides one measure of a lesbian identity. We must assume that women took these views seriously as descriptions of their own sexuality. But at the same time they were also continually reminded of the dire consequences of pregnancy, in terms of the cruel ostracism frequently heaped upon bastard-bearers, as well as the financial and social result. The conflict this must have created within women themselves should not be underestimated – and the extent to which lesbianism provided a physically safer and socially more acceptable (or at least socially opaque) alternative to non-marital heterosexuality should not be discounted.

By the end of our period, the rise of 'romantic friendship' had provided an alternative language in which to describe female relationships, and while it is certain that, for many, romantic friendship was simply the public face of a very physical love – without her journals, Anne Lister's relationships would look very much like 'romantic friendships' – we likewise need to take seriously the extent to which the ideology of romantic friendship created a set of categories in which upper-class women, in particular, could situate themselves. In part romantic friendship had the effect of legitimising same-sex relationships, but more than this it provided an identity for women who loved other women. At the same time, it created a link between lesbians and the broader female culture of the upper class and middling sort of the eighteenth century. In sharp contrast to the impact of the development of a male homosexual subculture, which starkly separated off gay men from their heterosexual contemporaries, the rise of romantic friendship ensured that lesbianism remained an acceptable facet of female society.

What begins to emerge is the possibility that the eighteenth century witnessed a broad transition from one sort of lesbianism to another, from lascivious woman to romantic friend, and although both are equally physical, they are not in fact the same.

* * *

Before attempting to describe this developmental process and its relationship to other types of sexualities we need to look at one final literature, which is at least tangentially involved in the development of lesbianism – that on female cross-dressing. The sheer numbers of women who chose to dress as men, and who were subsequently written about in popular pamphlet and newspaper accounts in the eighteenth century, is remarkable. In the Netherlands 119 cases have been identified, and while similar comprehensive research is yet to be undertaken in relation to England, anecdotal accounts suggests a similar number of cases could be found.[34] Equally remarkable is the high profile given to female cross-dressers in the public and popular culture of the eighteenth century. Female pirates, cross-dressed soldiers and false husbands were all the subjects of ballads, plays and pamphlets. In one twenty-year period, 1760–80, Antony Simpson has identified nine reports of different female cross-dressers, and while not all of these women cross-dressed in order to pursue lesbian relationships, their prominence and the positive way in which they are generally presented provided another category in which lesbians could place themselves.[35]

The historiography of this phenomenon in England has tended to stress the extent to which it is part of a literary genre in which heroines are given licence to perform feats of bravery, and in which a kind of theatrical transgression can be acted out without undermining the sharp divisions between the roles of the two genders. In the work of Julie Wheelwright and Dianne Dugaw a pantheon of characters is presented, each of whom seems calculated to valorise women while not attacking directly the structures of patriarchy. By extension this theatrical transgression has been related to the tradition of masquerade, and through that to the heart of eighteenth-century perceptions of the nature of order and disorder.[36]

Regardless of the literary role of this genre and the stories of which it is comprised, the lives of a number of women can be reconstructed through it. Ignoring the larger-than-life histories of people like Hannah Snell, the cross-dressed soldier and popular entertainer of mid-century, or the more problematic male/female/male cross-dresser, the Chevalier

D'Eon,[37] there were a number of very ordinary women who chose to live their lives in male attire.

One of the most successful of these women was Mary East, who, with a young friend and £30 of capital, decided in 1730 to create a 'marriage'. After the flip of a coin these friends decided that Mary East should become James How. The couple, now pretending to be man and wife, moved to Poplar and became inn-keepers. In this capacity they lived together for the next thirty-six years, James How serving in most of the parish offices and attracting only occasional comment.

Eventually someone from their home town recognised How and blackmailed her, but it was really only when the 'wife' died that the disguise and arrangement fell apart. The whole situation eventually came out in court at the trial of the would-be blackmailer.[38]

From the perspective of the twentieth century, the surprising thing about this story is that almost nobody suspected the disguise or, alternatively, nobody was willing to make a fuss about it.

Probably even more typical of the experience of women cross-dressers in the eighteenth century is the example of Theodora Verdion, a London book-dealer and exchange merchant. Born in Berlin, but having emigrated to London in her early twenties, Theodora Verdion lived for thirty-four years as a man until her death from breast cancer in 1802. The early-nineteenth-century account of her adoption of a male persona is plausible:

> During the seven years' war . . . she did a great deal of business, and was to be seen every day from one counting-house to another, all through the city. In dirty weather she began to wear boots, and with two large bags on each arm, though she had not then thrown by the dress of a female, cut a very remarkable figure. At the end of the war, she had more than doubled her capital: she then went again to Bayreuth, in Prussia; but when she returned, appeared altogether in man's attire, dressed like a huntsman: – This was in 1768 . . .

The gradual transformation, and her occupation on the very edge of the range of those acceptable for women, suggest at least one of the reasons cross-dressing might be popular. What is perhaps more important in this context is the fact that she seems to have been accepted as a local character, despite the fact that many of her acquaintances must have known her biological sex. On at least one occasion, while drunk, she allowed a group of companions to undress her, but she was likewise allowed to resume her disguise. The occasion for the publication of the account came only with her death from breast cancer and the public declaration her disease entailed.[39]

Rudolf Dekker and Lotte van de Pol, in their work on cross-dressing in early-modern Europe, have suggested that the adoption of male attire provided lesbians with an intellectual category through which to understand their sexual attraction to women. They have argued that in the process of changing their external appearance, cross-dressers were adopting a role which allowed them to pursue women.[40] In many ways this is a convincing argument that is supported by the internal logic of early-eighteenth-century medical thinking with its mutable gender categories and ambiguities. But there is another element of this phenomenon of which we must keep sight. For what is perhaps most remarkable about each of the numerous cases of cross-dressing in our period is that, first, so few people noticed and, second, so few people were upset about it. In an age when every new invention required a law in order to make its theft a capital crime, the complete absence of any attempt to legislate against cross-dressing is indicative of a degree of tolerance which later centuries would find difficult.[41] And while the ambiguous nature of early-eighteenth-century medical expectations around sexual division may explain some of the selective seeing involved, it cannot explain the experience of someone like Theodora Verdion.

After the turn of the nineteenth century the literature on cross-dressing goes into marked decline. And while we cannot be certain that large numbers of nineteenth-century women did not disguise themselves as men, it is clear that they were not caught at it and certainly were not celebrated for it. What one is left with, therefore, is a phenomenon, or a tolerance of a phenomenon, which dies out during a period which saw the rise of the 'passionless' woman, and of separate spheres ideology

* * *

It is, of course, impossible to chart the history of actual lesbian behaviour. We can gain almost no insight into the popularity or otherwise of lesbian sex from the information we have. What we can do, however, is begin to chart the ways in which patterns of tolerance and sexual assumption changed, in turn influencing the categories of identity available to lesbians. By simply juxtaposing the dominant ways of thinking about women's sexuality at the beginning and end of the century, a developmental process begins to emerge.

The popularity of cross-dressing, when combined with the 'one body' model of reproduction and women's bodies, suggests a highly physical and yet open and mutable set of categories within which both society and individual women could view lesbian behaviour. Hermaphrodites and tribades were 'normal', and if we can read a level of tolerance from the treatment of cross-dressers during much of the century, then they too were, at the very least, commonplace. These categories in turn would have the effect of pushing female sexuality in specific directions. Each of them gave credence to and placed emphasis upon quasi-heterosexual forms of love-making. The frequent mention of strap-on dildos and strongly gendered role-play within relationships amongst the few lesbians identified in the early part of the century would support this conclusion. In other words, following the ideas of historians such as Dekker and van de Pol, the intellectual categories available at the beginning of the century suggested that lesbian couples should in some ways mimic heterosexual sex. And precisely because early-eighteenth-century sexual behaviour was characterised by a strong non-penetrative emphasis, heterosexuality retained at least a passing relevance for women who loved women.

By the end of the century, with both the growing importance of romantic friendship and the idea of the 'passionless' woman, a new category and a new identity had become available. This new romantic lesbianism had the very modern characteristic of defining itself in opposition to heterosexuality. In the process it is likely (although not really demonstrable) that sexual behaviour changed, that mutual masturbation became more important and gendered role-play less so. In part, this development must be seen as a reaction to the changing nature of heterosexuality. As heterosex became more penetrative and more sharply characterised by extreme forms of gendered division, the applicability of its models and examples to lesbian love fell away.

In other words, the history of eighteenth-century lesbianism is one of a transition from mock-heterosexual to romantic forms, in the process of which change new varieties of self-identity were created. In part this was a response to changes in heterosexuality itself but, more importantly, it was part of a broader process of redefining both men and women, masculinity and femininity. In the end, lesbian relationships came to take on many of the characteristics increasingly imputed to women in general: sensitivity, emotional empathy and a deeply hidden sexuality.

The history of heterosexuality is characterised by the rise of phallocentric and mandatory marriage. It suggests that more people were encouraged to define themselves in terms of a sexuality dependent upon finding the other, 'opposite' sex attractive; a sexuality in which procreative, penetrative sex became the only allowable form of genital contact.

The more open heterosexual definitions and forms of the beginning of the century were being replaced by closed categories and strictly regulated activities.

As a result lesbian behaviour, at least imaginable within the context of early-eighteenth-century heterosexual models, was de-legitimised by the rise of a purely phallocentric and mandatory sexuality. Whereas at the beginning of the century it was possible for lesbians to think of their love-making in heterosexual terms, by the end this was no longer the case. Romantic friendship, therefore, became an important new category through which to express forms of sexual behaviour and feeling which could no longer be held within an increasingly sharply defined heterosexual framework.

7 Sexual Fear and the Regulation of Society

In late May 1748 Elizabeth Edwards was called before two Justices of the Peace for Middlesex to swear to the paternity of her bastard child. In response to the formulaic questions of her interlocutor Elizabeth did not retail the story of seduction and abandonment her audience wanted to hear. Instead she told them:

> ... that on the eleventh day of April last past she this Examinant was delivered of a male bastard child in the workhouse of the parish of Chelsea ... [who] was unlawfully begotten on her body by one Richard Jones of Chelsea Waterman, who had carnal knowledge of her body the first time, at the dwelling house of the said Richard Jones at Chelsea aforesd about three years agoe, at wch time this Examinant nursed his wife in her Lying-In – And this examinant says frequently afterwards in the said house and other places; and particularly at an apartment of her sister Mary's in Chelsea park, untill she proved with child by him and several times after – And this Examinant also says that the said Richard Jones is the true Father of the said Child and further says not. The mark of Elizabeth Edwards ... [1]

As a result of her honesty, Elizabeth was seldom able to coax the parish into providing her with the necessities she and her children needed. She entered the workhouse several times during the 1740s, but was ordered to quit the house on at least four occasions, and was never able to collect a pension in her own right. Even in the matter of a pair of shoes she requested four days before Christmas, a date which would argue for her need, she was turned down flat.[2] In a very real sense she had refused to conform to the model of female sexual passivity which lay at the heart of eighteenth-century social policy, and she paid a substantive price as a result.

This chapter will look at both the reality of one aspect of female plebeian sexual experience, prostitution, and the changing content of the highly emotive discourses surrounding prostitution, rape and the social policy of sexuality more generally. By contrasting the reality of women's experience with the changing stratagems and content of social policy this chapter will examine one mechanism through which femininity, masculinity and heterosexuality were transformed over the course of the eighteenth century. It will explore both the bitter reality of prostitution, and the dark chimera of social disorder created by middle-class reformers out of this raw material and which in turn impacted upon the lives and behaviour of women in general.

* * *

Of all eighteenth-century social problems prostitution seems the most familiar. Indeed, most of us owe our images of prostitution and prostitutes to eighteenth- and nineteenth-century literature. The bawd and libertine, the sympathetic tart and plush brothel are all stock elements of the eighteenth-century novel. But recent work on the history of prostitution has begun to force us to question these images, and to recognise the extent to which the literature which purports to explain the topic has traditionally been based either on images drawn from pornography, or else from the records and perspectives of, generally male, moralists set upon presenting a social problem, rather than examining the lives of individual women.[3] There have been until recently few attempts to examine prostitution from the perspective of the women and men for whom it formed either the basis of their economic existence or a major site of sexual activity.

Indeed, one can justifiably argue that the category of 'prostitute' is itself largely a construction of the sexual fantasies of pornographers and moral reformers. For, while there were certainly women who sold sex for money in most communities throughout the eighteenth century, it is much less certain that the women and communities involved would see themselves and these individuals in the stark light of a professional prostitute. In both rural and urban contexts the extent to which one sold sex as part of an economy of makeshifts – as a normal part of a wide-ranging set of economic and social activities – should not be underestimated. And while seventeenth- and eighteenth-century pornography is awash with professional women and brothels, these are increasingly coming to appear the standard and mythical backdrops to sexual fantasy, rather than the content of a realistic history of prostitution. In a similar way, the resolutely urban character of modern, and early-modern, images of prostitution should not blind us to the role of commercial sex in rural and provincial society.[4] We see urban prostitution distinctly because moral reformers have constructed it as a social problem. On reflection, however, few people would argue that the commodification of sex is somehow incompatible with rural society – especially in the highly capitalistic and moneyed countryside of eighteenth-century England.

The greater quantity of available evidence, regardless of its perhaps dubious origin, has, however, ensured that most work on the topic is about urban prostitution and, in Britain, about London. In a forthcoming book by Anthony Henderson a pattern of commercial sex in the capital has begun to emerge.[5] And while the metropolitan bias of this and similar works is frustrating, we can now begin to discern an outline of the experience of women for whom prostitution was an element of their economic existence. What Henderson and others have found is a more prosaic and believable world of commercial sex than that purveyed by moral reformers and pornographers.

Perhaps the most significant thing to note is that most prostitutes worked for themselves. Far from being organised by bawds and procuresses, prostitutes generally worked the streets in pairs, renting a room or using a quiet back street as and when required. Bagnios and bawdy houses were available, but the organisation of the trade was almost entirely left in the hands of the women involved. Pimping, in the modern sense of the term, was relatively uncommon, while the activities of the few procuresses who can be identified were deeply resented, at least by the broader public.[6] Indeed, when Mother Needham, one of the few procuresses who seem to fit the caricature, was exposed in the pillory in 1730 she was pelted to death by an angry crowd.[7]

In other words, prostitutes had a surprising degree of autonomy, and were quite capable of defending themselves against the depredations of the law and of social reformers. The sorts of attitudes and degree of self-confidence possessed by prostitutes is hinted at by the names recorded in watch books of the capital. When a watchman arrested a prostitute he had to record her name. The watchbooks of St James's Westminster list names like 'Ann Nothing', 'I'll tell you my name tomorrow', 'Won't tell you, damn my eyes' and the more prosaic 'Kis my Comekel'.[8] While this disrespect for authority may reflect desperation, it must also be a part of a broader self-confidence.

More than their autonomy and relative independence, prostitutes in the capital seem to have participated in a common life-cycle choice. The most reliable figures available suggest that most prostitutes were between the ages of fifteen and twenty-five.[9] They came from poverty stricken homes and were most likely to intersperse periods of life in service or in the largely female occupations of milliner, mantua-maker or haberdasher (trades which themselves were becoming increasingly uncertain as a result of the rise of the London season) with time spent on the street. Indeed Daniel Defoe came closest to an accurate description of the organisation of prostitution when he described the life-style as 'amphibious'.[10]

If we juxtapose these characteristics with what we know about poor women in the capital in general, the extent to which prostitution formed an element of the life experience of many women, or to which prostitutes were at least an integral part of plebeian society, becomes clear. The period in a woman's life when she was most likely to participate in prostitution, between fifteen and twenty-five years of age, was also the period of greatest economic insecurity for many women. Analyses of workhouse records, for example, demonstrate that while all women made substantive use of workhouse provisions, women in this younger group did so in circumstances that were particularly desperate, and at least tangentially connected to a world in which economic despair and sexual irregularity were the norm. Out of 4,400 entries into the Chelsea workhouse made between 1743 and 1766, some 468 represent adult women under the age of twenty-five, almost a quarter of whom were pregnant, generally with an illegitimate child – while many others were referred on to the Lock Hospital for the treatment of venereal disease. They spent, on average, longer in the workhouse than other equivalent groups, and were more likely to return to the house at a future date. All of this suggests the profound degree to which plebeian women in this age group were subject to deep economic insecurity.[11] Similarly, the upper end of the age range identified among London prostitutes fits very neatly with the average age of marriage for women throughout most of our period. In other words, prostitution must be seen as a response to elements of the life experience of the vast majority of plebeian women, and is probably better conceptualised as one outpost of female sexual and economic experience, than as the separate and well-defined status of the sort created in the mind's eye by the writings of social reformers and moralists.

Most women whom moral reformers labelled prostitutes probably went on to marry and set up households – disappearing into the mass of the plebeian population. They do not seem to have been ostracised by either their male or female contemporaries – and, indeed, they probably saved part of their earnings with marriage in mind. In Chapter 3 it was noted that sexual experience was no bar to plebeian women contracting successful marriages. And, indeed, even mothers with illegitimate children could, in London at least, expect to go on in many cases to both service and marriage.[12] These possibilities seem to have been equally open to prostitutes as to women whose sexual activities were driven by physical desire rather than financial need.

Having said this, it should be noted that plebeian culture was far from tolerant of promiscuity or indeed sexual laxity of any kind which might lead to pregnancy. Work on Church Court and Quarter Session records has fully demonstrated the extent to which sexual reputation remained an important part of eighteenth-century plebeian and middling-sort women's self- and public image. And among the panoply of insults which were flung at and between women in this period, 'whore' and its variants were perhaps the most common. In 1736, for instance, when Sarah Griffiths and Mary Payne, two fellow servants in the household of Samuel Underhill, began to argue, the accusation which seems to have really stuck was Payne's suggestion that Griffiths was a 'common strumpet'. In this instance, women whose life experience would have been very similar to that of the average prostitute are very actively and self-consciously using an expression which suggests prostitution to insult one another, and in the process apparently setting themselves apart from such women.[13]

What analysis of these Church Court records has suggested is a very complex set of attitudes. On the one hand, it is increasingly apparent from the work of Martin Ingram, Laura Gowing and, for the early eighteenth century, Tim Meldrum that sexual reputation was part and parcel of a broader set of qualities needed by women to maintain their social standing; and, moreover, that to be called a 'whore' brought in question one's honesty, probity and personal ability, as much as one's sexual behaviour. On the other hand, it is impossible to ignore the fact that professional prostitutes were moving in and out of this plebeian culture while actively contravening one element of its most basic moral code. And while the best material relating to these issues is seventeenth century in origin – the role of the Church Courts, and hence the evidence available, becoming increasingly restricted in the hundred years after the Restoration – there is little doubt that sexual reputation remained of central importance to plebeian women in particular throughout the eighteenth century.[14]

In a similar way the popular culture of both men and women frequently demonised both prostitutes and disorderly houses. Attacks on supposed brothels were a common element of the Lenten activities of London's apprentices, and likewise many of the assaults on both prostitutes and bawdy houses associated with the various Reformation of Manners Campaigns seem to have had the active support of a wide plebeian audience. And while it is certain that these attacks were more complex and politically motivated than they might at first sight appear, there is no doubt of the profound ambivalence felt towards the prostitute, and the much more difficult to define 'whore', by plebeian society.[15]

It is perhaps too much to ask that popular culture and attitudes should be internally consistent. And there is no avoiding the real contradiction between the evidence of the acceptance of prostitution implied in the demographic and criminal court records, and the obvious cultural antagonism that the idea of prostitution and the disorderly behaviour implied by the term 'whore' could inspire. But what the history of eighteenth-century sexual regulation reflects, perhaps more than anything else, is the extent to which there is very little necessary relationship between the way sex, sexuality and in this case prostitution worked and the intellectual and social discourses constructed around them. We should, perhaps, therefore not be too surprised to find individual prostitutes accepted as neighbours and friends, while at the same time 'whores' and 'strumpets' are demonised, and bawdy houses attacked. And if these apparent contradiction can be found in the beliefs and attitudes of plebeians who would of necessity be familiar with the reality of the lives of prostitutes, it should come as no surprise to find that elite discourses around prostitution are at even greater variance with reality than was plebeian culture.

* * *

While there is very little evidence that the content of most prostitutes' lives changed during the eighteenth century, this same period witnessed a profound transformation in the way in which the broader society constructed and responded to the idea of prostitution. Over the course of the century, literary and sociological depictions of prostitutes changed. Explanations for why women might become prostitutes were transformed, as were the range of civic responses deployed to deal with the reality of prostitution. In other words, although prostitution remained largely unchanged, and while prostitutes themselves continued to emerge from and submerge themselves in a more general plebeian culture, much as they had always done, the 'idea' of the prostitute was created and re-created.

At the beginning of the century to become a 'whore', and again the problem of definition arises, was in the eyes of social-policy reformers a product of individual moral failure. As we have seen in Chapter 4, women were believed to be peculiarly lustful and physically desirous of sex from which they gained the hot and dry essence of male semen.

Most commentators, while occasionally acknowledging the force of poverty, lay the blame for prostitution upon the weakness and moral turpitude of women. The prostitute had literally chosen, or been allowed to choose, sensuality over sensibility, sin over virtue, and her fate was therefore largely her in own hands. Or, in Peter Lake's words, 'In the person of the whore . . . [contemporaries found] the ultimate example of a sexuality freed from any of the constraining limits of familial or patriarchial power.'[16] Indeed, it is only in the 1730s that someone like Lady Mary Wortley Montagu could aver that 'Ladies of pleasure (very improperly so call'd) suffer more mortifications than any Nun of the most austere order that ever was instituted', and this in the context of a private letter rather than a public statement.[17] There was also a powerful belief that prostitutes had chosen idleness over industry, and Catholic luxury over Protestant frugality. These associations with both sin and idleness provide one explanation for why prostitution formed such a prominent target for the activities of the Societies for the Reformation of Manners in the 1690s and 1700s, which were, of course, themselves motivated by a providential religious understanding of social change.[18]

The significance of this early-eighteenth-century set of attitudes is profound. It ensured that prostitutes were viewed as aggressors. They were seen as criminals who deserved social retribution, rather than rehabilitation. It was not that their participation in illegal sex put them beyond the pale of normal society, but that their circumstance proved their own lack of moral worth. What an early-eighteenth-century attitude did was put prostitutes near an extreme end of a continuum of sins which encompassed the vast majority of the population and, in the process, ensured that they could be viewed both as deserving of imprisonment and corporal punishment, and at the same time as normal individuals similar to any other member of the general po-pulation.[19]

Gradually, however, over the course of the first half of the century, this set of stereotypes and assumptions began to change. The rise of the cult of seduction, changing understandings of female and male sexuality and a growing belief in the middle-class origins of many prostitutes all contributed to the creation of a new image of the 'fallen' woman.

Perhaps the most familiar element of these interlocking transforma-tions lies in the rise of the cult of seduction. Gradually over the course of the first half of the century the ideal history of the individual prostitute began to change. From being driven by lust, the prostitute became the victim of seduction at the hands of a generally upper-class man. Beginning life either as an innocent servant in a gentry household, or else as the impoverished, but middle-class, daughter of a half-pay officer or clergyman, the prostitute of mid-century and beyond was inevitably the victim of the honeyed words of a young rake who seduced and then abandoned the now ruined object of his attentions. The story is familiar from countless novels, Richardson's *Clarissa* forming a significant variation on the theme, but is also central to much of eighteenth-century pornography, and provides a major plot element of Cleland's *Fanny Hill* (see Chapter 2).[20]

In terms of social attitudes this represents a sea change in relation to female agency. From being an independent and lustful actor in her own tragedy, the story of seduction at the heart of the late-eighteenth-century stereotype turned women into passive foils for the activities of newly aggressive men. At the same time it transformed the social identity of the individual prostitute. From being an uppity servant, she became either the tragic daughter of a middle-class man or, at the least, the victim of the incompetence of the male head of household in which the seduction took place.[21]

Each of the components in this stereotype of seduction placed new onus on male activity and female passivity. Through the image of the seduced daughter of a half-pay officer or clergyman it made prostitution a social problem for the middling sort, while at the same time it helped to turn aggressive, sinful women into suitable objects of pity, charity and manipulation.

It is perhaps in this context that one can most clearly see the relative changes in masculinity and femininity which have formed a large part of the rest of this book. Within the concept of seduction lies the basic transformation which was to characterise the sexual self-image of all men and women. Gradually, over the course of the century women were encouraged to see themselves as passive, lacking sexual desire and instead focusing their whole sexual being on the one act of losing their virginity. Women went from a situation in which they were encouraged to believe themselves to be lustful and full of a barely controlled desire, to being sexually numb. At the same time, men who had begun the century being encouraged to believe that their own sexual desires could be easily controlled by their greater rationality and mental strength, who were being taught that they had a duty to be sexually responsible, ended the period being told that their sexual desires were largely beyond their control.

What the trope of seduction created was a situation in which it became increasingly possible to argue that women should be confined in the household in order to protect them from the newly rampant male sexuality. And while these stereotypes may have had their greatest impact on literature, their influence can likewise be found in the criminal and social construction of issues such as rape.

* * *

In the work of Anna Clark and Antony Simpson an historical account of the rise of a new attitude to rape is beginning to emerge. While there is no real evidence that the number or brutality of rapes actually changed, the courts' response to them appears to have done so, as did society's views of the victim. Anna Clark, in particular, has argued that fear of rape increased in the latter half of the eighteenth century; that from a situation in which rape was viewed as an equivalent to other forms of violent crime, it came to be set off to one side as a uniquely horrible event; and, more importantly, that this fear then ensured women remained in the household. Clark contends that because women in public came to be seen as possible victims of rape, and because male sexuality itself came to be seen as out of control, it could be thought justified to keep women off the streets in order to protect them. In other words, as with seduction, rape became a discursive mechanism through which female agency was limited. And although it was, of course, primarily working women who found themselves assaulted in the streets, or indeed elsewhere, as with seduction, it was in relation to women of the middling sort that these kinds of fears and expectations were worked out.[22]

Both of these changes are of a piece – the story of beliefs about prostitution and attitudes towards rape reflect similar attitudes towards masculinity and femininity, and by extension the power relationships contained within heterosexuality. But in order to develop a more detailed chronology of change, and to demonstrate some of the ways in which these changing intellectual currents impacted upon the lives of individual men and women, it is necessary to look at the changing pattern of institutional and legal responses to at least some of these forms of sexual, economic and violent behaviour. In London and most of the major provincial cities, and in the history of legislation, we can find a series of institutional and legal developments which reflect these changing discourses, and which likewise suggest one mechanism through which these elite nightmares of female danger were translated into social policy, and through social policy promulgated to women themselves.

* * *

The starting point for any history of the social policy of eighteenth-century sexuality must be the Reformation of Manners Campaign of the 1690s and early 1700s. Firmly established in the wake of the Glorious Revolution of 1688, Societies for the Reformation of Manners began to spring up first in London and then in most provincial cities from 1689. Motivated by religious millenarianism and a broader sense of urban crisis, and catalysed into existence by the accession of William and Mary, the societies were voluntary groupings of individuals set upon using the criminal justice system in order to prosecute blasphemy, Sabbath-breaking, disorderly houses and lewdness. Relying on the energy of both volunteers and paid informers, the societies actively persecuted and prosecuted thousands of primarily working people across urban Britain in the succeeding fifty years.[23]

In part, the nature of their objectives and activities was determined by the eighteenth-century criminal justice system. With no paid police and with prosecutions dependent upon individuals having sufficient time and wealth to pursue a malefactor, a society dedicated to prosecuting individuals made sense.[24] But what set these societies apart from later initiatives was their willingness to rely on Quarter Sessions and corporal punishment in order to discipline society. In other words, and this is particularly true in relationship to the persecution of prostitutes, the societies were more interested in punishment than reform, and hence were happy to rely on the creaking system of courts and bridewells to effect social discipline.

The other point that needs to be made about the societies is that they held a strong appeal for tradesmen and the lower-middling sort. These were not exclusively elite societies imposing their wishes on a distant urban problem. Instead, the societies were in some ways an outgrowth of the values and assumptions of a broad and inclusive London culture – a more organised version of the apprentice riots against bawdy houses.

If one looks at the societies through the lens of changing patterns of sexuality, what is significant is that they seem to have been attempting to order urban society, rather than transform the individuals involved. Likewise they were interested in a whole locus of interrelated problems which were less about sex *per se* and more about community. Like the definition of 'whore' or the seventeenth-century approach to sin itself, the societies analysed social problems as both inclusive and universal. They directed their efforts at the wide panoply of all sorts of sins, while at the same time seeming to assume that each individual had to be constantly on guard against their own sinful nature. The emphasis on disorderly houses and Sabbath-breaking, for example, was more about disciplining householders to participate in the main form of communal activity (the church) than about moral outrage at the sexual behaviour of individuals.

This early emphasis on social order changed significantly with the development of a range of voluntary organisations which came to take on the mantle of the societies. Where the societies had sought to discipline sinners, later organisations wanted to convert them.

It was noted in Chapter 4 that the Society for the Promotion of Christian Knowledge produced the first anti-masturbation tract in 1704. More than this, the Society, founded in 1698, represents the first successful voluntary reformatory organisation of a sort which was to dominate eighteenth-century social policy. Unlike the Societies for the Reformation of Manners, the SPCK was dedicated to the education of individuals in righteousness. A very secretive society made up of clergymen, gentry and merchants, the SPCK helped establish charity schools and workhouses, to reform prisons and to distribute cheap moralistic pamphlets. Throughout, there was a constant belief that once exposed to religion, prostitutes and idlers, blasphemers and drunkards would throw down the vices of their own oppression in order to grasp the self-evident rewards of virtue.[25]

But, in the process of adopting an actively reforming approach to individual sinners, the SPCK ensured that subsequent eighteenth-century social-policy initiatives would reflect the fears of social-policy reformers more completely than the reality of social disorder. By concentrating on the origin of sin, the Society gave new and vastly increased power to the stereotypes and discourses which characterised much of elite and middling-sort thinking about prostitution and sexual licence. In other words, the Society's assumption that individuals could be reformed ensured that later voluntary organisations would direct their efforts towards the mythical figure of the seduced virgin, rather than the real suffering (or indeed disorderly behaviour) of poverty stricken working women.

In the first instance, it was the SPCK's own favourite institutions which had the greatest impact on the lives of prostitutes. With the establishment of workhouses in most urban parishes throughout the country from the 1710s and 1720s, new institutional provision for the destitute was created. And although these houses were not designed with prostitutes in mind, there can be little doubt that many of the inmates had at some point sold sex for money. By 1776 a parliamentary inquiry could locate 1,916 workhouses, housing approximately 45,000 adult women, each institution attempting to teach religion and self-control to their inmates.[26]

* * *

While workhouses were in some ways the first substantive experiments in reform, the style for creating institutions which responded primarily to artificially created fear of particular types of social disorder reached its apotheosis at mid-century. There was, from around 1740 to the late 1750s, what might accurately be described as a crisis of social policy. A range of problems from gin to illegitimacy, from venereal disease to clandestine marriage seemed to hit society all at the same time, and at just the moment when new forms of charitable organisation became available. The responses elicited to these problems were various and substantial. The Lock Hospital, the Foundling Hospital and the Magdalen Hospital were all either founded or re-established in this period, while legislation directed at gin consumption, clandestine marriages and the suppression of bawdy houses was passed and implemented.[27]

There is little evidence, however, that gin was causing the kind of damage claimed for it. And while illegitimacy was certainly on the rise, as we have seen in Chapter 3, this was a gradual process which hardly merited the response it received. Likewise, with venereal disease and clandestine marriage – which were frequently associated with seduction – it was changing perception rather than a changing reality which brought these issues to boiling point.

One can, of course, point to growing urbanisation, the political insecurity associated with the Jacobite rising of 1745, imperial expansion and its attendant wars in order to explain these developments – a broader economic and political crisis made social problems seem worse.[28] But these influences seem to explain the timing of this crisis rather more effectively than its content. If we look briefly at some of these developments the shared and changing attitudes which underlay them will become clear.

The Foundling Hospital, established by Thomas Coram and opened in 1741, is perhaps the most typical example of these mid-century initiatives.[29] Supported by the great and good of London, the hospital was in part justified by a mercantilist analysis of the English economy – England needed a healthy population in order to export goods to the world. Illegitimate children were simply a readily available raw material to work with. But, as Ruth McClure has concluded, the children who were most likely to be admitted were those whose mothers conformed to a stereotype of seduction and abandonment – women like Mary Cole who applied on behalf of her child in 1768:

> The most humble Petition of Mary Cole, seduc'd & reduc'd and the Person who is the Cause of my Misfortunes has deceiv'd me and is gone abroad, by the best Intelligence I can have. He made me a promise of Marriage, with many Vows and Protestations, before I unhappily yielded to his Solicitations, by which I am now brought to this Miserable Condition, depriv'd of the Esteem and regard of my friends and relations, destitute of many Necessaries, ... Therefore, I humbly pray your Honours will have pity upon my unfortunate Case, and take my Child under your Protection, which will be means of preserving us both, for which Act of great Charity I shall ever in Duty be bound to pray. I am
>
> your Honours most unworthy and poor
distress'd hble. Servt.
Mary Cole.[30]

While raising healthy children may have been the hospital's justification, its impact was to give preferential treatment to women who could conform to a model of feminine behaviour in which seduction was the only justification for illegitimacy.

In a similar way, the Magdalen Hospital for Penitent Prostitutes, established in 1758, assumed and created a model of the prostitute largely at odds with reality.[31] And while this institution again justified itself in terms of the labour lost to the nation by the existence and degradation of prostitutes, it likewise appealed to and enforced a model of the prostitute as victim: 'A young creature perhaps is debauch'd at fifteen, soon abandon'd, quickly common, as quickly diseas'd, and as quickly loathsome and detested.'[32]

Once within the institution women were set a strict, monastic routine of silent labour and religious observation, which, in the view of the founders, would reinforce the penitence and humility that the objects of its charity were expected to possess already. Indeed, the first month or so in the hospital was spent in almost complete isolation, ensuring that the seductive forces which had driven these women to prostitution would be quickly forgotten. The reason this reformatory process was possible at all was that women had ceased to be the lustful actors on the urban stage they had been presented as half a century earlier, and instead had become the sexually numb victims of a combination of economics and a newly powerful male sexuality. By 1780 this development had progressed so far as to suggest to Martin Madan that male lust was so powerful, and female desire so quiescent, that polygamy was a workable solution to prostitution and adultery.[33]

The London Lying-In Hospital, the Asylum for Orphan Girls, the Lock Hospital and the Maternity Hospital were each founded in this period, and each contained this emphasis on women as victims or possible victims. Indeed, the resolutely female character of the vast majority of mid-century charitable foundations is noteworthy, and reflects, again, the extent to which women had come to be perceived as the new victims of society.

But this feminisation of social policy, and the fears which under-pinned it, was not restricted to the realm of voluntary charity. A brief examination of some of the legislation of the period will reveal a similar set of concerns and transformations.

Hardwicke's Marriage Act of 1753 is perhaps the best example of this. The effect of the Act was seriously to alter the nature of plebeian marriage. The Fleet and its provincial equivalents, which had been the location of choice for a high proportion of plebeian weddings, was set out of bounds at a stroke.[34] But the motivation behind the passage of the Act was less to do with the marriages of the poor, and much more to do with the seduction of the daughters of the middling sort and gentry. What comes through in clause after clause of the Act is a concern that the parents or guardians of the principles in a marriage should be given sufficient notice of and opportunity to object to a match. A single clause will suffice to give a sense of the purport of the Act as a whole:

> XI And it is hereby further enacted, That all marriages solemnised by licence ... where either of the parties ... shall be under the age of twenty one years, which shall be had without the consent of the father of such of the parties, so under age (if then living) first hath had and obtained, or if dead, of the guardian or guardians of the person of the party so under age, lawfully appointed, or one of them; and in case there shall be no such guardians or guardians, then of the mother (if living and unmarried) or if there shall be no mother living and unmarried, then of a guardian or guardians of the person appointed the court of *Chancery*; shall be absolutely null and void to all intents and purposes whatsoever.[35]

When it is considered that a simple statement of marriage by the principles had been sufficient to create a valid union under common law, the rigour of Hardwicke's Act and the extent to which it reflected real fear are apparent.[36]

In a similar way the Bawdy House, or Disorderly House, Act of 1752 was a profound over-reaction to a largely non-existent problem. In this instance the myth of the bawd and procuress seducing the daughters of the down-at-heel middle ranks became the driving force behind a substantive piece of legislation. As the prostitute herself was increasingly perceived as an innocent victim, the character of the bawd became more demonic. And while bawdy houses and brothels generally catered for the demand of the prostitutes themselves, rather than organising the trade, the keepers of these houses were the easy objects of middle-class fear. What the Bawdy House Act did was make it much easier to prosecute and regulate the owners of disorderly houses. It was renewed and made permanent in 1755, and at the time of its renewal it was praised for its effectiveness – although it is unclear who, if anyone, was actually prosecuted under its auspices.[37]

In one form or another all of the major innovations in eighteenth-century regulation of sexuality were in place by 1760. Prosecuting societies like the Societies for the Reformation of Manners were later re-established, under names such as the Proclamation Society and the Society for the Suppression of Vice. Institutions of various sorts were also founded throughout the latter half of the century, particularly provincial institutions following the model set by London at mid-century. But the fundamental transition which characterised the regulation of sexuality through social policy was the creation of the first half of the century, and amounted to the adoption of an image of women as victims.[38]

And while these developments were the product of the paranoid imaginations of the social-policy reformers, it must also be remembered that tens of thousands of women made use of these institutions, and hundreds of thousands more came into contact with their propaganda and diatribes. If, as in the case of Mary Cole, plebeian women knew the story their male audience wanted to hear, then it is little wonder if they chose to conform to it. And while it is impossible to gauge the extent to which they internalised the saccharin story of fallen womanhood demanded by charitable institutions, we should not underestimate the degree to which these institutional structures could impose behavioural norms on the population as a whole.

* * *

The experience of plebeian women, of prostitutes and the victims of rape did not change substantially over the course of the century. Prostitutes continued to be recruited from the poorest members of the female working class; driven by poverty and need to sell the one commodity for which they could get a reasonable price, their bodies. They continued to work largely for themselves, outside any organised system of brothels and pimps. Similarly, rape continued to be a domestic crime, in which the assailant and victim were known to each other and were likely to be of equal status. But above and beyond this a myth of victimhood was created, which, because of the changing nature of sin, could now be acted upon. Social-policy reformers paid little heed to the reality of the lives of working women and rape victims. But because they were possessed of the resources of eighteenth-century society, their myth was made real by the necessity of working people to conform to its lineaments and, in the process, begin to conform to a model of passive femininity which was both new and debilitating.

While eighteenth-century discourses concentrated on femininity, we should not forget that masculinity was also changing. Next to the story of increasingly passive, asexual womanhood, we must place that of the growing irresponsibility of male sexuality. Almost as a natural corollary to female lust, male probity had been assumed by early-eighteenth-century writers. Because men were rational beings, possessed of greater intellect and less subject to the vagaries of emotion, they were believed to be more able than women to control their sexual desires. But as women became the victims of seduction, men became the stooges of their own lust. Male desire gradually came to take on the characteristics of an uncontrollable natural force. A libertine ethic, combined with the creation of male sperm as the active physical force in reproduction, contributed to a set of ideologies which argued that individual men could in some ways no longer be held responsible for their own behaviour.

This, in turn, had at least one profound effect. It forced policy-makers and social commentators to abandon the idea that society could be ordered by reinforcing the probity of men, and instead encouraged the tendency to prevent sexual licence by policing the public roles of women. It is as yet unclear to what extent women's behaviour was actually constrained by these cultural and ideological developments on a day-to-day basis, but new restrictions on the lives of women could now be justified by pointing to the great danger women were supposed-ly under from the rampant sexuality of all men.

The sheer intellectual confusion which these transformations caused, the elision of desire and fear, of patronising order and social chaos, is perhaps best exemplified by the fictional description of Lord Baltimore's private brothel penned by Sophia Watson in 1768. In the midst of the signs of luxury – of alcohol and food, of plush fabrics and exotic dress – Watson lays out a set of rules and regulations. The times of waking and sleeping, of bathing and eating for each prostitute are set out in meticulous detail. To all intents and purposes this brothel had become a workhouse, with its diet sheets and reforming regimen. And, in the process, the varieties of order which social-policy reformers had sought to impose on the poor in general can be seen to have become so much a habit of mind that even the brothel, the site of greatest social disorder imaginable, can only be presented in their light.[39]

8 Conclusions

Summary [handwritten annotation]

In 1744 an isolated rural parish in colonial Massachusetts was rocked by scandal. The young men of the parish had obtained a copy of *Aristotle's Master-piece*, the quintessential eighteenth-century sex manual, and had used the information contained within it to huge and devastating effect. Calling the volume a 'Granny book', one of the young men, John Lancton, verbally assaulted three young women, Mary Downing, Moll Waters and Betty Jenks. Mary Downing later recounted how he had 'talked exceedingly uncleanly and Lasciviously so that [she] . . . had never heard any fellow Go so far' and 'after he was Gone We the young women that were there agree that we never heard any such talk come out of any mans mouth whatsoever . . .'.[1] What *Aristotle's Master-piece* had done, in this admittedly colonial example, was change the balance of sexual authority within this isolated community. A traditional form of female knowledge, the contents of a 'Granny book', had been given into the hands of a young man and, in the process, emboldened him to challenge the balance of authority and probity which had characterised sexual conduct and negotiation.

This book has been largely concerned with the conflicts and developments associated with this transfer of knowledge, and with the breakdown in traditional relationships which it caused. We have seen from a variety of perspectives the same kind of changes in the balance of sexual authority and behaviour.

In relation to the public discourses around sex, and to courtship behaviour, we have seen the early importance and relative decline of the role of the peer group in disciplining plebeian attitudes towards sex. In John Cannon's experience, for example, we saw the extent to which his sexual behaviour was profoundly circumscribed by both his friends and relatives and his own sense of sexual propriety. And, as importantly, we have seen how both the demographic record and the writings of later-eighteenth-century commentators suggest that forms of penetrative sex leading to pregnancy became more common. An exploitative sexual culture developed in which the risk of pregnancy for courting women became much more real.

110

Similarly, in relation to the body, we have seen how commentators gradually came to deny the significance of female physicality in reproduction. With the transition from a 'one body' to a 'two body' model, the nature of elite views of the role of both men and women changed. The female orgasm and sexual desire were essentially denied, while the importance of male sperm and lust was reified. In the process, men were liberated from the obligation to be responsible, while women were redefined as sexual victims, whose main interest should lie in reproduction rather than pleasure.

The reflection of these changes in the sexual relationships between men and women was likewise seen in the histories of both male homosexuality and lesbianism. The creation of a homosexual subculture and of rising homophobia provides evidence of a set of changing self-definitions, and of an increasingly defined and 'natural' set of heterosexual categories. As homosexual men came to adopt specific and generally effeminate forms of behaviour, newly heterosexual men were forced to eschew any form of activity which might cast doubt on their attraction towards women. Likewise, in the case of lesbian identities, we have seen the way in which the decline of female cross-dressing and the rise of romantic friendship can be seen as responses to the increasingly narrow set of behaviours available as a result of the rise of mandatory heterosexuality.

And finally, in relation to both prostitution and social policy we have seen the extent to which the irrational fears of the elite and middling sort were harnessed to transform sexual behaviour – helping to create a 'seduction myth' to which plebeian women were increasingly forced to appeal.

Each of these facets of the story of English sexualities in this period reflects a similar set of changes in the English culture of sex. And what emerges is a picture of eighteenth-century society which suggests that sex itself changed, and that people engaged in heterosexual activity increasingly restricted their behaviour to forms of phallocentric, penetrative sex which could be countenanced as procreative. In the process, the definitions of both 'masculinity' and 'femininity' changed. Both men and women were created as 'naturally' and biologically sexed, with an increasing onus, and this was particularly true for men, to restrict their behaviour to a heterosexual norm, and to find the other and now 'opposite' sex attractive. What occurred was not a liberation. For women it heralded a period of intense patriarchal oppression, but for men as well it reflected an increasingly restrictive form of masculinity, which was policed by a highly effective public and print culture.

Women were re-created as both socially and sexually passive, while men became sexually irresponsible and victims of their newly uncontrollable lust.

The outline of the story of this changing culture of sex is relatively clear. And while these transformations are a matter of degree rather than absolute and universal, we can confidently say that the early part of the century was characterised by a more negotiated set of sexual relationships, and the latter half by a more extreme, phallocentric culture. We have a much less clear idea why these transformations occurred.

Perhaps the most straightforward answer has been provided by demographic historians appealing to economic factors. Certainly, they have made a strong case for looking at the relationship between economic prosperity and industrial organisation, and age at marriage, bastardy rates and fecundity. This same kind of argument has also been made by historians working with anecdotal sources, such as Antony Simpson. He has argued that growing urbanisation and individual autonomy created many of the pressures which led to the rise of a homosexual subculture. But this kind of economic reductionism is not entirely satisfactory, and while it may provide the root force driving the essentially cultural transformations described in this volume, it cannot explain the panoply of fears, desires and memories from which a culture is constructed. Indeed, while making few claims for the relative importance of different explanatory strategies, this volume has identified two mechanisms through which economic and social change can be said to have transformed the content of English sexual culture, and hence behaviour. These are, first, the growth of a popular print literature in this period and, second, the rise of an urban philanthropy and social policy, largely built on literary and discursive practice, rather than experience.

In the case of the rise of a print culture, this undermined traditional forms of authority – women's authority in particular, but also the authority of parents, elders and peers. It waged war against the local community, and at the same time provided a mechanism through which the values and expectations of elite and middling-sort groups could be popularised to the poor. In the case of anti-masturbation diatribes and sex manuals, as much as religious pamphlets and homilies, a reformation of manners contributed to the replacement of assumptions based in oral culture with a new form of printed authority. And because the creators of this authority were generally men, and because men had greater access to it, this growing print culture had the effect of denigrating female knowledge and power.

In the case of John Lancton we have seen a rare example of evidence for the impact of this rising print culture, but we should not assume that this change was peculiarly characteristic of isolated communities and individuals. Adolescence, for both girls and boys, is largely about discovering and using forms of authority – especially in relation to sexual knowledge. In the case of this most intimate and frequently taboo subject, the impact of gaining knowledge through the well-thumbed pages of a copy of *Aristotle's Master-piece* or Culpeper's *Midwifery*, rather than from parents and friends, cannot be underestimated. And while no one would have drawn their views solely from printed sources, the addition of these new materials must have helped change the balance of knowledge and advice available to sexually active people in the eighteenth century.

The second agent in this social and cultural transformation identified in this volume is the rise of a more directed form of urban philanthropy and social policy. The Old Poor Law had, until the eighteenth century, been characterised by face-to-face relationships sited in the parish. This relationship changed as many urban parishes came to encircle populations numbering in the tens of thousands, as many large towns circumvented parochial authority to create city-wide institutions, and as philanthropists increasingly created hospitals and asylums with catchment areas covering whole sections of the country.

What had been a negotiated relationship, in which the behaviour and circumstances of each party were known, became a social policy in which an abstract ideal of virtuous behaviour was written into the rules of newly bureaucratic institutions. And while seventeenth-century overseers certainly had an opinion about the distinction between the deserving and undeserving, it was left to eighteenth-century projectors and bureaucrats to create detailed models of social victims. In the process, the victims they created were female. Increasingly, over the course of the century, resources were allocated to specific forms of victimhood. Bastard-bearers, reformed prostitutes and the syphilitic were catered for – encouraging poverty stricken women to present themselves as the people social policy was attempting to relieve. It is little wonder, if in the process these women came to believe the tales of seduction and denigration which were demanded of them by the middling-sort men who ran these institutions – forcing them to modify their behaviour as a result. And if the women believed them, it could provide nothing but encouragement to men to play their allotted role in the scene – to adopt the sexually irresponsible attitudes which were being urged on them from all sides, or, alternatively, and this seems particularly true in relation to evangelical masculinities, to construct their self-image around the ability to resist this increasingly powerful force leading men into sin and temptation.

Of course, these are only two additional explanatory strategies, neither of which is adequate in itself, and which do not replace the broader role of economic change in the explanation of historical transformation. And while they help to give some depth to the economic generalisations so often found in social history, or the simple description of discursive change which characterises so much of the modern literature associated with discourse theory, these suggestions are merely that. There are similar processes at work in relation to other facets of the linked set of transformations which characterise sexuality in this period. But, even given the preliminary and partial nature of the evidence currently available, we can confidently conclude that the nature of sex changed in the eighteenth century; and that a complex amalgam of economic and cultural forces, each individual strand of which affected all the others, created a kaleidoscopic pattern of seemingly coherent change in which phallocentrism and mandatory heterosexuality became increasingly dominant.

Notes

Chapter 1. Introduction: Sex before Discourse

1. *The French Prophetess Turned Adamite* (1707) pp. 21–2; quoted in H. Schwartz, *The French Prophets: The History of a Millenarian Group in Eighteenth-Century England* (Berkeley, Calif., 1980) p. 108. The original pamphlet description does not make clear the identity of the women involved, and the name of Elizabeth Gray is taken at the tentative suggestion of Hillel Schwartz.
2. A. Simpson, 'Masculinity and Control: The Prosecution of Sex Offenses in Eighteenth-Century London' (New York University, Ph.D. thesis, 1984) pp. 95–6.
3. For the best general account of the influence of psychoanalysis and the sexologists see J. Weeks, *Sex, Politics and Society: The Regulation of Sexuality since 1800*, 2nd edn (London, 1989) *passim*.
4. For significant contributions to the development of this literature see in particular D. Foxon, *Libertine Literature in England, 1660–1745* (New York, 1965); W.H. Epstein, *John Cleland, Images of a Life* (New York, 1974); R. Thompson, *Unfit for Modest Ears: A Study of Pornographic, Obscene and Bawdy Works Written or Published in England in the Second Half of the Seventeenth Century* (London, 1979); P. Wagner, *Eros Revived: Erotica of the Enlightenment in England and America* (London, 1988); L. Hunt, *The Invention of Pornography, 1500–1800* (New York, 1993). For an analysis of the development of pornography from a very different and imaginative perspective see W. Kendrick, *The Secret Museum: Pornography in Modern Culture* (New York, 1987).
5. The Cambridge Group itself adopts a 'cyclical' rather than 'whiggish' approach. Lawrence Stone's work on the family, however, represents a good example of a 'whig' approach: see his *The Family, Sex and Marriage in England, 1500–1800*, 1st edn (London, 1977); *Broken Lives: Separation and Divorce in England, 1660–1857* (Oxford, 1993); *Uncertain Unions: Marriage in England, 1660–1753* (Oxford, 1992); and *Road to Divorce: England, 1530–1987* (Oxford, 1990).

6. For a recent work on nineteenth-century sexuality see M. Mason, *The Making of Victorian Sexuality* (Oxford, 1994).
7. For Shorter's most substantive statement of this hypothesis see E. Shorter, *The Making of the Modern Family* (New York, 1975).
8. For the most accessible statement of Foucault's views on sexuality see M. Foucault, *The History of Sexuality: Volume 1: An Introduction* (London, 1976).

Chapter 2. The Public Cultures of Sex

1. Daniel Lysons, *Collectanea: or, a Collection of Advertisements and Paragraphs from the Newspapers, Relating to Various Subjects, Publick Exhibitions and Places of Amusement*, vol. IV (1840), British Library C.103.K.11., fol. 253.
2. *Records of the Most Ancient and Puissant Order of the Beggar's Benison and Merryland, Anstruther* (Anstruther, 1892) p. 9.
3. A typical pseudo-medical presentation was James Lunsdain's 'The Act of Generation' (1753) in which the mechanics of fertility are described, as well as a wide range of contraceptive techniques. Lunsdain concludes that fear of pregnancy is the main stumbling block to more widespread promiscuity. 'The Act of Generation' is reproduced in the *Supplement to the Historical Portion of the 'Records of the Most Ancient and Puissant Order of the Beggar's Benison and Merryland,' Being an Account of the Proceedings at the Meetings of the Society, Together with Excerpts from the Toasts, Recitations, Stories, Bon-Mots and Songs Delivered thereat* (Anstruther, 1892) pp. 45–54.
4. J.R. Gillis, *For Better, For Worse: British Marriages, 1600 to the Present* (Oxford, 1985), see in particular chapters 1 and 4.
5. *Ibid.*, pp. 175–7.
6. John Cannon, 'Memoirs of the Birth, Education, Life and Death of: Mr John Cannon. Sometime Officer of the Excise & Writing Master at Mere Glastenbury & West Lydford in the County of Somerset' (1743), Somerset Record Office MS DD/SAS C/1193/4, p. 53.
7. Written at the end of the first quarter of the nineteenth century, Francis Place's autobiography is full of self-righteous chagrin at his memory of the easy-going sexuality of the plebeian and artisanal London culture of his youth. See M. Thale, ed., *The Autobiography of Francis Place (1771–1854)* (Cambridge, 1972).
8. British Library, Place Papers, Add. MS 25144, fol. 182; quoted in J.R. Gillis, *For Better, For Worse*, op. cit., p. 176.

9. P. Clark, *The English Alehouse: A Social History, 1200–1830* (London, 1983), chapter 10, 'The Social World of the Alehouse: The Growth of Respectability 1660–1750'.

10. Greater London Record Office, 'St. Luke's Chelsea, Workhouse Register, 1743–1766', Microfilm, X/15/37, 'Rebecca Clements', 7 May 1748, 'Sarah Clements', 13 May 1748; Greater London Record Office, 'St. Luke's Chelsea, Settlement and Bastardy Examinations, 1733–1750', P74/Luk/121, 'Rebecca Clements', 29 April 1748.

11. M. Spufford, *Small Books and Pleasant Histories: Popular Fiction and its Readership in Seventeenth-Century England* (Cambridge, 1981).

12. *Ibid.*, see in particular chapter 7, 'Small Merry Books: Courtship, Sex and Songs', pp. 156–93.

13. Pepys' Library, Magdalen College, Cambridge, *Penny Merriments*, II (37), 'Cupid's Court of Salutations', fol. 898; quoted in M. Spufford, *Small Books and Pleasant Histories*, op. cit., p. 160.

14. For a discussion of Rousseau's attitudes towards sex see P.A. Weis, *Gendered Community, Rousseau, Sex, and Politics* (New York, 1993).

15. *Poor Robin's Intelligence, or, News from City and Country. On Fryday, July 17th. 1691* (London, 1691), number 2, British Library 816.m.19 (5). It should be noted that 'poor robin' was contemporary slang for a penis.

16. As a genre these works have been inappropriately ignored. For a recent treatment of them see P-G. Boucé, 'Chthonic and Pelagic Metaphorization in Eighteenth-Century English Erotica' in R.P. Maccubbin, ed., *'Tis Nature's Fault: Unauthorized Sexuality during the Enlightenment* (Cambridge, 1987).

17. *The Natural History of the Arborvitae, Tree of Life* (London, 1732), single sheet.

18. *Merryland Displayed: or, Plagiarism, Ignorance and Impudence, Detected. Being Observations upon a Pamphlet intituled A New Description of Merryland*, 2nd edn (Bath, 1741) p. 5.

19. While on this evidence Richard Manningham was an important popularizer of sexual knowledge, he is more frequently remembered as the founder of the first lying-in hospital in England in 1739. See A.H. Cash, 'The Birth of Tristram Shandy: Sterne and Dr Burton' in P-G. Boucé, ed., *Sexuality in Eighteenth-Century Britain* (Manchester, 1982) pp. 202 and 222 note 10.

20. *Merryland Displayed*, op. cit., pp. 36, 55.

21. *Flos Ingenii vel Evacuatio Discriptionis. Being an Exact Description of Epsam, and Epsam Wells* (1674), single sheet, British Library 816.m.19 (40).

22. P. Wagner, 'The Veil of Medicine and Mortality: Some Porno-graphic Aspects of the *Onania*', *The British Journal for Eighteenth-Century Studies*, VI (1983) 179–84.

23. P. Wagner, *Eros Revived: Erotica of the Enlightenment in England and America* (London, 1988) pp. 8–15.

24. John Cannon, 'Memoirs', op. cit., pp. 41–2. For an excellent American case of the impact of this kind of literature on an isolated com-munity see R. Thompson, *Unfit for Modest Ears: A Study of Porno-graphic, Obscene and Bawdy Works Written or Published in England in the Second Half of the Seventeenth Century* (London, 1979) pp. 163–4.

25. Porter has recently summarised his extensive article output on this subject in R. Porter and L. Hall, *The Facts of Life: The Creation of Sexual Knowledge in Britain, 1650–1950* (London, 1995).

26. P. Wagner, 'Trial Reports as a Genre of Eighteenth-Century Erotica', *The British Journal for Eighteenth-Century Studies*, V, 1 (1982) 117–23.

27. P. Wagner, *Eros Revived*, op. cit., pp. 120–1. See also C. Bingham, 'Seventeenth-Century Attitudes towards Deviant Sex, with a Com-ment by Bruce Mazlish', *The Journal of Interdisciplinary History*, I, 3 (1971) 447–72; A. Bray, *Homosexuality in Renaissance England* (London, 1982) pp. 29–30.

28. The most compact account of these is P. Wagner, 'Trial Reports as a Genre of Eighteenth-Century Erotica', op. cit., but for an account of part of this literature from a rather different perspective see P. Linebaugh, 'The Ordinary of Newgate and His Account' in J. S. Cockburn, ed., *Crime in England, 1550–1800* (London, 1977) pp. 246–69.

29. *Select Trials, for Murders . . . Rapes, Sodomy . . . .*, II (1734–5) p. 200; quoted in P. Wagner, *Eros Revived*, op. cit., p. 126.

30. Lawrence Stone's recent trilogy on the history of divorce is the best source for the legal elements of this transition. See his *Broken Lives: Separation and Divorce in England, 1660–1857* (Oxford, 1993); *Uncertain Unions: Marriage in England, 1660–1753* (Oxford, 1992); and *Road to Divorce: England, 1530–1987* (Oxford, 1990).

31. P. Wagner, *Eros Revived*, op. cit., p. 128.

32. *London and Paris*, vol. VIII (Weimar, 1800) pp. 242–3; quoted in P. Wagner, *Eros Revived*, op. cit., p. 128.

33. J.G. Turner has explored in detail the attitudes and sexual import of a range of eighteenth-century literary figures, including Love-lace. See his 'Pope's Libertine Self-Fashioning', *The Eighteenth Century*, XXIX, 2 (1988) 123–44; 'Lovelace and the Paradoxes of

Libertinism' in M.A. Doody and P. Sabor, eds, *Samuel Richardson* (Cambridge, 1989); 'The Libertine Sublime: Love and Death in Restoration England' in L.E. Brown and P. Craddock, eds, *Studies in Eighteenth-Century Culture*, 19 (1989) 99–115; and ' "Illustrious Depravity" and the Erotic Sublime' in P.J. Korshin, ed., *The Age of Johnson*, vol. II (New York, 1989).

34. *The Counterfeit Bridegroom* (n.d.), single sheet, British Library 816.m.19 (21).

35. While the search for a division between the erotic and the pornographic has consumed the intellectual energy of a small army of scholars, perhaps the best recent definition of pornography is Lynn Hunt's formulation: 'the explicit depiction of sexual organs and sexual practices with the aim of arousing sexual feelings'. L. Hunt, *The Invention of Pornography, 1500–1800* (New York, 1993) p. 10.

36. There are a number of excellent studies which trace in great detail the history of pornography. While P. Wagner's *Eros Revived* is the most recent comprehensive survey, older works of value include: D. Foxon, *Libertine Literature in England, 1660–1745* (New York, 1965); H.M. Hyde, *A History of Pornography* (London, 1964); P. Kearney, *A History of Erotic Literature* (London, 1982); G. Legman, *The Horn Book: Studies in Erotic Folklore and Bibliography* (New York, 1964); D. Loth, *The Erotic in Literature: A Historical Survey of Pornography as Delightful as it is Indiscreet* (London, 1962); R. Thompson, *Unfit for Modest Ears: A Study of Pornographic, Obscene and Bawdy Works Written or Published in England in the Second Half of the Seventeenth Century* (London, 1979).

37. P. Kearney, *A History of Erotic Literature*, op. cit., pp. 24, 34.

38. See P. Wagner, *Eros Revived*, op. cit., pp. 72–99.

39. See R. Darnton, *The Literary Underground of the Old Regime* (Cambridge, Mass., 1982); R. Darnton, 'Sex for Thought', *New York Review of Books*, XXXXI, 21 (22 Dec. 1994) 65–74. See also L. Hunt, *The Invention of Pornography*, op. cit., in particular 'Introduction: Obscenity and the Origins of Modernity, 1500–1800', pp. 9–45. For a valuable alternative reading which focuses on the discovery of sexually explicit classical materials see W. Kendrick, *The Secret Museum: Pornography in Modern Culture* (New York, 1987).

40. For a selection of recent work specifically on Cleland and *Fanny Hill* see: J.G. Basker, ' "The Wages of Sin": The Later Career of John Cleland', *Etude Anglaises*, XL (1987) 178–94; L. Braudy, '*Fanny Hill* and Materialism', *Eighteenth Century Studies*, 4 (1970) 21–40; J. Epstein, 'Fanny's Fanny: Epistolarity, Eroticism and the Transsexual' in E.C. Goldsmith, ed., *The Female Voice: Essays on Epistolary*

Literature (London, 1989); W.H. Epstein, *John Cleland: Images of a Life* (New York, 1974); D.H. Mengay, 'The Sodomitical Muse: *Fanny Hill* and the Rhetoric of Crossdressing', *Journal of Homosexuality*, XXIII, 1/2 (1991) 185–98; R. Roussel, *The Conversation of the Sexes: Seduction and Equality in Selected Seventeenth- and Eighteenth-Century Texts* (New York, 1986), chapter 2, 'Fanny Hill and the Androgynous Reader'; P. Sabor, 'The Censor Censured: Expurgating *Memoirs of a Woman of Pleasure*' in R.P. Maccubbin, ed., *'Tis Nature's Fault*, op. cit.

41. L. Stone, 'Libertine Sexuality in Post-Restoration England: Group Sex and Flagellation among the Middling Sort in Norwich in 1706–07', *Journal of the History of Sexuality*, II, 4 (1992) 511–26.

42. A full account of these incidents may be found in P. Aries and G. Duby, eds, *History of Private Life*, vol. III: *Passions of the Renaissance*, R. Chartier *et al.*, eds (Cambridge, 1989) p. 143.

43. W.H. Epstein, *John Cleland*, op. cit., p. 5.

44. A comprehensive account of Edmund Curll's career may be found in H.M. Hyde, *A History of Pornography*, op. cit., pp. 156–62.

45. For Griffith's relationship with John Cleland see W.H. Epstein, *John Cleland*, op. cit.

46. For a selection of various approaches to libertinism see L.C. Jones, *The Clubs of the Georgian Rakes* (New York, 1942); D. Foxon, *Libertine Literature in England*, op. cit.; B. Ivker, 'Towards a Definition of Libertinism in Eighteenth-Century French Fiction', *Studies on Voltaire and the Eighteenth Century*, LXXIII (1970) 221–39; D.P. Mannix, *The Hell-Fire Club* (New York, 1959); R. Trumbach, 'Sodomy Transformed: Aristocratic Libertinage, Public Reputation and the Gender Revolution of the Eighteenth-Century', *Journal of Homosexuality*, XIX (1990) 105–24; J.G. Turner, 'Lovelace and the Paradoxes of Libertinism', op. cit.; J.G. Turner, 'The Libertine Sublime', op. cit.; J.G. Turner, ' "Illustrious Depravity" and the Erotic Sublime', op. cit.

47. While his definition of libertine clubs is rather generous, L.C. Jones would claim there were dozens of these societies throughout the country. See L.C. Jones, *The Clubs of the Georgian Rakes*, op. cit., p. 5.

48. For an extensive account of the activities of Sir Francis Dashwood and the Medmenham Monks see L.C. Jones, *The Clubs of the Georgian Rakes*, op. cit., pp. 84–115.

49. For an excellent account of some of the displays prostitutes were paid to undertake in this period, primarily as evidenced in literature, see T.G.A. Nelson, 'Women of Pleasure', *Eighteenth-Century Life*, XI, n.s., 1 (1987) 181–98.

50. C. Walker, *Authentick Memoirs of the Life Intrigues and Adventures of the Celebrated Sally Salisbury*, facs. edn (New York, 1975) p. 262; quoted in T.G.A. Nelson, 'Women of Pleasure', op. cit., p. 192.

51. For the association of radicalism and pornography in an English context see I. McCalman, 'Unrespectable Radicalism, Infidels and Pornography in Early 19th Century London', *Past and Present*, 104 (1984) 74–110; I. McCalman, *Radical Underworld: Prophets, Revolutionaries and Pornographers in London, 1795–1840* (Cambridge, 1988).

52. For an excellent discussion of eighteenth-century responses to Tahiti see R. Porter, 'The Exotic as Erotic: Captain Cook at Tahiti' in G.S. Rousseau and R. Porter, eds, *Exoticism in the Enlightenment* (Manchester, 1990).

Chapter 3. Marriage, Courtship and Sexuality

1. *A Dialogue of Courtship between Jockey and Maggy as They Were Coming from the Market, Giving Excellent Instructions How to Court a Young Girl* (1775); quoted in B. Hill, *Women, Work and Sexual Politics in Eighteenth-Century England* (London, 1989) p. 183.

2. John Cannon, 'Memoirs of the Birth, Education, Life and Death of: Mr John Cannon. Sometime Officer of the Excise & Writing Master at Mere Glastenbury & West Lydford in the County of Somerset' (1743), Somerset Record Office MS DD/SAS C/1193/4, pp. 460–1.

3. For material on eighteenth-century demography see P. Laslett, K. Oosterveen and R. Smith, eds, *Bastardy and Its Comparative History* (London, 1980); D. Levine, *Family Formation in an Age of Nascent Capitalism* (New York, 1977); D. Levine, ' "For Their Own Reasons": Individual Marriage Decisions and Family Life', *Journal of Family History* (1982) 255–64; B. Meteyard, 'Illegitimacy and Marriage in Eighteenth-Century England', *Journal of Interdisciplinary History*, X, 3 (1980) 479–89; also the following debate between L. Stone and B. Meteyard, 'Illegitimacy in Eighteenth-Century England: Again', *Journal of Interdisciplinary History*, XI, 3 (1981) 507–14; R. Schofield, 'English Marriage Patterns Revisited', *Journal of Family History* (1985) 2–20; P. Sharpe, 'Locating the "Missing Marryers" in Colyton, 1660–1750', *Local Population Studies*, 48 (1992) 49–59; P. Sharpe, 'Marital Separation in the Eighteenth and Early Nineteenth Centuries', *Local Population Studies*, 45 (1990) 66–70; R. Wall, 'Leaving Home and the Process of Household Formation in Pre-Industrial England', *Continuity and Change*, II, 1 (1987) 77–101; D.R.

Weir, 'Rather Never than Late: Celibacy and Age at Marriage in English Cohort Fertility, 1541–1871', *Journal of Family History* (1984) 340–54; A. Wilson, 'Illegitimacy and Its Implications in Mid-Eighteenth-Century London: The Evidence of the Foundling Hospital', *Continuity and Change*, IV, 1 (1989) 103–64; E.A. Wrigley and R.S. Schofield, *The Population History of England, 1541–1871* (London, 1981); E.A. Wrigley, 'The Growth of Population in Eighteenth-Century England: A Conundrum Resolved', *Past and Present*, 98 (1983) 121–50; E.A. Wrigley, 'Marriage, Fertility and Population Growth in Eighteenth-Century England' in R.B. Outhwaite, ed., *Marriage and Society: Studies in the Social History of Marriage* (London, 1981); G. Wyatt, 'Bastardy and Prenuptial Pregnancy in a Cheshire Town during the Eighteenth Century', *Local Population Studies*, 49 (1992) 38–50.

4. For alternative views of the relative importance of celibacy in the overall rate of population change see D.R. Weir, 'Rather Never than Late', op. cit., and R. Schofield, 'English Marriage Patterns Revisited', op. cit.

5. These figures are quoted in A. Macfarlane, *Marriage and Love in England, 1300–1840* (Oxford, 1986) p. 25.

6. P. Laslett, 'Introduction: Comparing Illegitimacy over Time and between Cultures' in P. Laslett *et al.*, eds, *Bastardy and Its Comparative History*, op. cit., see Table I.1(a), pp. 14–15.

7. E.A. Wrigley, 'Marriage, Fertility and Population Growth', op. cit., p. 156.

8. *Ibid.*, see Table I, p. 139.

9. *Ibid.*, see Table III, p. 147; A. Macfarlane, *Marriage and Love in England*, op. cit., p. 25; P. Laslett, 'Introduction: Comparing Illegitimacy', op. cit., see Table I.1(a), pp. 14–15, and Table I.3, p. 23.

10. E.A. Wrigley, 'The Growth of Population in Eighteenth-Century England', op. cit.

11. For a powerful critique of the analysis of the demographers see B. Hill, 'The Marriage Age of Women and the Demographers', *History Workshop*, 28 (1989) 129–47.

12. For an article expressing the frustration of demographic historians attempting to establish a set of economic reasons for the transitions see D. Levine, ' "For Their Own Reasons" ', op. cit.

13. E. Shorter, *The Making of the Modern Family* (New York, 1975). For critiques of Shorter's analysis see C. Fairchilds, 'Female Sexual Attitudes and the Rise of Illegitimacy: A Case Study', *Journal of*

Interdisciplinary History, 4 (1978) 627–67; P. Laslett, 'Introduction: Comparing Illegitimacy', op. cit., pp. 26–9.

14. See L. Stone, *The Family, Sex and Marriage in England, 1500–1800*, 1st edn (London, 1977). For a more recent rendition of Stone's views see L. Stone, *Road to Divorce: England, 1530–1987* (Oxford, 1990).

15. For a critique of Stone's early work on the family see R.T. Vann, 'Review Essay', *Journal of Family History*, Fall (1979) pp. 308–15.

16. H. Abelove, 'Some Speculations on the History of Sexual Intercourse during the Long Eighteenth Century in England', *Genders*, 6 (1989) 125–30.

17. T. Laqueur, 'Sex and Desire in the Industrial Revolution' in P. O'Brien and R. Quinault, eds, *The Industrial Revolution and British Society* (Cambridge, 1993).

18. For an excellent overview of Cannon's life see J. Money, 'Teaching in the Market-Place, or "Caesar Adsum Jam Forte: Pompey Aderat": The Retailing of Knowledge in Provincial England during the Eighteenth Century' in J. Brewer and R. Porter, *Consumption and the World of Goods* (London, 1993).

19. John Cannon, 'Memoirs', op. cit., p. 29.

20. J. Gillis, *For Better, For Worse: British Marriages 1600 to the Present* (Oxford, 1985) pp. 21–2.

21. For an account of the publishing history and content of *Aristotle's Master-piece* see R. Porter, ' "The Secrets of Generation Display'd": *Aristotle's Masterpiece* in Eighteenth-Century England' in R.P. Maccubbin, ed., *'Tis Nature's Fault: Unauthorized Sexuality during the Enlightenment* (Cambridge, 1987).

22. John Cannon, 'Memoirs', op. cit., p. 41.

23. *Ibid.*, p. 53.

24. *Ibid.*, p. 53.

25. *Ibid.*, p. 54.

26. *Ibid.*, p. 57.

27. Except in the context of trial reports relating to sodomy I have been unable to locate any creditable accounts of oral sex in the eighteenth century. For an analysis of one example of extreme sexual behaviour among a group of middling-sort people in the early eighteenth century which nonetheless excludes oral sex see L. Stone, 'Libertine Sexuality in Post-Restoration England: Group Sex and Flagellation among the Middling Sort in Norwich in 1706–07', *Journal of the History of Sexuality*, II (1992) 511–26.

28. John Cannon, 'Memoirs', op. cit., p. 57.

29. *Ibid.*, p. 64.

30. *Ibid.*, p. 57.
31. E.A. Wrigley, 'Marriage, Fertility and Population Growth', op. cit., and A. Wilson, 'Illegitimacy and Its Implications', op. cit.
32. John Cannon, 'Memoirs', op. cit., p. 87.
33. *Ibid.*, p. 103.
34. J. Money, 'Teaching in the Market-Place', op. cit., p. 350.
35. John Cannon, 'Memoirs', op. cit., p. 89.
36. For an excellent account of the role of reputation in women's lives during the seventeenth century see M. Ingram, *Church Courts, Sex and Marriage in England, 1570–1640* (Cambridge, 1987), in particular chapter 10 'Sexual Slander'.
37. E. Shorter, *The Making of the Modern Family*, op. cit. For an account of a similar set of experiences for a slightly later date as set down by William Hutton in his autobiography see J.F.C. Harrison, *The Common People: A History from the Norman Conquest to the Present* (London, 1984) pp. 146–54.
38. John Cannon, 'Memoirs', op. cit., p. 111. The roles and nature of clandestine marriage have attracted an increasing amount of historical attention, as has Hardwicke's Marriage Act of 1753, which was designed to prevent it. For the most recent and comprehensive account of the Act see R.B. Outhwaite, *Clandestine Marriage in England 1500–1850* (London, 1995). See also J. Boulton, 'Clandestine Marriages in London: An Examination of a Neglected Urban Variable', *Urban History*, XX, 2 (1993) 191–210; R.L. Brown, 'The Rise and Fall of the Fleet Marriages' in R.B. Outhwaite, ed., *Marriage and Society*, op. cit.; J. Gillis, *For Better, For Worse*, op. cit.; P. Sharpe, 'Locating the "Missing Marryers" in Colyton', op. cit.; T.C. Smout, 'Scottish Marriage, Regular and Irregular, 1500–1940' in R.B. Outhwaite, ed., *Marriage and Society*, op. cit.; L. Stone, *Uncertain Unions: Marriage in England, 1660–1753* (Oxford, 1992).
39. John Cannon, 'Memoirs', op. cit., pp. 114–15.
40. A. Wilson, 'Illegitimacy and Its Implications', op. cit.
41. E.A. Wrigley, 'Marriage, Fertility and Population Growth', op. cit.
42. See M. Thale, ed., *The Autobiography of Francis Place* (Cambridge, 1972). For an account of the opinions and actions of James Boswell see L. Stone, *The Family, Sex and Marriage in England*, 1st edn, op. cit., pp. 572–98; for Boswell's own account see F.A. Pottle, *Boswell's London Journal, 1762–63* (New York, 1950).
43. L. Stone, *The Family, Sex and Marriage in England*, 1st edn, op. cit., p. 581.

44. N. McKendrick, 'Introduction: The Birth of a Consumer Society: The Commercialization of Eighteenth-Century England' in N. McKendrick, J. Brewer and J.H. Plumb, *The Birth of a Consumer Society* (London, 1983) pp. 1–8.

45. R. Porter, ' "The Secrets of Generation Display'd" ', op. cit.

46. L. Stone, 'Libertine Sexuality in Post-Restoration England', op. cit.

Chapter 4. The Body, Medicine and Sexual Difference

1. F.A. Illingworth, *A Just Narrative or Account of the Man whose Hands and Legs Rotted Off: in the Parish of Swinford, in Staffordshire, Where He Died, June 21, 1677* (London, 1678).

2. For Galenic medicine and its relationship to sex and gender and the history of the body see P. Crawford, 'Attitudes to Menstruation in Seventeenth-Century England', *Past and Present*, 91 (1981) 47–73; D. Jacquart and C. Thomasset, eds, *Sexuality and Medicine in the Middle Ages* (Cambridge, 1988); T. Laqueur, *Making Sex: Body and Gender from the Greeks to Freud* (Cambridge, Mass., 1990); T. Laqueur, 'Orgasm, Generation and the Politics of Reproductive Biology' in C. Gallagher and T. Laqueur, eds, *The Making of the Modern Body: Sexuality and Society in the Nineteenth Century* (Berkeley, Calif., 1987); I. Maclean, *The Renaissance Notion of Woman* (Cambridge, 1980); R. Martensen, 'The Transformation of Eve: Women's Bodies, Medicine and Culture in Early Modern England' in R. Porter and M. Teich, *Sexual Knowledge, Sexual Science: The History of Attitudes to Sexuality* (Cambridge, 1994); A. McLaren, *Reproductive Rituals. The Perception of Fertility in England from the Sixteenth Century to the Nineteenth Century* (London, 1984). For an invaluable guide to the literature on the history of the body see B. Duden, 'A Repertory of Body History' in M. Feher, ed., *Fragments for a History of the Human Body*, part three (New York, 1989).

3. P. Mack, *Visionary Women: Ecstatic Prophecy in Seventeenth-Century England* (Berkeley, Calif., 1992).

4. For a discussion of the history of the clitoris see T. Laqueur, 'Amor Veneris, vel Dulcedo Appeletur' in M. Feher, ed., *Fragments for a History*, part three, op. cit., pp. 90–131.

5. For a brief description of conception and the development of the foetus see A. Eccles, *Obstetrics and Gynaecology in Tudor and Stuart England* (Kent, Ohio, 1982) pp. 26–57.

6. Daniel Lysons, *Collectanea: or, a Collection of Advertisements and Paragraphs from the Newspapers, Relating to Various Subjects, Publick Exhibitions and Places of Amusement*, vol. I (1840), British Library C.103.K.11., fol. 82.

7. For information on Mary Toft see S. Bruce, 'The Flying Island and Female Anatomy: Gynaecology and Power in *Gulliver's Travels*', *Genders*, 2 (1988) 60–76; L. Cody, 'The Doctor's in Labour: or, a New Whim Wham from Guildford', *Gender and History*, I, 4 (1992); M. Nicolson and G.S. Rousseau, *This Long Disease, My Life: Alexander Pope and the Sciences* (Princeton, 1968) pp. 109–15; G. Leslie, 'Cheat and Imposter: Debate Following the Case of the Rabbit Breeder', *The Eighteenth Century: Theory and Interpretation*, XXVII, 3 (1986) 269–86.

8. For general material on menstruation and the impact of the imagination see P-G. Boucé, 'Imagination, Pregnant Women, and Monsters in Eighteenth-Century England and France' in G.S. Rousseau and R. Porter, eds, *Sexual Underworlds of the Enlightenment* (Manchester, 1987); P. Crawford, 'Sexual Knowledge in England, 1500–1750' in R. Porter and M. Teich, '*Sexual Knowledge, Sexual Science*, op. cit., pp. 82–106; P. Crawford, 'Attitudes to Menstruation', op. cit.; A. Eccles, *Obstetrics and Gynaecology*, op. cit.; K. Park and L.J. Daston, 'Unnatural Conceptions: The Study of Monsters', *Past and Present*, 92 (1981) 20–54.

9. For a discussion of beliefs about 'quickening' see A. McLaren, *Reproductive Rituals*, op. cit., pp. 107–11; A. Eccles, *Obstetrics and Gynaecology*, op. cit., p. 45.

10. For a discussion of prostitution and biology see T. Laqueur, 'The Social Evil, the Solitary Vice and Pouring Tea' in M. Feher, ed., *Fragments for a History*, part three, op. cit.

11. See E. Donoghue, *Passions between Women: British Lesbian Culture, 1688–1801* (London, 1993) pp. 4–5. For a discussion of clitoral enlargement as evidence in a legal context see T. van der Meer, 'Tribades on Trial: Female Same-Sex Offenders in Late Eighteenth-Century Amsterdam', *Journal of the History of Ideas*, I, 3 (1991) 424–45.

12. T. Laqueur, *Making Sex*, op. cit.

13. For information specifically on the role of the female orgasm see T. Laqueur, 'Orgasm, Generation and the Politics of Reproductive Biology', op. cit., and T. Laqueur, 'Amor Veneris', op. cit.

14. For examples of work following Laqueur's lead see A. Fletcher, 'Men's Dilemma: The Future of Patriarchy in England, 1560–

1660', *Royal Historical Society, Transactions*, IV, 6th ser. (1994) 61–82, and R. Martensen, 'The Transformation of Eve', op. cit. See also A. Fletcher, *Gender, Sex and Subordination in England 1500–1800* (New Haven, Conn., 1995).

15. For a concise statement of Roper's views see L. Roper, *Oedipus and the Devil: Witchcraft, Sexuality and Religion in Early Modern Europe* (London, 1994), 'Introduction', pp. 1–34.

16. R. Martensen, 'The Transformation of Eve' op. cit. R. Martensen, ' "Habit of Reason": Anatomy and Anglicanism in Restoration England', *Bulletin of the History of Medicine*, 66 (1992) 511–35.

17. M. Fissell, 'Gender and Generation: Representing Reproduction in Early Modern England', *Gender and History*, VII, 3 (1995) 433–56.

18. I. Maclean, *The Renaissance Notion of Woman*, op. cit., see in particular chapter 3, 'Medicine, Anatomy, Physiology'.

19. L. Schiebinger, 'Skeletons in the Closet: The First Illustrations of the Female Skeleton in Eighteenth-Century Anatomy' in C. Gallagher and T. Laqueur, eds, *The Making of the Modern Body*, op. cit. For a careful discussion of the various points of view associated with the observation of sperm and eggs see A. McLaren, *Reproductive Rituals*, op. cit., pp. 22–7.

20. For a subtle account of these transitions see M. Fissell, *Patients, Power, and the Poor in Eighteenth-Century Bristol* (Cambridge, 1991).

21. For a discussion of the work of Jane Sharp and of female authority in relation to midwifery see M. Fissell, 'Gender and Generation', op. cit.

22. An extensive literature has developed on the history of midwifery and the rise of the male mid-wife, some examples of which are J. Donnison, *Midwives and Medical Men: A History of Inter-professional Rivalries and Women's Rights* (New York, 1977); A. Eccles, *Obstetrics and Gynaecology*, op. cit.; T. Forbes, 'The Regulation of English Midwives in the Sixteenth and Seventeenth Centuries', *Medical History*, 8 (1964) 235–44; R. Porter, 'A Touch of Danger: The Man-Midwife as Sexual Predator' in G.S. Rousseau and R. Porter, eds, *Sexual Underworlds*, op. cit.; and A. Wilson, *The Making of Man-Midwifery: Childbirth in England, 1660–1770* (Cambridge, Mass., 1995).

23. For discussion of the impact of these medical changes on women's lives see R. Perry, 'Colonizing the Breast: Sexuality and Maternity in Eighteenth-Century England', *Journal of the History of Sexuality*, II, 2 (1991) 204–34. For an intriguing analysis of how scientific thought in its broadest formulation interacted with these social and

medical transitions see L. Schiebinger, 'Mammals, Primatology and Sexology' in R. Porter and M. Teich, *Sexual Knowledge, Sexual Science*, op. cit.

24. For an excellent recent survey of the history of early nineteenth-century masculinity see J. Tosh, 'What Should Historians do with Masculinity? Reflections on Nineteenth-Century Britain', *History Workshop*, 38 (1994) 179–202.

25. See R. Perry, 'Colonizing the Breast', op. cit.; see also V. Fildes, *Wet Nursing: A History from Antiquity to the Present* (Oxford, 1988), especially chapter 8, 'Wet Nursing in the Eighteenth Century'. For an analysis of the development of separate spheres see L. Davidoff and C. Hall, *Family Fortunes: Men and Women of the English Middle Class, 1780–1850* (London, 1987).

26. The ascription of the work to Aristotle was entirely apocryphal.

27. R. Porter, 'The Literature of Sexual Advice before 1800' in R. Porter and M. Teich, *Sexual Knowledge, Sexual Science*, op. cit., p. 136.

28. R. Porter, 'Spreading Carnal Knowledge or Selling Dirt Cheap? Nicolas Venette's *Tableau de l'amour conjugal* in Eighteenth-Century England', *Journal of European Studies*, 14 (1984) p. 237.

29. For an analysis of Graham's appeal see R. Porter, 'The Sexual Politics of James Graham', *British Journal for Eighteenth-Century Studies*, V, 2 (1982) 199–206.

30. For an excellent discussion of the problem of analysing the readership of popular health texts in this period see M. Fissel, 'Readers, Texts and Contexts: Vernacular Medical Works in Early Modern England' in R. Porter, ed., *The Popularization of Medicine, 1650–1850* (London, 1992).

31. M. Thale, ed., *The Autobiography of Francis Place* (Cambridge, 1972) p. 45.

32. For a discussion of its role in Sterne see R. Porter, ' "The Whole Secret of Health": Mind, Body and Medicine in *Tristram Shandy*' in J. Christie and S. Shuttleworth, eds, *Nature Transfigured* (Manchester, 1989).

33. R. Porter, 'The Literature of Sexual Advice before 1800', op. cit.

34. O.T. Beall, Jr, *'Aristotle's Masterpiece* in America: A Landmark in the Folklore of Medicine', *William and Mary Quarterly*, XX (1963) 207–22; P. Crawford, 'Sexual Knowledge in England', op. cit.; M. Fissel, 'Readers, Texts and Contexts', op. cit. Roy Porter's substantial number of articles on the topic of popular health texts have recently been superseded by R. Porter and L. Hall, *The Facts of Life:*

The Creation of Sexual Knowledge in Britain, 1650–1950 (New Haven and London, 1995).

35. Quoted in R. Porter, ' "The Secrets of Generation Display'd": *Aristotle's Masterpiece* in Eighteenth-Century England' in R.P. Maccubin, ed., *'Tis Natures Fault: Unauthorized Sexuality during the Enlightenment* (Cambridge, 1987) p. 6.
36. A. McLaren, *Reproductive Rituals*, op. cit., p. 80, and R. Porter, 'The Literature of Sexual Advice before 1800', op. cit.
37. A. McLaren, *Reproductive Rituals*, op. cit., and A. McLaren, *A History of Contraception from Antiquity to the Present Day* (Oxford, 1990), especially chapter 5, 'Fertility Control in Early Modern Europe'.
38. Daniel Lysons, *Collectanea: or, a Collection of Advertisements and Paragraphs from the Newspapers, Relating to Various Subjects*, vol. I, part two (1828), British Library 1881.b.6., fol. 117.
39. A. McLaren, *Reproductive Rituals*, op. cit., pp. 135–6.
40. For a broader discussion of this process see *ibid.*, chapter 5, ' "Converting this Measure of Security into a Crime": The Early Nineteenth-Century Abortion Laws'.
41. Quoted in *ibid.*, p. 81.
42. For examples of contemporary references to the use of condoms see F.A. Pottle, ed., *Boswell's London Journal, 1762–1763* (New York, 1950) pp. 49, 227, 255, 262.
43. A. McLaren, *Reproductive Rituals*, op. cit.
44. E.H. Hare, 'Masturbatory Insanity: The History of an Idea', *Journal of Mental Science*, 108 (1962) 12.
45. For accounts of the publishing activities of the SPCK see L.W. Cowie, *Henry Newman: An American in London, 1708–1743* (London, 1956), and M.G. Jones, *The Charity School Movement: A Study of Eighteenth-Century Puritanism in Action* (Cambridge, 1938). For the Societies for the Reformation of Manners see R.B. Shoemaker, 'Reforming the City: The Reformation of Manners Campaign in London, 1690–1738' in L. Davison, T. Hitchcock, T. Kiern and R.B. Shoemaker, eds, *Stilling the Grumbling Hive: The Response to Social and Economic Problems in England, 1688–1750* (Stroud, Glos., 1992); D.W.R. Bahlman, *The Moral Revolution of 1688* (New Haven, 1957); T.C. Curtis and W.A. Speck, 'The Societies for the Reformation of Manners: a Case Study in the Theory and Practice of Moral Reform', *Literature and History*, 3 (1976) 45–7; A.G. Craig, 'The Movement for the Reformation of Manners, 1688–1715' (Edinburgh University Ph.D. thesis, 1980); T.B. Isaacs, 'Moral Crime, Moral Reform and the State in Eighteenth-Century England: a

Study of Piety and Politics' (University of Rochester Ph.D. thesis, 1979); J. Spurr, ' "Virtue, Religion and Government" the Anglican Uses of Providence' in T. Harris, P. Seaward, and M. Goldie, eds, *The Politics of Religion in Restoration England* (Oxford, 1990).

46. P. Wagner, 'The Veil of Medicine and Mortality: Some Pornographic Aspects of the *Onania*', *The British Journal for Eighteenth Century Studies*, VI (1983) 179.

47. R.H. MacDonald, 'The Frightful Consequences of Onanism: Notes on the History of a Delusion', *Journal of the History of Ideas*, XXVIII, 3 (1967) p. 425.

48. P. Wagner, 'The Veil of Medicine and Mortality', op. cit.

49. *Onania, or, The Heinous Sin of Self-Pollution, and All its Frightful Consequences in Both Sexes*, 15th edn with the 6th edn of *A Supplement to the Onania* (1730), *Supplement*, pp. 48–50.

50. *Ibid.*, p. 51.

51. R.P. Neuman, 'Masturbation, Madness, and the Modern Concepts of Childhood and Adolescence', *Journal of Social History*, VIII (1975) 2.

52. E.H. Hare, 'Masturbatory Insanity', op. cit.

53. See respectively R.P. Neuman, 'Masturbation, Madness, and the Modern Concepts of Childhood and Adolescence', op. cit., and L. Jordanova, 'The Popularisation of Medicine: Tissot on Onanism', *Textual Practice*, I, 1 (1987) 68–80.

Chapter 5. The Development of Homosexuality

1. M. McIntosh, 'The Homosexual Role', *Social Problems*, XVI, 2 (1968) 182–92, reprinted in K. Plummer, ed., *The Making of the Modern Homosexual* (London, 1981); A. Bray, *Homosexuality in Renaissance England* (London, 1982); A. Bray, 'Homosexuality and the Signs of Male Friendship in Elizabethan England', *History Workshop*, 29 (1990) 1–19; R. Trumbach, 'Sodomitical Subcultures, Sodomitical Roles, and the Gender Revolution of the Eighteenth Century: The Recent Historiography' in R.P. Maccubbin, *'Tis Nature's Fault: Unauthorized Sexuality during the Enlightenment* (Cambridge, 1987); R. Trumbach, 'London's Sodomites: Homosexual Behaviour and Western Culture in the Eighteenth Century', *Journal of Social History*, XI, 1 (1977) 1–33; R. Trumbach, 'Sex, Gender, and Sexual Identity in Modern Culture: Male Sodomy and Female Prostitution in Enlightenment London', *Journal of the History of Sexuality*, II, 2

(1991) 186–203; R. Trumbach, 'The Birth of the Queen: Sodomy and the Emergence of Gender Equality in Modern Culture, 1660–1750' in M. Duberman, M. Vicinus and G. Chauncy Jr, eds, *Hidden from History: Reclaiming the Gay and Lesbian Past* (London, 1991); R. Trumbach, 'Sodomitical Assaults, Gender Roles, and Sexual Development in Eighteenth-Century London', *Journal of Homosexuality*, XVI, 1/2 (1989) 407–29; A. Simpson, 'Masculinity and Control: The Prosecution of Sex Offenses in Eighteenth-Century London' (New York University Ph.D. thesis, 1984). For a recent synthesis of this material see R. Norton, *Mother Clap's Molly House: The Gay Subculture in England, 1700–1830* (London, 1992).

2. R. Trumbach, 'London's Sodomites', op. cit., p. 23.

3. For a selection of the literature proposing this alternative analysis see M. Foucault, *The History of Sexuality: Volume 1: An Introduction* (London, 1976); J. Weeks, 'Foucault for Historians', *History Workshop*, 14 (1982) 106–19; J. Weeks, 'Invented Moralities', *History Workshop*, 32 (1991) 151–66; J. Weeks, *Sex, Politics and Society: Regulation of Sexuality since 1800*, 2nd edn (London, 1989).

4. L. Crompton, 'Homosexuals and the Death Penalty in Colonial America', *Journal of Homosexuality*, I, 3 (1976) 277–94; L. Crompton, '*Don Leon*, Byron, and Homosexual Law Reform', *Journal of Homosexuality*, VIII, 3/4 (1983) 53–72; L. Crompton, 'The Myth of Lesbian Impunity: Capital Laws from 1270 to 1791', *Journal of Homosexuality*, XVI, 1/2 (1980/81) 11–26; A.N. Gilbert, 'Buggery and the British Navy, 1700–1861', *Journal of Social History*, X, 1 (1976) 72–98; A.N. Gilbert, 'Conceptions of Homosexuality and Sodomy in Western History', *Journal of Homosexuality*, VI, 1/2 (1980/81) 57–68; A.N. Gilbert, 'Sexual Deviance and Disaster during the Napoleonic Wars', *Albion*, IX, 1 (1977) 98–113. Other works concerning the same issues include: P. Morris, 'Sodomy and Male Honor: The Case of Somerset, 1740–1850', *Journal of Homosexuality*, XVI, 1/2 (1989) 383–406; C. Bingham, 'Seventeenth-Century Attitudes towards Deviant Sex, with a Comment by Bruce Mazlish', *The Journal of Interdisciplinary History*, I, 3 (1971) 447–72; R.F. Oaks, ' "Things Fearful to Name": Sodomy and Buggery in Seventeenth-Century New England', *Journal of Social History*, XII, 2 (1978) 268–81; R.F. Oaks, 'Defining Sodomy in Seventeenth-Century Massachusetts', *Journal of Homosexuality*, VI, 1/2 (1980/81) 79–83; R.F. Oaks, 'Perceptions of Homosexuality by Justices of the Peace in Colonial Virginia', *Journal of Homosexuality*, V, 1/2 (1979/80) 35–42.

5. L. Crompton, 'Gay Genocide: From Leviticus to Hitler' in L. Crew, ed., *The Gay Academic* (Palm Springs, Calif., 1978). For an overview of the development of this literature see P. Higgins, *A Queer Reader* (London, 1993) pp. 6–8.

6. B.R. Burg, ' "Ho Hum, Another Work of the Devil": Buggery and Sodomy in Early Stuart England', *Journal of Homosexuality*, VI, 1/2 (1980/81) 70.

7. *Ibid.*, p. 71.

8. For a discussion of the nature of the evidence needed to gain a conviction for sodomy in an eighteenth-century court see A.N. Gilbert, 'Buggery and the British Navy', op. cit., pp. 74–6.

9. A. Simpson, 'Masculinity and Control', op. cit., see Tables 5 and 11, pp. 819–22, 828–31.

10. B. Eriksson, trans., 'A Lesbian Execution in Germany, 1721, Trial Records', *Journal of Homosexuality*, VI, 1/2 (1980/81) pp. 31, 37.

11. For example see E.W. Monter, 'Sodomy and Heresy in Early Modern Switzerland', *Journal of Homosexuality*, VI, 1/2 (1980/81) 41–57.

12. See P. Lake, 'Anti-Popery: The Structure of a Prejudice' in R. Cust and A. Hughes, eds, *Conflict in Early Stuart England: Studies in Religion and Politics, 1603–1642* (London, 1989). See also A. Bellany, ' "Raylinge Rymes and Vaunting Verse": Libellous Politics in Early Stuart England, 1603–1628' in K. Sharpe and P. Lake, eds, *Culture and Politics in Early Stuart England* (London, 1994).

13. B.R. Burg, 'Ho Hum, Another Work of the Devil', op. cit., pp. 71–2.

14. For a discussion of attitudes towards bestiality and its treatment by the courts see P. Morris, 'Sodomy and Male Honor', op. cit., pp. 387–90. For material on seventeenth-century American colonial attitudes see R.F. Oaks, ' "Things Fearful to Name" ', op. cit.

15. The prosecution of sexual assault and rape of children must be understood in the context of contemporary beliefs about venereal disease. It was popularly believed that sex with a virgin would cure the disease and it is this belief which must lie behind the series of rape cases involving young infected children prosecuted at the Old Bailey in the eighteenth century, the almost invariable outcome of which was execution of the perpetrator. For example see *Select Trials for Murder, Robbery, Burglary, Rapes . . . and Other Offences and Misdemeanours at the Sessions House in the Old Bailey*, vol. I (London, 1764) 129, 130, 214. I would like to thank Susan Dart for this reference.

16. A. Bray, *Homosexuality in Renaissance England*, op. cit., p. 68; and for a general discussion of the nature of sexual intolerance in the eighteenth-century see P-G. Boucé, 'Aspects of Sexual Tolerance and Intolerance in XVIIIth-Century England', *The British Journal for Eighteenth-Century Studies*, III (1980) 173–91.

17. For discussions of the nature of sin in the seventeenth century see C.B. Herrup, 'Law and Morality in Seventeenth-Century England', *Past and Present*, 106 (1985) 102–23; P. Lake, 'Anti-Popery', op. cit.; and P. Lake, 'Deeds against Nature: Cheap Print, Protestantism and Murder in Early Seventeenth-Century England' in K. Sharpe and P. Lake, eds, *Culture and Politics*, op. cit.

18. Quoted in P. Morris, 'Sodomy and Male Honor', op. cit., p. 386.

19. A.N. Gilbert, 'The "Africane" Courts-Martial: A Study of Buggery in the Royal Navy', *Journal of Homosexuality*, I (1974) 111–22.

20. G.S. Rousseau, ' "In the House of Madam Vander Tasse, on the Long Bridge": A Homosocial University Club in Early Modern Europe', *Journal of Homosexuality*, XVI, 1/2 (1989) 330–1.

21. Quoted in P. Higgins, *A Queer Reader*, op. cit., p. 92.

22. See for example A.L. Rowse, *Homosexuals in History: Ambivalence in Society, Literature and the Arts* (New York, 1977).

23. For a discussion of the case of William III see S.O. Murray, 'Homosexual Acts and Selves in Early Modern Europe', *Journal of Homosexuality*, XVI, 1/2 (1989) 458–9. For a powerful discussion of the changing nature of the ways in which homosexuality and male friendship were used in a political context during the seventeenth century see A. Bray, 'Homosexuality and the Signs of Male Friendship in Elizabethan England', op. cit.

24. C. Bingham, 'Seventeenth-Century Attitudes towards Deviant Sex', op. cit., pp. 447–72.

25. A. Bray, *Homosexuality in Renaissance England*, op. cit., p. 72.

26. *Ibid.*, p. 14.

27. Quoted in *ibid.*, p. 82.

28. R. Trumbach, 'Sodomitical Assaults, Gender Roles, and Sexual Development', op. cit., p. 409.

29. See A. Bray, *Homosexuality in Renaissance England*, op. cit., p. 85, and A. Simpson, 'Masculinity and Control', op. cit., pp. 484–90.

30. Quoted in A. Bray, *Homosexuality in Renaissance England*, op. cit., p. 87.

31. For a valuable discussion of the internal workings of the subculture see R. Trumbach, 'London's Sodomites', op. cit., pp. 15–21.

32. Quoted in *ibid.*, p. 15.

33. *Ibid.*, pp. 18–19; see also A. Simpson, 'Masculinity and Control', op. cit.

34. A. Bray, *Homosexuality in Renaissance England*, op. cit., p. 99.

35. Corporation of London Record Office, 'Courts of the President and Governors for the Poor of London, 1702–1705', 32B, fol. 65v. 20 October 1703 (Report 19 Oct.); fol. 99v. ct. 23 Feb. (Report 17 Feb.) 1703/4.

36. Bridewell Hospital Archives (Beckenham), 'Bridewell Court Book, 1701–1713. Court of Governors', 25 May 1705, p. 251. I would like to thank Tim Wales for this and the previous reference.

37. Daniel Lysons, *Collectanea: or, a Collection of Advertisements and Paragraphs from the Newspapers, Relating to Various Subjects*, vol. II, part two (1828), British Library 1881.b.6., fol. 183. The information contained here dates the advent of street signs to 1742, in contradiction to Dan Cruickshank who suggests this development must be dated from 1765. D. Cruickshank, *Life in the Georgian City* (London, 1990) p. 19.

38. R. Trumbach, 'Sodomitical Assaults, Gender Roles, and Sexual Development', op. cit., pp. 407–8.

39. For an excellent discussion of this transition in relation to the theatre see L. Senelick, 'Mollies or Men of Mode? Sodomy and the Eighteenth-Century London Stage', *Journal of the History of Sexuality*, I, 1 (1990) 33–67.

40. See R.B. Shoemaker, 'Reforming the City: The Reformation of Manners Campaign in London, 1690–1738' in L. Davison, T. Hitchcock, T. Kiern and R.B. Shoemaker, eds, *Stilling the Grumbling Hive: The Response to Social and Economic Problems in England, 1688–1750* (Stroud, Glos., 1992). For further discussion of the Reformation Societies see D.W.R. Bahlman, *The Moral Revolution of 1688* (New Haven, Conn., 1957); T.C. Curtis and W.A. Speck, 'The Societies for the Reformation of Manners: A Case Study in the Theory and Practice of Moral Reform', *Literature and History*, 3 (1976) 45–7; A.G. Craig, 'The Movement for the Reformation of Manners, 1688–1715' (Edinburgh University Ph.D. thesis, 1980); T.B. Isaacs, 'Moral Crime, Moral Reform and the State in Eighteenth-Century England: A Study of Piety and Politics' (University of Rochester Ph.D. thesis, 1979).

41. A. Bray, *Homosexuality in Renaissance England*, op. cit., pp. 81–4, 90–1.

42. *The Tryal and Condemnation of Mervin, Lord Audley Earl of Castle-Haven* (1699).

43. For the Moorfields persecutions see A. Simpson, 'Masculinity and Control', op. cit., pp. 484–90. For information on the persecutions around 1810 see A.N. Gilbert, 'Sexual Deviance and Disaster', op. cit.

44. A. Simpson, 'Masculinity and Control', op. cit., pp. 760–70.

45. Quoted in *ibid.*, p. 774.

46. *Ibid., passim.*

47. For the most concise statement of Trumbach's views see R. Trumbach, 'Sex, Gender, and Sexual Identity in Modern Culture', op. cit.

48. A. Bray, *Homosexuality in Renaissance England*, op. cit., pp. 104–14. For a critique of Bray's views see K. Gerard's review in *Journal of Homosexuality*, XVI, 1/2 (1989) 479–82.

Chapter 6. Tribades, Cross-Dressers and Romantic Friendship

1. Greater London Record Office, 'St. Luke's Chelsea, Settlement and Bastardy Examinations, 1750–1766', P74/Luk/122/RI104, Ann Carrack, 25 March 1761. For an account of the legal, social and economic circumstances experienced by feme sole businesses in the eighteenth century see M. Hunt, *The Middling Sort: Commerce, Gender and the Family in England, 1680–1780* (Berkeley, Calif., 1996), especially chapter 3, 'Daughters in the Family Economy', and chapter 5, 'Eighteenth-Century Middling Women and Trade'.

2. Economic arguments have been most frequently deployed and debated in relation to the decision-making of widows. See for example J. Boulton, 'London Widowhood Revisited: The Decline of Female Remarriage in the Seventeenth and Early Eighteenth Centuries', *Continuity and Change*, V, 3 (1990) 323–55; B.J. Todd, 'Demographic Determinism and Female Agency: The Remarrying Widow Reconsidered ... Again', *Continuity and Change*, IX, 3 (1994) 421–50; and B. Hill, 'The Marriage Age of Women and the Demographers', *History Workshop*, 28 (1989) 129–47. For material on 'spinster clustering' see O. Hufton, 'Women without Men: Widows and Spinsters in England and France in the Eighteenth Century', *Journal of Family History*, Winter (1984) 361–2.

3. The most comprehensive work on 'romantic friendship' is L. Faderman, *Surpassing the Love of Men* (London, 1981). For other

works on the same theme see G.E. Haggerty, ' "Romantic Friendship" and Patriarchal Narrative in Sarah Scott's *Millennium Hall'*, *Genders*, 13 (1992) 108–22; E. Mavor, *The Ladies of Llangollen: A Study in Romantic Friendship* (London, 1973); and C. Smith-Rosenburg, 'A Study of Erotic Rhetoric in 18th and 19th C. Women's Friendships', *Signs*, 1 (1975) 1–29.

4. For examples of this second historiographical tradition see T. Castle, *The Apparitional Lesbian: Female Homosexuality and Modern Culture* (New York, 1993), particularly chapter 5, 'The Diaries of Anne Lister'; E. Donaghue, *Passions between Women: British Lesbian Culture, 1668–1801* (London, 1993); M. Vicinus, ' "They Wonder to Which Sex I Belong": The Historical Roots of the Modern Lesbian Identity' in H. Abelove, M.A. Barale, and D.M. Halperin, eds, *The Lesbian and Gay Studies Reader* (London, 1993). For an example of the level of discord these disparate traditions can engender see B. Cook, 'The Historical Denial of Lesbianism', *Radical History Review*, 20 (1979) 60–5.

5. For an analysis of the idea of a 'lesbian continuum' see Adrienne Rich, 'Compulsory Heterosexuality and the Lesbian Experience' in H. Abelove, *et al.*, eds, *The Lesbian and Gay Studies Reader*, op. cit.

6. For information on the treatment of lesbians by the various criminal justice systems of Europe see L. Crompton, 'The Myth of Lesbian Impunity: Capital Laws from 1270 to 1791', *Journal of Homosexuality*, VI, 1/2 (1980/81) 11–26. For an excellent treatment of the legal situation in the Netherlands see R.M. Dekker and L.C. van de Pol, *The Tradition of Female Transvestism in Early Modern Europe* (London, 1989) pp. 76–80.

7. See B. Eriksson, trans., 'A Lesbian Execution in Germany, 1721: The Trial Records', *Journal of Homosexuality*, VI, 1/2 (1980/81) 27–40.

8. A. Simpson, 'Masculinity and Control: The Prosecution of Sex Offences in Eighteenth-Century London' (New York University Ph.D. thesis, 1984) pp. 364–5. This case is also discussed in E. Donaghue, *Passions between Women*, op. cit., p. 69.

9. Greater London Record Office, 'Sealy vs Hollingsworth', MS DL/C/146, London Consistory Court, fol. 531. For treatment of a more complex marital case involving two women see P. Crawford and S. Mendelson, 'Sexual Identities in Early Modern England: The Marriage of Two Women in 1680', *Gender and History*, VII, 3 (1995) 362–77.

10. E. Donaghue, *Passions between Women*, op. cit., p. 18, and T. Castle, *The Apparitional Lesbian*, op. cit., p. 6.

11. See E.P. Thompson, *Whigs and Hunters: The Origin of the Black Act* (London, 1975); for a general treatment of the criminal justice system see J. Beattie, *Crime and the Courts in England, 1660-1800* (Oxford, 1986).

12. Quoted in P. Wagner, *Eros Revived: Erotica of the Enlightenment in England and America* (London, 1987) pp. 17-18.

13. For a historical account of the medical history of the clitoris see T. Laqueur, 'Amor Veneris, vel Dulcedo Appeletur' in M. Feher, ed., *Fragments for a History of the Human Body*, part three (New York, 1989).

14. For an overview of the medical discourses surrounding these issues see T. Laqueur, *Making Sex: Body and Gender from the Greeks to Freud* (Cambridge., Mass., 1990).

15. P.M. Spacks, ' "Ev'ry Woman is at Heart a Rake" ', *Eighteenth-Century Studies*, VIII, 1 (1974) 27-46.

16. See above, Chapter 2, for material on John Cleland and *Memoirs of a Woman of Pleasure*. For a discussion of the way in which eighteenth-century writers presented this transition from lesbian sex to heterosexuality see D. Kraakman, 'Reading Pornography Anew: A Critical History of Sexual Knowledge for Girls in French Erotic Fiction, 1750-1840', *Journal of the History of Sexuality*, IV, 4 (1994) 517-48, and E. Marks, 'Lesbian Intertextuality' in E. Marks and G. Stambolian, eds, *Homosexualities and French Literature* (Ithaca, N.Y., 1979).

17. See above, Chapter 4. For an overview of this as it relates to women's bodies see R. Perry, 'Colonizing the Breast: Sexuality and Maternity in Eighteenth-Century England', *Journal of the History of Sexuality*, II, 2 (1991) 204-34.

18. L. Faderman, *Surpassing the Love of Men*, op. cit.

19. E. Mavor, *The Ladies of Llangollen*, op. cit., p. 88. For a rather different analysis of the 'Ladies of Llangollen' see T. Castle, *Apparitional Lesbian*, op. cit., pp. 93-6.

20. For Hester Thrale Piozzi see L. Faderman, *Surpassing the Love of Men*, op. cit., p. 125.

21. For discussions of the historical development of romantic friendship in a Dutch and American context respectively see M. Everard, 'Lesbian History: A History of Change and Disparity' in M. Kehoe, ed., *Historical, Literary, and Erotic Aspects of Lesbianism* (London, 1986), and C. Smith-Rosenberg, 'The Female World of Love and Ritual:

Relations between Women in Nineteenth-Century America' in E. Abel and E.K. Abel, eds, *The Signs Reader: Women, Gender and Scholarship* (Chicago, 1983).

22. E. Donaghue, *Passions between Women*, op. cit.

23. For a more detailed study of the life of Charlotte Charke see K. Straub, 'The Guilty Pleasures of Female Theatrical Cross-Dressing and the Autobiography of Charlotte Charke' in J. Epstein and K. Straub, *Body Guards: The Cultural Politics of Gender Ambiguity* (London, 1991).

24. Quoted in E. Donaghue, *Passions between Women*, op. cit., p. 146.

25. For a further discussion of this issue see R. Norton, *Mother Clap's Molly House: The Gay Subculture in England, 1700– 1830* (London, 1992), chapter 15, 'Tommies and the Game of Flats'.

26. H. Whitbread, ed., *I Know My Own Heart: The Diaries of Anne Lister, 1791–1840* (London, 1988); H. Whitbread, ed., *No Priest but Love: The Journals of Anne Lister from 1824–1826* (Otley, W. Yorks, 1992); and T. Castle, *The Apparitional Lesbian*, op. cit., chapter 5, 'The Diaries of Anne Lister'.

27. H. Whitbread, ed., *No Priest but Love*, op. cit., p. 20.

28. *Ibid.*, pp. 64–5.

29. E. Donaghue, *Passions between Women*, op. cit., pp. 19–22.

30. For an excellent discussion of the relationship between class, romantic friendship and sex in a Dutch context see M. Everard, 'Lesbian History', op. cit.

31. See T. van der Meer, 'Tribades on Trial: Female Same-Sex Offenders in Late Eighteenth-Century Amsterdam', *Journal of the History of Sexuality*, I, 3 (1991) 424–45.

32. Throughout the whole panoply of the literature on sexuality there is an unspoken assumption that while the rich and literate have sexualities the poor are driven by economic necessity. While the sexuality of the independent labouring poor, particularly in a rural context, has received some attention, I know of no attempt to address this issue in relation to the inmates of the plethora of poor law and criminal justice institutions of the eighteenth century. For a discussion of the sexuality of women caught up in the poor law system in London see T. Hitchcock, ' "Unlawfully Begotten on Her Body": Illegitimacy and the Parish Poor in St. Luke's Chelsea' in T. Hitchcock, P. King and P. Sharpe, eds, *Chronicling Poverty: The Voices and Strategies of the English Poor, 1640–1840* (London, 1996).

33. In relation to the middling sort Lawrence Stone has suggested that the practice of having women sleep two to a bed was a 'common precaution against fornication or rape'. L. Stone, *Uncertain Unions: Marriage in England, 1660–1753* (Oxford, 1992) p. 51.

34. R.M. Dekker and L.C. van de Pol, *The Tradition of Female Transvestism*, op. cit., p. 1. Cross-dressing has produced a larger and more sophisticated literature than most topics associated with eighteenth-century sexuality. See for example D. Dugaw, *Warrior Women and Popular Balladry, 1650–1850* (Cambridge, 1989); L. Friedli, ' "Passing Women": A Study of Gender Boundaries in the Eighteenth Century' in G.S. Rousseau and R. Porter, eds, *Sexual Underworlds of the Enlightenment* (Manchester, 1987); M. Garber, *Vested Interests: Cross-Dressing and Cultural Anxiety* (London, 1992); P. Rogers, 'The Breeches Part' in P-G. Boucé, *Sexuality in Eighteenth-Century Britain* (Manchester, 1982); K. Straub, 'The Guilty Pleasures of Female Theatrical Cross-Dressing', op. cit.; J. Wheelwright, *Amazons and Military Maids: Women Who Dressed as Men in Pursuit of Life, Liberty and Happiness* (London, 1989).

35. A. Simpson, 'Masculinity and Control', op. cit., p. 366. For an excellent analysis of the public presentation of cross-dressing see D. Dugaw, *Warrior Women and Popular Balladry*, op. cit.

36. See J. Wheelwright, *Amazons and Military Maids*, op. cit., and D. Dugaw, *Warrior Women and Popular Balladry*, op. cit For examples of the treatment of cross-dressing and lesbianism in the context of both the theatre and masquerade see T. Castle, 'Eros and Liberty at the English Masquerade, 1710–90', *Eighteenth-Century Studies*, XVII, 2 (1983–84) 156–76; T. Castle, *Masquerade and Civilisation: The Carnivalesque in Eighteenth-Century English Culture and Fiction* (London, 1986); K. Kendall, 'From Lesbian Heroine to Devoted Wife: or, What the Stage Would Allow', *Journal of Homosexuality*, XII, 3/4 (1986) 9–22; P. Rogers, 'The Breeches Part', op. cit.

37. The best recent treatment of D'Eon is G. Kates, 'D'Eon Returns to France: Gender and Power in 1777' in J. Epstein and K. Straub, *Body Guards*, op. cit.

38. E. Donaghue, *Passions between Women*, op. cit., pp. 70–3.

39. Several unattributed accounts of the history of Theodora Verdion are interleaved in Daniel Lysons, *Collectanea: or, a Collection of Advertisements and Paragraphs from the Newspapers, Relating to Various Subjects*, vol. I, part one (1828), British Library 1881.b.6., fol. 30.

40. R.M. Dekker and L.C. van de Pol, *The Tradition of Female Transvestism*, op. cit., p. 100.

41. M. Goldstein, 'Some Tolerant Attitudes toward Female Homosexuality throughout History', *Journal of Psychohistory*, IX (1982) 437–60.

Chapter 7. Sexual Fear and the Regulation of Society

1. Greater London Record Office, 'St. Luke's Chelsea, Settlement and Bastardy Examinations, 1733–1750', MS P74/Luk/121, Microfilm X15/39, 'Elizabeth Edwards', 21 May 1748.
2. For a wider discussion of Elizabeth Edwards' experience see T. Hitchcock, ' "Unlawfully Begotten on Her Body": Illegitimacy and the Parish Poor in St. Luke's Chelsea' in T. Hitchcock, P. King and P. Sharpe, eds, *Chronicling Poverty: The Voices and Strategies of the English Poor, 1640–1840* (London, 1996).
3. For an example of an account of prostitution based largely on these dubious sources see E.J. Burford, *Wits, Wenchers and Wantons: London's Low Life: Covent Garden in the Eighteenth Century* (London, 1986).
4. For a suggestive account of sexual relations and commercial sex in a rural context covering a period slightly before our own see G.R. Quaife, *Wanton Wenches and Wayward Wives: Peasants and Illicit Sex in Early Seventeenth-Century England* (London, 1979).
5. This volume is due out from Longman's Press in 1997, and is based on his excellent doctoral thesis: A. Henderson, 'Female Prostitution in London, 1730–1830' (University of London Ph.D. thesis, Royal Holloway and Bedford New College, 1992). Other recent works which deal with prostitution include V.L. Bullough, 'Prostitution and Reform in Eighteenth-Century England' in R.P. Maccubbin, ed., *'Tis Nature's Fault: Unauthorized Sexuality during the Enlightenment* (Cambridge, 1987); A.D. Harvey, *Sex in Georgian England: Attitudes and Prejudices from the 1720s to the 1820s* (London, 1994); S. Nash, 'Prostitution and Charity: The Magdalen Hospital, a Case Study', *Journal of Social History*, 17 (1974) 617–28; T.G.A. Nelson, 'Women of Pleasure', *Eighteenth-Century Life*, XI, n.s., 1 (1987) 181–98; W.A. Speck, 'The Harlot's Progress in Eighteenth-Century England', *British Journal for Eighteenth-Century Studies*, 3 (1980) 127–39; R. Trumbach, 'Sex, Gender, and Sexual Identity in Modern Culture: Male Sodomy and Female Prostitution in Enlightenment London', *Journal of the History of Sexuality*, II, 2 (1991) 186–203.
6. A. Henderson, 'Female Prostitution in London', op. cit., chapters 2 and 3.

7. E.J. Bristow, *Vice and Vigilance, Purity Movements in Britain since 1700* (Dublin, 1977) p. 25.

8. Westminster City Archive, 'Charge Books of the Parish of St. James Piccadilly', MS D2105-D2108, *passim*; quoted in A. Henderson, 'Female Prostitution in London', op. cit., p. 233.

9. For a discussion of the evidence for the age of London's prostitutes see A. Henderson, 'Female Prostitution in London', op. cit., pp. 48-50. See also A.D. Harvey, *Sex in Georgian England*, op. cit., pp. 95-6.

10. Quoted in A. Henderson, 'Female Prostitution in London', op. cit., p. 38.

11. Out of 468 women in this age group, 107 entered the house because of pregnancy; thirty were referred on to hospital, and on average they stayed in the workhouse for ninety days. Greater London Record Office, 'St. Luke's Chelsea, Workhouse Register, 1743-1766', Microfilm, X/15/37. For an extended discussion of the relationship between plebeian women and workhouse provision see T. Hitchcock, ' "Unlawfully Begotten on Her Body" ', op. cit.

12. See *ibid.*; see also N. Rogers, 'Carnal Knowledge: Illegitimacy in Eighteenth-Century Westminster', *Journal of Social History*, XXIII, 2 (1989) 355-75; A. Wilson, 'Illegitimacy and Its Implications in Mid-Eighteenth-Century London: The Evidence of the Foundling Hospital', *Continuity and Change*, IV, 1 (1989) 103-64; and D.A. Kent, ' "Gone for a Soldier": Family Breakdown and the Demography of Desertion in a London Parish, 1750-91', *Local Population Studies*, 45 (1990) 27-42. For an alternative view of the economic position of female servants see D.A. Kent, 'Ubiquitous but Invisible: Female Domestic Servants in Mid-Eighteenth-Century London', *History Workshop*, 28 (1989) 111-28.

13. Quoted in T. Meldrum, 'A Woman's Court in London: Defamation at the Bishop of London's Consistory Court, 1700-1745', *The London Journal*, XIX, 1 (1994) 1.

14. Material on defamation of sexual honour is growing at a tremendous rate. For some recent contributions see A. Clark, 'Whores and Gossips: Sexual Reputation in London, 1770-1825' in A. Angerman et al., eds, *Current Issues in Women's History* (London, 1989); T. Meldrum, 'A Woman's Court in London', op. cit., pp. 1-20; P. Morris, 'Sodomy and Male Honor: The Case of Somerset, 1740-1850', *Journal of Homosexuality*, XVI, 1/2 (1989) 383-406. For material on sixteenth- and seventeenth-century defamation see M. Ingram, *Church Courts, Sex and Marriage in England, 1570-1640*

(Cambridge, 1987), and L. Gowing, 'Gender and the Language of Insult in Early Modern London', *History Workshop*, 35 (1993) 1–21. For an excellent recent discussion of plebeian women's culture and attitudes towards sexual licence drawn from a different set of sources see J. Wiltenburg, *Disorderly Women and Female Power in the Street Literature of Early Modern England and Germany* (Charlottesville, Virg., 1992).

15. See, for example, T. Harris, 'The Bawdy House Riots of 1688', *Historical Journal*, XXIX, 3 (1986) 537–56. For a general discussion of the 'mob' see R.B. Shoemaker, 'The London 'Mob' in the Early Eighteenth Century' in P. Borsay, ed., *The Eighteenth-Century Town, 1688–1820* (Harlow, Essex, 1990).

16. P. Lake, 'Deeds against Nature: Cheap Print, Protestantism and Murder in Early Seventeenth-Century England' in K. Sharpe and P. Lake, eds, *Culture and Politics in Early Stuart England* (London, 1994) p. 264.

17. R. Halsband, ed., *The Complete Letters of Lady Mary Wortley Montagu* (Oxford, 1966) vol. II, p. 488.

18. For a discussion of attitudes towards prostitutes see V.L. Bullough, 'Prostitution and Reform', op. cit.; A.D. Harvey, *Sex in Georgian England*, op. cit.; T.G.A. Nelson, 'Women of Pleasure', op. cit.; R. Trumbach, 'Sex, Gender, and Sexual Identity', op. cit. For an important example of work on French prostitution see C. Jones, 'Prostitution and the Ruling Class in Eighteenth-Century Montpellier', *History Workshop*, 6 (1978) 7–28.

19. For two insightful analyses of the meaning of sin in seventeenth-century thought see C.B. Herrup, 'Law and Morality in Seventeenth-Century England', *Past and Present*, 106 (1985) 102–23, and P. Lake, 'Deeds against Nature', op. cit.

20. For a discussion of the role of seduction in *Fanny Hill* see R. Roussel, *The Conversation of the Sexes: Seduction and Equality in Selected Seventeenth- and Eighteenth-Century Texts* (New York, 1986), chapter 2, 'Fanny Hill and the Androgynous Reader'.

21. For two more general discussions of the history of seduction in the eighteenth century see A. Clark, 'The Politics of Seduction in English Popular Culture, 1748–1848' in J. Radford, ed., *The Progress of Romance: The Politics of Popular Fiction* (London, 1986), and S. Staves, 'British Seduced Maidens', *Eighteenth-Century Studies*, XIV (1980–81) 109–34.

22. A. Clark, *Women's Silence, Men's Violence: Sexual Assault in England, 1770–1845* (London, 1987); A. Simpson, 'Masculinity and Control:

The Prosecution of Sex Offences in Eighteenth-Century London' (New York University Ph.D. thesis, 1984); A. Simpson, 'Vulnerability and the Age of Female Consent: Legal Innovation and its Effect on Prosecution for Rape in Eighteenth-Century London' in G.S. Rousseau and R. Porter, eds, *Sexual Underworlds of the Enlightenment* (Manchester, 1987). For a well-argued response to Clark's contentions see R. Porter, 'Rape – Does it Have a Historical Meaning?' in S. Tomaselli and R. Porter, eds, *Rape: An Historical and Cultural Enquiry* (Oxford, 1986); and for a recent, more sophisticated approach to the history of rape see M. Chaytor, 'Husband(ry): Narratives of Rape in the Seventeenth Century', *Gender and History*, VII, 3 (1995) 378–407.

23. For examples of the extensive literature on the societies see D.W.R. Bahlman, *The Moral Revolution of 1688* (New Haven, Conn., 1957); E.J. Bristow, *Vice and Vigilance*, op. cit.; T. Isaacs, 'The Anglican Hierarchy and the Reformation of Manners, 1688–1738', *Journal of Ecclesiastical History*, XXXIII, 3 (1982) 391–411; R.B. Shoemaker, 'Reforming the City: The Reformation of Manners Campaign in London, 1690–1738' in L. Davison, T. Hitchcock, T. Kiern and R.B. Shoemaker, eds, *Stilling the Grumbling Hive: The Response to Social and Economic Problems in England, 1688–1750* (Stroud, Glos., 1992); R.B. Shoemaker, *Prosecution and Punishment: Petty Crime and the Law in London and Rural Middlesex, c.1660–1725* (Cambridge, 1991). For a discussion of later reformation movements see J. Innes, 'Politics and Morals: The Reformation of Manners Movement in Later Eighteenth-Century England' in E. Hellmuth, ed., *The Transformation of Political Culture: England and Germany in the Late Eighteenth Century* (Oxford, 1990).

24. For a comprehensive account of the workings of the eighteenth-century criminal justice system see J.M. Beattie, *Crime and the Courts in England 1660–1800* (Oxford, 1986).

25. The two most comprehensive and now rather elderly accounts of the SPCK are M.G. Jones, *The Charity School Movement: A Study in Eighteenth-Century Puritanism in Action* (Cambridge, 1938), and L.W. Cowie, *Henry Newman: An American in London, 1708–1743* (London, 1956). For more recent work see E. Duffy, '*Correspondance fraternelle*: The SPCK, the SPG, and the Churches of Switzerland in the War of the Spanish Succession' in D. Baker, ed., *Reform and Reformation: England and the Continent, c. 1500–1750* (Oxford, 1979); C.M. Haydon, 'The Anti-Catholic Activity of the S.P.C.K., c.1698–1740', *Recusant History*, XVIII, 4 (1987) 418–21; T. Hitchcock, 'Paupers

and Preachers: The SPCK and the Parochial Workhouse Movement' in L. Davison et al., eds, *Stilling the Grumbling Hive*, op. cit.

26. For national totals for the workhouse population see House of Lords Record Office, 'Poor Rate Returns, 1777', Parchment Collection, Box 162. For a brief published account of the parochial workhouse movement see T. Hitchcock, 'Paupers and Preachers', op. cit. The figure for adult women represents 50 per cent of the total number of workhouse inmates, a proportion derived from an analysis of 1,312 paupers housed by St Luke's, Chelsea, between 1743 and 1766 (the approximate equivalent for adult men is 20 per cent, and for children under sixteen years, 30 per cent). Greater London Record Office, 'St. Luke's Chelsea, Workhouse Register, 1743–1766'.

27. The best general account of the full range of voluntary foundations of this period is D.T. Andrew, *Philanthropy and Police: London Charity in the Eighteenth Century* (Princeton, N.J., 1989).

28. Donna Andrew bases her analysis of these foundations on the role of both these influences and the rise of a mercantilist approach to social policy. See D.T. Andrew, *Philanthropy and Police*, op. cit.

29. For material on the Foundling Hospital see D.T. Andrew, *Philanthropy and Police*, op. cit., pp. 57–64, 98–101; R. McClure, *Coram's Children: The London Foundling Hospital in the Eighteenth-Century* (New Haven, Conn., 1981); A. Wilson, 'Illegitimacy and Its Implications', op. cit. For a discussion of the relationship between the social and sexual strategies of plebeian women and the Foundling Hospital see T. Hitchcock, ' "Unlawfully Begotten on Her Body" ', op. cit.

30. Quoted in R. McClure, *Coram's Children*, op. cit., p. 140.

31. See D.T. Andrew, *Philanthropy and Police*, op. cit., pp. 119–26; A.D. Harvey, *Sex in Georgian England*, op. cit.; A. Henderson, 'Female Prostitution in London', op. cit.; S. Nash, 'Prostitution and Charity', op. cit.; T.G.A. Nelson, 'Women of Pleasure', op. cit.; W.A. Speck, 'The Harlot's Progress', op. cit.

32. Quoted in A.D. Harvey, *Sex in Georgian England*, op. cit., p. 96.

33. See V.L. Bullough, 'Prostitution and Reform', op. cit., pp. 68–9.

34. The most recent and comprehensive treatment of Fleet marriages and Hardwicke's Act is R.B. Outhwaite, *Clandestine Marriage in England, 1500–1850* (London, 1995). For further material see J. Boulton, 'Clandestine Marriages in London: An Examination of a Neglected Urban Variable', *Urban History*, XX, 2 (1993) 191–210; R.L. Brown, 'The Rise and Fall of the Fleet Marriages' in R.B. Outhwaite, ed., *Marriage and Society: Studies in the Social History of*

Marriage (London, 1981); L. Stone, *Road to Divorce: England, 1530–1987* (Oxford, 1990). For a Scottish perspective on this material see T.C. Smout, 'Scottish Marriage, Regular and Irregular, 1500–1940' in R.B. Outhwaite, ed., *Marriage and Society*, op. cit.

35. 26 George II, chapter xxxiii.

36. See in particular J. Gillis, 'Married but not Churched: Plebeian Sexual Relations and Marital Nonconformity in Eighteenth-Century Britain' in R.P. Maccubbin, 'Tis Nature's Fault, op. cit.; J. Gillis, *For Better, For Worse: British Marriages 1600 to the Present* (Oxford, 1985) pp. 90–8.

37. 25 George II, chapter xxxvi. See A. Henderson, 'Female Prostitution in London', op. cit., chapter 6.

38. For accounts of later institutional and legal developments see J. Bettley, '*Post Voluptatem Misericordia*: The Rise and Fall of the London Lock Hospital', *The London Journal*, X, 2 (1984) 167–75; E.J. Bristow, *Vice and Vigilance*, op. cit.; V.L. Bullough, 'Prostitution and Reform', op. cit.; J. Innes, 'Politics and Morals', op. cit.; S. Pederson, 'Hannah More Meets Simple Simon: Tracts, Chapbooks and Popular Culture in Late Eighteenth-Century England', *The Journal of British Studies*, 25 (1986) 84–113; M.J.D. Roberts, 'The Society for the Suppression of Vice and Its Early Critics, 1802–1812', *The Historical Journal*, XXVI, 1 (1983) 159–76.

39. [(Sophia) Watson], *Memoirs of the Seraglio of the Bashaw of Merryland* [alias Lord Baltimore] (1768).

Chapter 8. Conclusions

1. Quoted in P. Wagner, *Eros Revived: Erotica of the Enlightenment in England and America* (London, 1988) p. 295.

Further Reading

General, Introductory and Theoretical

Abelove, H., 'Some Speculations on the History of Sexual Intercourse during the Long Eighteenth Century in England', *Genders*, 6 (1989) 125–30.

Aries, P. and Duby, G., eds, *History of Private Life* vol. 3, Chartier, R., et al., eds, *Passions of the Renaissance* (Cambridge, 1989).

Barker-Benfield, G.J., *The Culture of Sensibility: Sex and Society in Eighteenth-Century Britain* (Chicago, Mich., 1992).

Bennett, P. and Rosario, V.A., eds, *Solitary Pleasures: The Historical, Literary, and Artistic Discourses of Autoeroticism* (New York, 1995).

Boucé, P-G., ed., *Sexuality in Eighteenth-Century Britain* (Manchester, 1982).

Clark, A., *The Struggle for the Breeches: Gender and the Making of the British Working Class* (Berkeley, Calif., 1995).

Donoghue, E., *Passions between Women: British Lesbian Culture, 1668–1801* (London, 1993).

Duberman, M., Vicinus, M. and Chauncy, G. Jr, eds, *Hidden from History: Reclaiming the Gay and Lesbian Past* (London, 1991).

Epstein, J. and Straub, K., eds, *Body Guards: The Cultural Politics of Gender Ambiguity* (London, 1991).

Fletcher, A., *Gender, Sex and Subordination in England, 1500–1800* (New Haven, Conn., 1995).

Foucault, M., *The History of Sexuality: Volume 1: An Introduction* (London, 1976).

Gillis, J., *For Better, For Worse: British Marriages 1600 to the Present* (Oxford, 1985).

Hitchcock, T., 'Redefining Sex in Eighteenth-Century England', *History Workshop*, 41 (1996) 72–90.

Hunt, L., 'Foucault's Subject in *The History of Sexuality*' in Stanton, D.C., ed., *Discourses of Sexuality from Aristotle to Aids* (Ann Arbor, Mich., 1992).

Jordanova, L., *Sexual Visions: Images of Gender in Science and Medicine between the Eighteenth and Twentieth Centuries* (New York, 1989).

Laqueur, T., *Making Sex: Body and Gender from the Greeks to Freud* (Cambridge, Mass., 1990).

Laqueur, T., 'Sex and Desire in the Industrial Revolution' in O'Brien, P. and Quinault, R., eds, *The Industrial Revolution and British Society* (Cambridge, 1993).

Norton, R., *Mother Clap's Molly House: The Gay Subculture in England, 1700–1830* (London, 1992).

Porter, R., 'Is Foucault Useful for Understanding Eighteenth- and Nineteenth-Century Sexuality?', *Contention: Debates in Society, Culture and Science*, I, 1 (1991) 62–81; also M. Poster, 'A Response to Roy Porter on Foucault', 83–8.

Porter, R. and Hall, L., *The Facts of Life: The Creation of Sexual Knowledge in Britain, 1650–1950* (New Haven and London, 1995).

Trumbach, R., 'London's Sapphists: From Three Sexes to Four Genders in the Making of Modern Culture' in Epstein, J. and Straub, K., eds, *Body Guards: The Cultural Politics of Gender Ambiguity* (London, 1991).

Weeks, J., *Sex, Politics and Society: The Regulation of Sexuality since 1800*, 2nd edn (London, 1989).

Pornography and the Public Cultures of Sex

Basker, J.G., ' "The Wages of Sin": The Later Career of John Cleland', *Etude Anglaises*, XL (1987) 178–94.

Boucé, P-G., 'Chthonic and Pelagic Metaphorization in Eighteenth-Century English Erotica' in Maccubbin, R.P., ed., *'Tis Nature's Fault: Unauthorized Sexuality during the Enlightenment* (Cambridge, 1987).

Boucé, P-G., 'The Secret Nexus: Sex and Literature in Eighteenth-Century Britain' in Bold, A., ed., *The Sexual Dimension in Literature* (London, 1982).

Brady, F., '*Tristram Shandy*: Sexuality, Morality and Sensibility', *Eighteenth-Century Studies*, 1 (1970) 41–56.

Braudy, L., '*Fanny Hill* and Materialism', *Eighteenth-Century Studies*, 4 (1970) 21–40.

Carter, A., *The Sadeian Woman: An Exercise in Cultural History* (New York, 1978).

Castle, T., 'Eros and Liberty at the English Masquerade, 1710–90', *Eighteenth-Century Studies*, XVII, 2 (1983/4) 156–76.

Clarke, N., 'Refining Tastes: Literacy and Consumerism in the Eighteenth Century', *Gender and History*, VI, 2 (1994) 275–80.

Darnton, R., *The Kiss of Lamourette: Reflections in Cultural History* (London, 1990), particularly chapter 9, 'First Steps Toward a History of Reading'.

Darnton, R., *The Literary Underground of the Old Regime* (Cambridge, Mass., 1982).

DeJean, J., *Fictions of Sappho, 1546–1937* (Chicago, Mich., 1989).

Epstein, J., 'Fanny's Fanny: Epistolarity, Eroticism and the Transsexual' in Goldsmith, E.C., ed., *The Female Voice: Essays on Epistolary Literature* (London, 1989).

Epstein, W.H., *John Cleland: Images of a Life* (New York, 1974).

Farley-Hills, D., ed., *Rochester: The Critical Heritage* (New York, 1972).

Ferguson, F., 'Sade and the Pornographic Legacy' in *Representations*, 36 (1991) 1–21.

Foxon, D., *Libertine Literature in England, 1660–1745* (New York, 1965).

Hagstrum, J.H., *Sex and Sensibility: Ideal and Erotic Love from Milton to Mozart* (Chicago, Mich., 1980).

Hess, T.B. and Nochlin, L., eds, *Women as Sex Object: Studies in Erotic Art, 1730–1970* (New York, 1972).

Hunt, L., ed., *The Invention of Pornography, 1500–1800* (New York, 1993).

Hyde, H.M., *A History of Pornography* (London, 1964).

Isherwood, R.M., *Farce and Fantasy: Popular Entertainment in Eighteenth-Century Paris* (New York, 1986).

Ivker, B., 'Towards a Definition of Libertinism in Eighteenth-Century French Fiction', *Studies on Voltaire and the Eighteenth-Century*, LXXIII (1970) 221–39.

Jones, L.C., *The Clubs of the Georgian Rakes* (New York, 1942).

Kahn, M., *Narrative Transvestism: Rhetoric and Gender in the Eighteenth-Century English Novel* (Ithaca, N.Y., 1991).

Kearney, P., *A History of Erotic Literature* (London, 1982).

Kendrick, W., *The Secret Museum: Pornography in Modern Culture* (New York, 1987).

Kraakman, D., 'Reading Pornography Anew: A Critical History of Sexual Knowledge for Girls in French Erotic Fiction, 1750–1840', *Journal of the History of Sexuality*, IV, 4 (1994) 517–48.

Legman, G., *The Horn Book: Studies in Erotic Folklore and Bibliography* (New York, 1964).

Loth, D., *The Erotic in Literature: A Historical Survey of Pornography as Delightful as it is Indiscreet* (London, 1962).

Mannix, D.P., *The Hell-Fire Club* (New York, 1959).

Mannsaker, F., 'Elegancy and Wildness: Reflections of the East in the Eighteenth-Century Imagination' in Rousseau, G.S. and Porter, R., eds, *Exoticism in the Enlightenment* (Manchester, 1990).

McCalman, I., *Radical Underworld: Prophets, Revolutionaries and Pornographers in London, 1795–1840* (Cambridge, 1988).

McCalman, I. 'Unrespectable Radicalism, Infidels and Pornography in Early 19th Century London', *Past and Present*, 104 (1984) 74–110.

Mengay, D.H., 'The Sodomitical Muse: *Fanny Hill* and the Rhetoric of Crossdressing', *Journal of Homosexuality*, XXIII, 1/2 (1991) 185–98.

Mills, J., *Bloomsbury Guide to Erotic Literature* (London, 1993).

Nussbaum, F.A., *The Brink of All We Hate* (Lexington, Ken., 1984).

Porter, R., 'The Exotic as Erotic: Captain Cook at Tahiti' in Rousseau, G.S. and Porter, R., eds, *Exoticism in the Enlightenment* (Manchester, 1990).

Porter, R., 'The Sexual Politics of James Graham', *British Journal for Eighteenth-Century Studies*, V, 2 (1982) 199–207.

Rousseau, G.S. and Porter, R., 'Introduction: Approaching Enlightenment Exoticism' in Rousseau, G.S. and Porter, R., eds, *Exoticism in the Enlightenment* (Manchester, 1990).

Roussel, R., *The Conversation of the Sexes: Seduction and Equality in Selected Seventeenth- and Eighteenth-Century Texts* (New York, 1986), chapter 2, 'Fanny Hill and the Androgynous Reader'.

Sabor, P., 'The Censor Censured: Expurgating *Memoirs of a Woman of Pleasure*' in Maccubbin, R.P., ed., *'Tis Nature's Fault: Unauthorized Sexuality during the Enlightenment* (Cambridge, 1987).

Said, E.W., *Orientalism* (London, 1978).

Smith, N., 'Sexual Mores in the Eighteenth Century: Robert Wallace's "Of Venery" ', *Journal of the History of Ideas*, XXXIX, 3 (1978) 419–34.

Spack, P.M., ' "Ev'ry Woman is at Heart a Rake" ', *Eighteenth-Century Studies*, VIII, 1 (1974) 27–46.

Spufford, M., *Small Books and Pleasant Histories: Popular Fiction and its Readership in Seventeenth-Century England* (Cambridge, 1981).

Stone, L., 'Libertine Sexuality in Post-Restoration England: Group Sex and Flagellation among the Middling Sort in Norwich in 1706–07', *Journal of the History of Sexuality*, II, 4 (1992) 511–26.

Thompson, R., *Unfit for Modest Ears: A Study of Pornographic, Obscene and Bawdy Works Written or Published in England in the Second Half of the Seventeenth Century* (London, 1979).

Turner, J.G., ' "Illustrious Depravity" and the Erotic Sublime' in Korshin, P.J., ed., *The Age of Johnson*, vol. II (New York, 1989) 1–38.

Turner, J.G., 'Lovelace and the Paradoxes of Libertinism' in Doody, M.A. and Sabor, P., eds, *Samuel Richardson* (Cambridge, 1989).

Turner, J.G., 'Pope's Libertine Self-Fashioning', *The Eighteenth Century*, XXIX, 2 (1988) 123–44.

Turner, J.G., 'The Libertine Sublime: Love and Death in Restoration England' in Brown, L.E. and Craddock, P., eds, *Studies in Eighteenth-Century Culture*, 19 (1989) 99–115.

Turner, J.G., ed., *Sexuality and Gender in Early Modern Europe: Institutions, Texts, Images* (Cambridge, 1993).

Vartanian, A., 'La Mettrie, Diderot, and Sexology in the Enlightenment' in Macary, J., ed., *Essays on the Age of Enlightenment in Honor of Ira O. Wade* (Geneva, 1977).

Wagner, P., *Eros Revived: Erotica of the Enlightenment in England and America* (London, 1988).

Wagner, P., 'The Veil of Medicine and Mortality: Some Pornographic Aspects of the *Onania*', *The British Journal for Eighteenth-Century Studies*, VI (1983) 179–84.

Wagner, P., 'Trial Reports as a Genre of Eighteenth-Century Erotica', *The British Journal for Eighteenth-Century Studies*, V, 1 (Spring 1982) 117–23.

Wagner, P., ed., *Erotica in the Enlightenment* (Frankfurt, 1991).

Marriage, Courtship and Heterosex

Abelove, H., 'Some Speculations on the History of Sexual Intercourse during the Long Eighteenth Century in England', *Genders*, 6 (1989) 125–30.

Ben-Amos, I.K., *Adolescence and Youth in Early Modern England* (New Haven, Conn., 1994).

Blom, I., 'The History of Widowhood: A Bibliographic Overview', *Journal of Family History*, XVI, 2 (1991) 191–210.

Bonfield, L., 'Marriage Settlements, 1660–1740: The Adoption of the Strict Settlement in Kent and Northamptonshire' in Outhwaite, R.B., ed., *Marriage and Society: Studies in the Social History of Marriage* (London, 1981).

Boulton, J., 'Clandestine Marriages in London: An Examination of a Neglected Urban Variable', *Urban History*, XX, 2 (1993) 191–210.

Boulton, J., 'London Widowhood Revisited: The Decline of Female Remarriage in the Seventeenth and Early Eighteenth Centuries', *Continuity and Change*, V, 3 (1990) 323–55.

Brown, R.L., 'The Rise and Fall of the Fleet Marriages' in Outhwaite, R.B., ed., *Marriage and Society: Studies in the Social History of Marriage* (London, 1981).

Clark, P., *The English Alehouse: A Social History 1200–1830* (London, 1983).

Cooper, S.M., 'Intergenerational Social Mobility in Late-Seventeenth- and Early-Eighteenth-Century England', *Continuity and Change*, VII, 3 (1992) 283–301.

Earle, P., *The Making of the English Middle Class: Business, Society and Family Life in London, 1660–1730* (London, 1989).

Gillis, J., *For Better, For Worse: British Marriages 1600 to the Present* (Oxford, 1985).

Gillis, J., 'Married but not Churched: Plebeian Sexual Relations and Marital Nonconformity in Eighteenth-Century Britain' in Maccubbin, R.P., *'Tis Nature's Fault: Unauthorized Sexuality during the Enlightenment* (Cambridge, 1987).

Hill, B., 'The Marriage Age of Women and the Demographers', *History Workshop*, 28 (1989) 129–47.

Hill, B., *Women, Work and Sexual Politics in Eighteenth-Century England* (London, 1989).

Houlbrooke, R., *The English Family, 1450–1700* (Harlow, Essex, 1984).

Hufton, O., 'Women Without Men: Widows and Spinsters in Britain and France in the Eighteenth Century', *Family History* (1984) 355–76.

Ingram, M., *Church Courts, Sex and Marriage in England, 1570–1640* (Cambridge, 1987).

Kent, D.A., ' "Gone for a Soldier": Family Breakdown and the Demography of Desertion in a London Parish, 1750–91', *Local Population Studies*, 45 (1990) 27–42.

Kent, D.A., 'Ubiquitous but Invisible: Female Domestic Servants in Mid-Eighteenth-Century London', *History Workshop*, 28 (1989) 111–28.

Laqueur, T., 'Sex and Desire in the Industrial Revolution' in O'Brien, P. and Quinault, R., eds, *The Industrial Revolution and British Society* (Cambridge, 1993).

Laslett, P., Oosterveen, K. and Smith, R., eds, *Bastardy and Its Comparative History* (London, 1980).

Leneman, L., 'The Study of Illegitimacy from Kirk Session Records: Two Eighteenth-Century Perthshire Parishes', *Local Population Studies*, 31 (1983) 29–33.

Levine, D., *Family Formation in an Age of Nascent Capitalism* (New York, 1977).

Levine, D., ' "For Their Own Reasons": Individual Marriage Decisions and Family Life', *Journal of Family History* (1982) 255–64.

Macfarlane, A., *Marriage and Love in England, 1300–1840* (Oxford, 1986).

McLaren, A., *A History of Contraception from Antiquity to the Present Day* (Oxford, 1990).

McLaren, A., 'The Pleasures of Procreation: Traditional and Bio-medical Theories of Conception' in Bynum, W.F. and Porter, R., eds, *William Hunter and the Eighteenth-Century Medical World* (Cambridge, 1985).

Meteyard, B., 'Illegitimacy and Marriage in Eighteenth-Century England', *Journal of Interdisciplinary History*, X, 3 (1980) 479–89; also the following debate between Stone, L. and Meteyard, B., 'Illegitimacy in Eighteenth-Century England: Again', *Journal of Interdisciplinary History*, XI, 3 (1981) 507–14.

Outhwaite, R.B., *Clandestine Marriage in England, 1500–1850* (London, 1995).

Parfitt, G. and Houlbrooke, R., eds, *The Courtship Narrative of Leonard Wheatcroft* (Reading, 1986).

Potter, R.G. and Millman, S.R., 'Fecundability and the Frequency of Marital Intercourse: A Critique of Nine Models', *Population Studies*, 39 (1985) 461–70.

Rendall, J., *Women in an Industrializing Society: England, 1750–1880* (Oxford, 1990).

Rogers, N., 'Carnal Knowledge: Illegitimacy in Eighteenth-Century Westminster', *Journal of Social History*, XXIII, 2 (1989) 355–75.

Schofield, R., 'English Marriage Patterns Revisited', *Journal of Family History* (1985) 2–20.

Sharpe, P., 'Locating the "Missing Marryers" in Colyton, 1660–1750', *Local Population Studies*, 48 (1992) 49–59.

Sharpe, P., 'Marital Separation in the Eighteenth and Early Nineteenth Centuries', *Local Population Studies*, 45 (1990) 66–70.

Shorter, E., *The Making of the Modern Family* (New York, 1975).

Smout, T.C., 'Scottish Marriage, Regular and Irregular, 1500–1940' in Outhwaite, R.B., ed., *Marriage and Society: Studies in the Social History of Marriage* (London, 1981).

Snell, K.D.M., *Annals of the Labouring Poor: Social Change and Agrarian England, 1660–1900* (Cambridge, 1985).

Stone, L., *Broken Lives: Separation and Divorce in England, 1660–1857* (Oxford, 1993).

Stone, L., *Road to Divorce: England, 1530–1987* (Oxford, 1990).

Stone, L., *The Family, Sex and Marriage in England, 1500–1800*, 1st edn (London, 1977).

Stone, L., *Uncertain Unions: Marriage in England, 1660–1753* (Oxford, 1992).

Wall, R., 'Leaving Home and the Process of Household Formation in Pre-Industrial England', *Continuity and Change*, II, 1 (1987) 77–101.

Weir, D.R., 'Rather Never than Late: Celibacy and Age at Marriage in English Cohort Fertility, 1541–1871', *Journal of Family History* (1984) 340–54.

Wilson, A., 'Illegitimacy and Its Implications in Mid-Eighteenth-Century London: The Evidence of the Foundling Hospital', *Continuity and Change*, IV, 1 (1989) 103–64.

Wilson, A., *The Making of Man-Midwifery: Childbirth in England, 1660–1770* (Cambridge, Mass., 1995).

Wrigley, E.A., 'Marriage, Fertility and Population Growth in Eighteenth-Century England' in Outhwaite, R.B., ed., *Marriage and Society: Studies in the Social History of Marriage* (London, 1981).

Wrigley, E.A., 'The Growth of Population in Eighteenth-Century England: A Conundrum Resolved', *Past and Present*, 98 (1983) 121–50.

Wrigley, E.A. and Schofield, R.S., *The Population History of England, 1541–1871* (London, 1981).

Wyatt, G., 'Bastardy and Prenuptial Pregnancy in a Cheshire Town during the Eighteenth Century', *Local Population Studies*, 49 (1992) 38–50.

The Body, Medicine and Sexual Difference

Beall, O.T., Jr, '*Aristotle's Masterpiece* in America: A Landmark in the Folklore of Medicine', *William and Mary Quarterly*, XX (1963) 207–22.

Bennett, P. and Rosario, V.A., II, eds, *Solitary Pleasures: The Historical, Literary and Artistic Discourses of Autoeroticism* (New York, 1995).

Boucé, P-G., 'Imagination, Pregnant Women, and Monsters, in Eighteenth-Century England and France' in Rousseau, G.S. and Porter, R., eds, *Sexual Underworlds of the Enlightenment* (Manchester, 1987).

Boucé, P-G., 'Some Sexual Beliefs and Myths in Eighteenth-Century Britain' in Boucé, P-G., ed., *Sexuality in Eighteenth-Century Britain* (Manchester, 1982).

Cash, A.H., 'The Birth of Tristram Shandy: Sterne and Dr Burton' in Boucé, P-G., ed., *Sexuality in Eighteenth-Century Britain* (Manchester, 1982).

Crawford, P., 'Attitudes to Menstruation in Seventeenth-Century England', *Past and Present*, 91 (1981) 47–73.

Crawford, P., 'Attitudes to Pregnancy from a Woman's Spiritual Diary, 1687–8', *Local Population Studies*, 21 (1978) 43–5.

Crawford, P., 'Printed Advertisements for Women Medical Practitioners in London, 1670–1710', *Society for the Social History of Medicine, Bulletin*, 35 (1984) 66–70.

Crawford, P., 'Sexual Knowledge in England, 1500–1750' in Porter, R. and Teich, M., *'Sexual Knowledge, Sexual Science: The History of Attitudes to Sexuality* (Cambridge, 1994).

Donnison, J., *Midwives and Medical Men: A History of Inter-professional Rivalries and Women's Rights* (New York, 1977).

Duden, B., 'A Repertory of Body History' in Feher, M., ed., *Fragments for a History of the Human Body*, part three (New York, 1989).

Eccles, A., *Obstetrics and Gynaecology in Tudor and Stuart England* (Kent, Ohio, 1982).

Engelhardt, T., 'The Disease of Masturbation: Values and Concepts of Disease', *Bulletin of the History of Medicine*, 48 (1974) 234–48.

Erickson, R.A., ' "The Books of Generation": Some Observations on the Style of the English Midwife Books, 1671–1764' in Boucé, P-G., ed., *Sexuality in Eighteenth-Century Britain* (Manchester, 1982).

Fildes, V., *Wet Nursing: A History from Antiquity to the Present* (Oxford, 1988).

Fissell, M., 'Gender and Generation: Representing Reproduction in Early Modern England', *Gender and History*, VII, 3 (1995) 433–56.

Fissell, M., 'Readers, Texts and Contexts: Vernacular Medical Works in Early Modern England' in Porter, R., ed., *The Popularization of Medicine, 1650–1850* (London, 1992).

Forbes, T., 'The Regulation of English Midwives in the Sixteenth and Seventeenth Centuries', *Medical History*, 8 (1964) 235–44.

Gallagher, C. and Laqueur, T., eds, *The Making of the Modern Body: Sexuality and Society in the Nineteenth Century* (Berkeley, Calif., 1987).

Hare, E.H., 'Masturbatory Insanity: The History of an Idea', *Journal of Mental Science*, 108 (1962) 2–25.

Jacquart, D. and Thomasset, C., eds, *Sexuality and Medicine in the Middle Ages* (Cambridge, 1988).

Jordanova, L., *Sexual Visions: Images of Gender in Science and Medicine between the Eighteenth and Twentieth Centuries* (London, 1989).

Jordanova, L., 'The Popularization of Medicine: Tissot on Onanism', *Textual Practice*, I, 1 (1987) 68–80.

Keller, E.F., *Reflections on Gender and Science* (New Haven, Conn., 1985).

Laqueur, T., 'Amor Veneris, vel Dulcedo Appeletur' in Feher, M., ed., *Fragments for a History of the Human Body*, part three (New York, 1989).

Laqueur, T., 'Bodies of the Past', *Bulletin of the History of Medicine*, 67 (1993) 155–61.

Laqueur, T., *Making Sex: Body and Gender from the Greeks to Freud* (Cambridge, Mass., 1990).

Laqueur, T., 'Orgasm, Generation and the Politics of Reproductive Biology' in Gallagher, C. and Laqueur, T., eds, *The Making of the Modern Body: Sexuality and Society in the Nineteenth Century* (Berkeley, Calif., 1987).

Laqueur, T., 'The Social Evil, the Solitary Vice and Pouring Tea' in Feher, M., ed., *Fragments for a History of the Human Body*, part three (New York, 1989).

Leslie, G., 'Cheat and Imposter: Debate Following the Case of the Rabbit Breeder', *The Eighteenth Century: Theory and Interpretation*, XXVII, 3 (1986) 269–86.

MacDonald, R.H., 'The Frightful Consequences of Onanism: Notes on the History of a Delusion', *Journal of the History of Ideas*, XXVIII, 3 (1967) 423–31.

Maclean, I., *The Renaissance Notion of Woman* (Cambridge, 1980).

Martensen, R., ' "Habit of Reason": Anatomy and Anglicanism in Restoration England', *Bulletin of the History of Medicine*, 66 (1992) 511–35.

Martensen, R., 'The Transformation of Eve: Women's Bodies, Medicine and Culture in Early Modern England' in Porter, R. and Teich, M., *Sexual Knowledge, Sexual Science: The History of Attitudes to Sexuality* (Cambridge, 1994).

McLaren, A., *A History of Contraception from Anitiquity to the Present Day* (Oxford, 1990).

McLaren, A., *Reproductive Rituals: The Perception of Fertility in England from the Sixteenth-Century to the Nineteenth-Century* (London, 1984).

Merchant, C., *The Death of Nature: Women, Ecology and the Scientific Revolution* (New York, 1980).

Mort, F., *Dangerous Sexualities: Medical-Moral Politics in England* (London 1987).

Neuman, R.P., 'Masturbation, Madness, and the Modern Concepts of Childhood and Adolescence', *Journal of Social History*, VIII (1975) 1–27.

Perry, R., 'Colonizing the Breast: Sexuality and Maternity in Eighteenth-Century England', *Journal of the History of Sexuality*, II, 2 (1991) 204–34.

Porter, R., 'A Touch of Danger: The Man-Midwife as Sexual Predator' in Rousseau, G.S. and Porter, R., eds, *Sexual Underworlds of the Enlightenment* (Manchester, 1987).

Porter, R., 'Love, Sex and Medicine: Nicolas Venette and His *Tableau de l'amour conjugal* ' in Wagner, P., ed., *Erotica and the Enlightenment* (Frankfurt, 1990).

Porter, R., 'Spreading Carnal Knowledge or Selling Dirt Cheap? Nicolas Venette's *Tableau de l'amour conjugal* in Eighteenth-Century England', *Journal of European Studies*, 14 (1984) 233–56.

Porter, R., 'The Literature of Sexual Advice before 1800' in Porter, R. and Teich, M., *Sexual Knowledge, Sexual Science: The History of Attitudes to Sexuality* (Cambridge, 1994).

Porter, R., ' "The Secrets of Generation Display'd": *Aristotle's Masterpiece* in Eighteenth-Century England' in Maccubin, R.P., ed., *'Tis Natures Fault: Unauthorized Sexualities during the Enlightenment* (Cambridge, 1987).

Porter, R., 'The Sexual Politics of James Graham', *British Journal for Eighteenth-Century Studies*, V, 2 (1982) 199–206.

Porter, R., ' "The Whole Secret of Health": Mind, Body and Medicine in *Tristram Shandy*' in Christie, J. and Shuttleworth, S., eds, *Nature Transfigured* (Manchester, 1989).

Porter, R. and Hall, L., *The Facts of Life: The Creation of Sexual Knowledge in Britain, 1650–1950* (New Haven and London, 1995).

Roper, L., *Oedipus and the Devil: Witchcraft, Sexuality and Religion in Early Modern Europe* (London, 1994).

Schiebinger, L., 'Mammals, Primatology and Sexology' in Porter, R. and Teich, M., *Sexual Knowledge, Sexual Science: The History of Attitudes to Sexuality* (Cambridge, 1994).

Schiebinger, L., *Nature's Body: Sexual Politics and the Making of Modern Science* (London, 1994).

Schiebinger, L., 'Skeletons in the Closet: The First Illustrations of the Female Skeleton in Eighteenth-Century Anatomy' in Gallagher, C. and Laqueur, T., eds, *The Making of the Modern Body: Sexuality and Society in the Nineteenth Century* (Berkeley, Calif., 1987).

Schiebinger, L., *The Mind Has No Sex? Women in the Origins of Modern Science* (Cambridge, Mass., 1989).

Smith, H., 'Gynecology and Ideology in Seventeenth-Century England' in Caroll, B., *Liberating Women's History* (Westport, Conn., 1978).

Veith, I., *Hysteria: The History of a Disease* (Chicago, 1965).

The Development of Homosexuality

Bingham, C., 'Seventeenth-Century Attitudes towards Deviant Sex, with a Comment by Bruce Mazlish', *The Journal of Interdisciplinary History*, I, 3 (1971) 447–72.

Boon, L.J., 'Those Damned Sodomites: Public Images of Sodomy in the Eighteenth-Century Netherlands', *Journal of Homosexuality*, XVI, 1/2 (1989) 237–48.

Boucé, P-G., 'Aspects of Sexual Tolerance and Intolerance in XVIIIth-Century England', *The British Journal for Eighteenth-Century Studies*, III (1980) 173–91.

Bray, A., 'Homosexuality and the Signs of Male Friendship in Elizabethan England', *History Workshop*, 29 (1990) 1–19.

Bray, A., *Homosexuality in Renaissance England* (London, 1982).

Burg, B.R., ' "Ho Hum, Another Work of the Devil": Buggery and Sodomy in Early Stuart England', *Journal of Homosexuality*, VI, 1/2 (1980/81) 69–78.

Corber, R.J., 'Representing the "Unspeakable": William Godwin and the Politics of Homophobia', *Journal of the History of Sexuality*, I (1990–91) 85–101.

Crompton, L., '*Don Leon*, Byron, and Homosexual Law Reform', *Journal of Homosexuality*, VIII, 3/4 (1983) 53–72.

Crompton, L., 'Homosexuals and the Death Penalty in Colonial America', *Journal of Homosexuality*, I, 3 (1976) 277–94.

Crompton, L., 'Jeremy Bentham's Essay on "Paederasty": An Introduction', *Journal of Homosexuality*, III, 4 (1978) 383–8.

Crompton, L., ed., 'Jeremy Bentham's Essay on "Paederasty" (Part 2)', *Journal of Homosexuality*, IV, 1 (1978) 91–107.

Crompton, L., ed., 'Offences against One's Self: Paederasty (Part 1)', *Journal of Homosexuality*, III, 4 (1978) 389–405.

Duberman, M., Vicinus, M. and Chauncy, G., Jr, eds, *Hidden from History: Reclaiming the Gay and Lesbian Past* (London, 1991).

Gilbert, A.N., 'Buggery and the British Navy, 1700–1861', *Journal of Social History*, X, 1 (1976) 72–98.

Gilbert, A.N., 'Conceptions of Homosexuality and Sodomy in Western History', *Journal of Homosexuality*, VI, 1/2 (1980/81) 57–68.

Gilbert, A.N., 'Sexual Deviance and Disaster during the Napoleonic Wars', *Albion*, IX, 1 (1977) 98–113.

Hekma, G., 'Sodomites, Platonic Lovers, Contrary Lovers: The Backgrounds of the Modern Homosexual', *Journal of Homosexuality*, XVI, 1/2 (1989) 433–55.

Herrup, C.B., 'Law and Morality in Seventeenth-Century England', *Past and Present*, 106 (1985) 102–23.

Higgins, P., *A Queer Reader* (London, 1993).

Howson, G., *The Thief-Taker General: The Rise and Fall of Jonathan Wild* (London, 1970).

Huusen, A.H., Jr, 'Sodomy in the Dutch Republic during the Eighteenth Century' in Maccubbin, R.P., *'Tis Nature's Fault: Unauthorized Sexuality during the Enlightenment* (Cambridge, 1987).

Juussen, A.H., 'Prosecution of Sodomy in Eighteenth-Century Frisia, Netherlands', *Journal of Homosexuality*, XVI, 1/2 (1989) 249–62.

Kopelson, K., 'Seeing Sodomy: *Fanny Hill's* Blinding Vision', *Journal of Homosexuality*, XXIII, 1/2 (1992) 173–83.

Lake, P., 'Deeds against Nature: Cheap Print, Protestantism and Murder in Early Seventeenth-Century England' in Sharpe, K. and Lake, P., eds, *Culture and Politics in Early Stuart England* (London, 1994).

Monter, E.W., 'Sodomy and Heresy in Early Modern Switzerland', *Journal of Homosexuality*, VI, 1/2 (1980/81) 41–57.

Morris, P., 'Sodomy and Male Honor: The Case of Somerset, 1740–1850', *Journal of Homosexuality*, XVI, 1/2 (1989) 383–406.

Murray, S.O., 'Homosexual Acts and Selves in Early Modern Europe', *Journal of Homosexuality*, XVI, 1/2 (1989) 457–77.

Noordam, D.J., 'Sodomy in the Dutch Republic, 1600–1725', *Journal of Homosexuality*, XVI, 1/2 (1989) 207–28.

Norton, R., *Mother Clap's Molly House: The Gay Subculture in England, 1700–1830* (London, 1992).

Oaks, R.F., 'Defining Sodomy in Seventeenth-Century Massachusetts', *Journal of Homosexuality*, VI, 1/2 (1980/81) 79–83.

Oaks, R.F., 'Perceptions of Homosexuality by Justices of the Peace in Colonial Viginia', *Journal of Homosexuality*, V, 1/2 (1979/80) 35–42.

Oaks, R.F., ' "Things Fearful to Name": Sodomy and Buggery in Seventeenth-Century New England', *Journal of Social History*, XII, 2 (1978) 268–81.

Oosterhoff, J., 'Sodomy at Sea and at the Cape of Good Hope during the Eighteenth Century', *Journal of Homosexuality*, XVI, 1/2 (1989) 229–35.

Parker, W., 'Homosexuality in History: An Annotated Bibliography', *Journal of Homosexuality*, VI, 1/2 (1980/81) 191–210.

Rey, M., 'Parisian Homosexuals Create a Lifestyle, 1700–1750: The Police Archives' in Maccubbin, R.P., ed., *'Tis Nature's Fault: Unauthorized Sexuality during the Enlightenment* (Cambridge, 1987).

Rey, M., 'Police and Sodomy in Eighteenth-Century Paris: From Sin to Disorder', *Journal of Homosexuality*, XVI, 1/2 (1989) 129–46.

Rousseau, G.S., 'The Pursuit of Homosexuality in the Eighteenth Century: "Utterly Confused Category" and/or Rich Repository?' in Maccubbin, R.P., ed., *'Tis Nature's Fault: Unauthorized Sexuality during the Enlightenment* (Cambridge, 1987).

Rousseau, G.S., ' "In the House of Madam Vader Tasse, on the Long Bridge": A Homosocial University Club in Early Modern Europe', *Journal of Homosexuality*, XVI, 1/2 (1989) 311–47.

Rubini, D., 'Sexuality and Augustan England: Sodomy, Politics, Elite Circles and Society', *Journal of Homosexuality*, XVI, 1/2 (1989) 349–82.

Senelick, L., 'Mollies or Men of Mode? Sodomy and the Eighteenth-Century London Stage', *Journal of the History of Sexuality*, I, 1 (1990) 33–67.

Smith, N., 'Sexual Mores in the Eighteenth-Century: Robert Wallace's "Of Venery" ', *Journal of the History of Ideas*, XXXIX, 3 (1978) 419–34.

Spencer, C., *Homosexuality: A History* (London, 1995).

Sprague, G.A., 'Male Homosexuality in Western Culture: The Dilemma of Identity and Subculture in Historical Research', *Journal of Homosexuality*, X, 3/4 (1984) 29–43.

Trumbach, R., 'London's Sodomites: Homosexual Behaviour and Western Culture in the Eighteenth Century', *Journal of Social History*, XI, 1 (1977) 1–33.

Trumbach, R., 'Sex, Gender, and Sexual Identity in Modern Culture: Male Sodomy and Female Prostitution in Enlightenment London', *Journal of the History of Sexuality*, II, 2 (1991) 186–203.

Trumbach, R., 'Sodomitical Assaults, Gender Roles, and Sexual Development in Eighteenth Century London', *Journal of Homosexuality*, XVI, 1/2 (1989) 407–29.

Trumbach, R., 'Sodomitical Subcultures, Sodomitical Roles, and the Gender Revolution of the Eighteenth Century: The Recent Historiography' in Maccubbin, R.P., ed., *'Tis Nature's Fault: Unauthorized Sexuality during the Enlightenment* (Cambridge, 1987).

Trumbach, R., 'The Birth of the Queen: Sodomy and the Emergence of Gender Equality in Modern Culture, 1660–1750' in Duberman, M., Vicinus, M. and Chauncy, G., Jr, eds, *Hidden from History: Reclaiming the Gay and Lesbian Past* (London, 1991).

van der Meer, T., 'The Persecution of Sodomites in Eighteenth-Century Amsterdam: Changing Perceptions of Sodomy', *Journal of Homosexuality*, XVI, 1/2 (1989) 263–307.

Tribades, Cross-Dressers and Romantic Friendship

Brown, J.C., *Immodest Acts: The Life of a Lesbian Nun in Renaissance Italy* (Oxford, 1986).

Brown, J.C., 'Lesbian Sexuality in Medieval and Early Modern Europe' in Duberman, M., Vicinus, M. and Chauncy, G., Jr, eds, *Hidden from History: Reclaiming the Gay and Lesbian Past* (London, 1991).

Brown, J.C., 'Lesbian Sexuality in Renaissance Italy: The Case of Sister Benedetta Carline', *Signs*, 9 (1984) 751–58.

Castle, T., 'Eros and Liberty at the English Masquerade, 1710–90', *Eighteenth-Century Studies*, XVII, 2 (1983–84) 156–76.

Castle, T., 'Marie Antoinette Obsession', *Representations*, 38 (1992), 1–38, also reproduced as chapter 4 in Castle, T., *The Apparitional Lesbian: Female Homosexuality and Modern Culture* (New York, 1993).

Castle, T., *Masquerade and Civilization: The Carnivalesque in Eighteenth-Century English Culture and Fiction* (London, 1986).

Castle, T., 'Matters Not Fit to Be Mentioned: Fielding's *The Female Husband*', *English Literary History*, XLIX, 3 (1982) 602–23.

Castle, T., *The Apparitional Lesbian: Female Homosexuality and Modern Culture* (New York, 1993).

Clark, A., 'Queen Caroline and the Sexual Politics of Popular Culture in London 1820', *Representations*, 31 (1990) 47–68.

Cook, B., 'The Historical Denial of Lesbianism', *Radical History Review*, 20 (1979) 60–5.

Cott, N.F., 'Passionless: An Interpretation of Victorian Sexual Ideology, 1790–1850', *Signs*, 4 (1978) 237–52.

Crawford, P. and Mendelson, S., 'Sexual Identities in Early Modern England: The Marriage of Two Women in 1680', *Gender and History*, VII, 3 (1995) 362–77.

Crompton, L., 'The Myth of Lesbian Impunity: Capital Laws from 1270 to 1791', *Journal of Homosexuality*, VI, 1/2 (1980/81) 11–26.

DeJean, J., *Fictions of Sappho, 1546–1937* (Chicago, Mich., 1989).

Dekker, R.M. and van de Pol, L.C., *The Tradition of Female Transvestism in Early Modern Europe* (London, 1989).

Donaghue, E., *Passions between Women: British Lesbian Culture, 1668–1801* (London, 1993).

Duberman, M., Vicinus, M. and Chauncy, G., Jr, eds, *Hidden from History: Reclaiming the Gay and Lesbian Past* (London, 1991).

Dugaw, D., *Warrior Women and Popular Balladry, 1650–1850* (Cambridge, 1989).

Duyfhuizen, B., ' "That Which I Dare Not Name": Aphra Behn's "The Willing Mistress" ', *English Literary History*, LVIII (1991) 63–82.

Eriksson, B., trans., 'A Lesbian Execution in Germany, 1721: The Trial Records', *Journal of Homosexuality*, VI, 1/2 (1980/81) 27–40.

Faderman, L., *Surpassing the Love of Men* (London, 1981).

Friedli, L., ' "Passing Women": A Study of Gender Boundaries in the Eighteenth Century' in Rousseau, G.S. and Porter, R., eds, *Sexual Underworlds of the Enlightenment* (Manchester, 1987).

Frith, W., 'Sex, Smallpox and Seraglios: A Monument to Lady Mary Wortley Montagu' in Perry G. and Rossington, M., eds, *Femininity and Masculinity in Eighteenth-Century Art and Culture* (Manchester, 1994).

Garber, M., *Vested Interests: Cross-Dressing and Cultural Anxiety* (London, 1992).

Goldstein, Melvin, 'Some Tolerant Attitudes toward Female Homosexuality throughout History', *Journal of Psychohistory*, IX (1982) 437–60.

Goreau, A., 'Two English Women in the Seventeenth Century: Notes for an Anatomy of Feminine Desire' in Aries, P. and Bejin, A., eds, *Western Sexuality: Practice and Precept in Past and Present Times* (Oxford, 1985).

Haggerty, G.E., ' "Romantic Friendship" and Patriarchal Narrative in Sarah Scott's *Millenium Hall* ', *Genders*, 13 (1992) 108–22.

Hill, B., 'A Refuge from Men: The Idea of a Protestant Nunnery', *Past and Present*, 117 (1987) 107–30.

Hobby, E. and White, C., eds, *What Lesbians Do in Books* (London, 1991).

Hufton, O., 'Women without Men: Widows and Spinsters in England and France in the Eighteenth Century', *Journal of Family History* (1984) 355–76.

Jones, V., *Women in the Eighteenth Century: Constructions of Femininity* (London, 1990).

Kates, G., 'D'Eon Returns to France: Gender and Power in 1777' in Epstein, J. and Straub, K., eds, *Body Guards: The Cultural Politics of Gender Ambiguity* (London, 1991).

Kehoe, M., ed., *Historical, Literary and Erotic Aspects of Lesbianism* (New York, 1986).

Kendall, K., 'From Lesbian Heroine to Devoted Wife: or, What the Stage Would Allow', *Journal of Homosexuality*, XII, 3/4 (1986) 9–22.

Kent, D.A., 'Ubiquitous but Invisible: Female Domestic Servants in Mid-Eighteenth-Century London', *History Workshop*, 28 (1989) 111–28.

King, K.R., 'The Unaccountable Wife and Other Tales of Female Desire in Jane Barker's *A Patch-Work Screen for the Ladies*', *The Eighteenth Century: Theory and Interpretation*, XXXV, 2 (1994) 155–72.

Kraakman, D., 'Reading Pornography Anew: A Critical History of Sexual Knowledge for Girls in French Erotic Fiction, 1750–1840', *Journal of the History of Sexuality*, IV, 4 (1994) 517–48.

Liddington, J., 'Anne Lister of Shibden Hall, Halifax (1791–1840): Her Diaries and the Historians', *History Workshop*, 35 (1993) 45–77.

Mavor, E., *The Ladies of Llangollen: A Study in Romantic Friendship* (London, 1973).

Mendelson, S.H., *The Mental World of Stuart Women: Three Studies* (Brighton, 1987).

Norton, R., *Mother Clap's Molly House: The Gay Subculture in England, 1700–1830* (London, 1992).

Nussbaum, F.A., *The Brink of All We Hate: English Satires on Women, 1660–1750* (Lexington, Ken., 1984).

Perry, R., 'Colonizing the Breast: Sexuality and Maternity in Eighteenth-Century England', *Journal of the History of Sexuality*, II, 2 (1991) 204–34.

Rogers, K.M., *Feminism in Eighteenth-Century England* (Brighton, 1982).

Rogers, P., 'The Breeches Part' in Boucé, P-G., ed., *Sexuality in Eighteenth-Century Britain* (Manchester, 1982).

Smith-Rosenburg, C., 'A Study of Erotic Rhetoric in 18th and 19th C. Women's Friendships', *Signs*, 1 (1975) 1–29.

Spacks, P.M., ' "Ev'ry Woman is at Heart a Rake" ', *Eighteenth-Century Studies*, VIII, 1 (1974) 27–46.

Stanley, L., 'Epistemological Issues in Researching Lesbian History: The Case of Romantic Friendship' in Hinds, H. et al., eds, *Working Out: New Directions for Women's Studies* (Falmer, Penn., 1992).

Stiebel, A., 'Not Since Sappho: The Erotic in Poems of Katherine Philips and Aphra Behn', *Journal of Homosexuality*, XXIII, 1/2 (1992) 153–72.

Straub, K., 'The Guilty Pleasures of Female Theatrical Cross-Dressing and the Autobiography of Charlotte Charke' in Epstein, J. and Straub, K., eds, *Body Guards: The Cultural Politics of Gender Ambiguity* (London, 1991).

Trumbach, R., 'London's Sapphists: From Three Sexes to Four Genders in the Making of Modern Culture' in Epstein, J. and Straub, K., eds, *Body Guards: The Cultural Politics of Gender Ambiguity* (London, 1991).

Turner, M., 'Two Entries from the Marriage Register of Taxal, Cheshire', *Local Population Studies*, 21 (1978) 64.

van der Meer, T., 'Tribades on Trial: Female Same-Sex Offenders in Late Eighteenth-Century Amsterdam', *Journal of the History of Sexuality*, I, 3 (1991) 424–45.

Vicinus, M., ' "They Wonder to Which Sex I Belong": The Historical Roots of the Modern Lesbian Identity' in Abelove, H., Barale, M.A.

and Halperin, D.M., eds, *The Lesbian and Gay Studies Reader* (London, 1993).

Wheelwright, J., *Amazons and Military Maids: Women Who Dressed as Men in Pursuit of Life, Liberty and Happiness* (London, 1989).

Whitbread, H., ed., *I Know My Own Heart: The Diaries of Anne Lister, 1791–1840* (London, 1988).

Whitbread, H., ed., *No Priest but Love: The Journals of Anne Lister from 1824–1826* (Otley, W. Yorks, 1992).

Williams, C., 'The Changing Face of Change: Fe/male In/constancy', *British Journal for Eighteenth-Century Studies*, XII (1989) 13–28.

The Regulation of Sexuality

Abelove, H., *Evangelist of Desire: John Wesley and the Methodists* (Palo Alto, Calif., 1991).

Andrew, D.T., *Philanthropy and Police: London Charity in the Eighteenth Century* (Princeton, N.J., 1989).

Bahlman, D.W.R., *The Moral Revolution of 1688* (New Haven, Conn., 1957).

Barker-Benfield, G.J., *The Culture of Sensibility: Sex and Society in Eighteenth-Century Britain* (Chicago, Mich., 1992).

Beattie, J.M., *Crime and the Courts in England 1660–1800* (Oxford, 1986).

Bettley, J., '*Post Voluptatem Misericordia*: The Rise and Fall of the London Lock Hospital', *The London Journal*, X, 2 (1984) 167–75.

Black, J., 'The Language of Licentiousness', *The Scriblerian and the Kit-Cats*, XXVI, 2 (1994) 1–7.

Boucé, P-G., 'Aspects of Sexual Tolerance and Intolerance in XVIIIth-Century England', *The British Journal for Eighteenth-Century Studies*, III (1980) 173–91.

Bristow, E.J., *Vice and Vigilance: Purity Movements in Britain since 1700* (Dublin, 1977).

Brown, R.L., 'The Rise and Fall of the Fleet Marriages' in Outhwaite, R.B., ed., *Marriage and Society: Studies in the Social History of Marriage* (London, 1981).

Bullough, V.L., 'Prostitution and Reform in Eighteenth-Century England' in Maccubbin, R.P., ed., *'Tis Nature's Fault: Unauthorized Sexuality during the Enlightenment* (Cambridge, 1987).

Burford, E.J., *Wits, Wenches and Wantons: London's Low Life: Covent Garden in the Eighteenth Century* (London, 1986).

Chaytor, M., 'Husband(ry): Narratives of Rape in the Seventeenth Century', *Gender and History*, VII, 3 (1995) 378–407.

Clark, A., 'Humanity or Justice? Wifebeating and the Law in the Eighteenth and Nineteenth Centuries' in Smart, C., ed., *Regulating Womanhood: Historical Writings on Marriage, Motherhood and Sexuality* (London, 1992).

Clark, A., 'The Politics of Seduction in English Popular Culture, 1748–1848' in Radford, J., ed., *The Progress of Romance: The Politics of Popular Fiction* (London, 1986).

Clark, A., 'Whores and Gossips: Sexual Reputation in London, 1770–1825' in Angerman, A. et al., eds, *Current Issues in Women's History* (London, 1989).

Clark, A., *Women's Silence, Men's Violence: Sexual Assault in England, 1770–1845* (London, 1987).

Cowie, L.W., *Henry Newman: An American in London, 1708–1743* (London, 1956).

Fissell, M., *Patients, Power, and the Poor in Eighteenth-Century Bristol* (Cambridge, 1991).

Gatrell, V.A.C., *The Hanging Tree: Execution and the English People 1770–1868* (Oxford, 1994).

Gillis, J., *For Better, For Worse: British Marriages 1600 to the Present* (Oxford, 1985).

Gowing, L., 'Gender and the Language of Insult in Early Modern London', *History Workshop*, 35 (1993) 1–21.

Harris, T., 'The Bawdy House Riots of 1668', *Historical Journal*, XXIX, 3 (1986) 537–56.

Harvey, A.D., *Sex in Georgian England: Attitudes and Prejudices from the 1720s to the 1820s* (London, 1994).

Herrup, C.B., 'Law and Morality in Seventeenth-Century England', *Past and Present*, 106 (1985) 102–23.

Hill, B., *Women, Work and Sexual Politics in Eighteenth-Century England* (London, 1989).

Hitchcock, T., ' "Unlawfully Begotten on Her Body": Illegitimacy and the Parish Poor in St. Luke's Chelsea' in Hitchcock, T., King, P. and Sharp, P., eds, *Chronicling Poverty: The Voices and Strategies of the English Poor, 1640–1840* (London, 1996).

Howson, G., *Thief-Taker General: The Rise and Fall of Jonathn Wild* (London, 1970).

Hunt, M., 'Wife Beating, Domesticity and Women's Independence in Eighteenth-Century London', *Gender and History*, I, 1 (1992) 10–33.

Ingram, M., *Church Courts, Sex and Marriage in England, 1570–1640* (Cambridge, 1987).

Innes, J., 'Politics and Morals: The Reformation of Manners Movement in Later Eighteenth-Century England' in Hellmuth, E., ed., *The Transformation of Political Culture: England and Germany in the Late Eighteenth Century* (Oxford, 1990).

Isaacs, T., 'The Anglican Hierarchy and the Reformation of Manners, 1688–1738', *Journal of Ecclesiastical History*, XXXIII, 3 (1982) 391–411.

Jones, C., 'Prostitution and the Ruling Class in Eighteenth-Century Montpellier', *History Workshop*, 6 (1978) 7–28.

Jones, M.G., *The Charity School Movement: A Study in Eighteenth-Century Puritanism in Action* (Cambridge, 1938).

Linebaugh, P., *The London Hanged: Crime and Civil Society in the Eighteenth Century* (London, 1991).

McClure, R., *Coram's Children: The London Foundling Hospital in the Eighteenth Century* (New Haven, Conn., 1981).

Meldrum, T., 'A Woman's Court in London: Defamation at the Bishop of London's Consistory Court, 1700–1745', *The London Journal*, XIX, 1 (1994) 1–20.

Mitchison, R. and Leah L., *Sexuality and Society Control: Scotland 1660–1780* (Oxford, 1989).

Nash, S., 'Prostitution and Charity: The Magdalen Hospital, a Case Study', *Journal of Social History*, 17 (1974) 617–28.

Nelson, T.G.A., 'Women of Pleasure', *Eighteenth-Century Life*, XI, n.s., 1 (1987) 181–98.

Outhwaite, R.B., *Clandestine Marriage in England, 1500–1850* (London, 1995).

Pederson, S., 'Hannah More Meets Simple Simon: Tracts, Chapbooks and Popular Culture in Late Eighteenth-Century England', *The Journal of British Studies*, 25 (1986) 84–113.

Porter, R., 'Rape – Does it have a Historical Meaning?' in Tomaselli, S. and Porter, R., eds, *Rape: An Historical and Cultural Enquiry* (Oxford, 1986).

Quaife, G.R., *Wanton Wenches and Wayward Wives: Peasants and Illicit Sex in Early Seventeenth-Century England* (London, 1979).

Roberts, M.J.D., 'The Society for the Suppression of Vice and Its Early Critics, 1802–1812', *The Historical Journal*, XXVI, 1 (1983) 159–76.

Rogers, N., 'Carnal Knowledge: Illegitimacy in Eighteenth-Century Westminster', *Journal of Social History*, XXIII, 2 (1989) 355–75.

Shoemaker, R.B., *Prosecution and Punishment: Petty Crime and the Law in London and Rural Middlesex, c.1660–1725* (Cambridge, 1991).

Shoemaker, R.B., 'Reforming the City: The Reformation of Manners Campaign in London, 1690–1738' in Davison, L., Hitchcock, T.,

Kiern, T. and Shoemaker, R.B., eds, *Stilling the Grumbling Hive: The Response to Social and Economic Problems in England, 1688–1750* (Stroud, Glos., 1992).

Simpson, A., 'Vulnerability and the Age of Female Consent: Legal Innovation and its Effect on Prosecution for Rape in Eighteenth-Century London' in Rousseau, G.S. and Porter, R., eds, *Sexual Underworlds of the Enlightenment* (Manchester, 1987).

Smout, T.C., 'Scottish Marriage, Regular and Irregular, 1500–1940' in Outhwaite, R.B., ed., *Marriage and Society: Studies in the Social History of Marriage* (London, 1981).

Spacks, P.M., ' "Ev'ry Woman is at Heart a Rake" ', *Eighteenth-Century Studies*, XIII, 1 (1974) 27–46.

Speck, W.A., 'The Harlot's Progress in Eighteenth-Century England', *British Journal for Eighteenth-Century Studies*, 3 (1980) 127–39.

Staves, S., 'British Seduced Maidens', *Eighteenth-Century Studies*, XIV (1980–81) 109–34.

Trumbach, R., 'Sex, Gender, and Sexual Identity in Modern Culture: Male Sodomy and Female Prostitution in Enlightenment London', *Journal of the History of Sexuality*, II, 2 (1991) 186–203.

Wilson, A., 'Illegitimacy and Its Implications in Mid-Eighteenth-Century London: The Evidence of the Foundling Hospital', *Continuity and Change*, IV, 1 (1989) 103–64.

Wiltenburg, J., *Disorderly Women and Female Power in the Street Literature of Early Modern England and Germany* (Charlottesville, Virg., 1992).

Wyatt, G., 'Bastardy and Prenuptial Pregnancy in a Cheshire Town during the Eighteenth Century', *Local Population Studies*, 9 (1992) 38–50.

INDEX

Abelove, Henry, 27–8
abortion and abortifacients, 52–3
adolescence, 14, 113
adultery, 16; *see also* criminal
    conversation
advertisements, 13, 52
alcohol/drunkenness, 104
    in courting, 34, 35
alehouses/inns, 8
    as sites of courting, 10, 34–5
Aretino, *Ragionamenti*, 18; *see also*
    pornography
Aries, Phillipe, 57
Aristotelian medicine, 47
Aristotle's Master-piece, 14, 29, 40, 49,
    50, 51, 53, 110, 113
Asylum for Orphan Girls, London,
    106
Atherton, John, Bishop of
    Waterford, 66

Barlow, Mrs, 85
bastardy rate, 25, 26
Beggar's Benison, 8, 21
Belling, Susannah, 78
bestiality, 42, 62
biological essentialism, 4
birth control, *see* abortion; coitus
    interruptus; condoms;
    contraception
bisexuality, 65
blackmail, 89
Bond, Ann, 15–16
Boswell, James, 39
Bougainville, Louis de, 23
Bray, Alan, 58, 63, 74
brothels, 20, 71, 94, 107, 108–9
    attacks on, 97–8
Brown, Mary, 31
Buchan, William, 50

buggery, 42; *see also* sodomy
Burg, B.R., 61
Burke, Edmund, and lesbianism, 82
Butler, Eleanor, 82

Cambridge Group for the History
    of Population and Social
    Structure, 3; *see also* demo-
    graphy
Cannon, John, 9–10, 24, 28–38, 48,
    50, 110
Carrack, Ann, 76
Castle, Terry, 77, 78, 83
Castlehaven, Earl of, 15, 66
Catholicism, *see* Roman Catholicism
celibacy, 26
censorship, 21; *see also* Curll,
    Edmund
chapbooks, 8, 10–12
charity schools, 103
Charke, Charlotte, 83
Charteris, Colonel Francis, 15–16
Chelsea, 1, 10, 76, 96
child abuse, 61, 62
childhood, 57
Chorier, Nicolas, *Satyra Sotadica*, 18
church courts, 28, 78, 97
Clark, Anna, 101
Cleland, John, *Memoirs of a Woman of
    Pleasure*, 9, 17, 19, 20, 21, 81,
    100
Clements, Rebecca, 10
clitoris, 43, 45, 47, 79
clubs, 22, 75
Clutterbuck, Thomas, 1
coitus interruptus, 52, 53
Coke, Edward, on sodomy, 60
Cole, Mary, 105
companionate marriage, 3, 27
condoms, 53

contraception, 51, 52–4; *see also* abortion; coitus interruptus; condoms

Cook, Capt. Thomas, 23

Cooper, John, 73

Coram, Thomas, 104

Counterfeit Bridegroom, 17

courting, 24–41 *passim*, 110, 150–3
  adult oversight of, 30
  role of peer group, 34
  see also marriage

Coustos, John, 10

creationist school of the history of sexuality, 4–6

criminal conversation, 16–17; *see also* adultery

Crompton, Louis, 59

cross-dressing, female, 83, 88–90, 159–63; *see also* effeminacy

Culpeper, Nicholas, *Midwifery*, 29, 50, 113

Curll, Edmund, 21; *see also* censorship

Damer, Anne, 83–4

Darnton, Robert, 18

Deane, Susannah (née Cannon), 37

Defoe, Daniel, 96

Dekker, Rudolf, 90, 91

demography, 3, 25–7, 39, 112, 150–3; *see also* bastardy rate; illegitimacy; marriage

Diderot, Denis, 23

dildos, 83, 91

Disorderly House Act (1752), 107; *see also* brothels

divorce, 16; *see also* criminal conversation

doctor/patient relationship, 48

domestic servants/service, 35–6, 86, 96–7

domesticity, and pornography, 19, 23

Donaghue, Emma, 77, 78, 83, 85

Donne, John, 12

Dowdeny, George, 61

Dugaw, Dianne, 88

East, Mary (James How), 89; *see also* cross-dressing

economic reductionism, 112

economies of makeshift, 94

Edwards, Elizabeth, 93

effeminacy, 68

eggs, 46

ejaculation, 43

elite, as audience for pornography, 20–31

Ellis, Havelock, 2

Enlightenment, 2, 6, 18–19

Erick, Mary, 76

Essay on Woman, 19, 22

European marriage pattern, 25; *see also* demography

Faderman, Lillian, 76–7, 82–3

fairs as site of courting, 9–10

family, history of the, 3
  formation, 24–5
  role in courting, 31–3
  see also companionate marriage

Farren, Elizabeth, 84

female agency, 100

femininity, 91, 100–1, 111–12, 108

Fissell, Mary, 46

flagellation, 40

foetus
  development of, 43, 44
  position of in womb, 44

Foucault, Michel, 4–5, 59

Foundling Hospital, London, 39, 104–5; *see also* illegitimacy

Foxon, David, 2, 17

French, William, 64

French Prophets, 1

Galen of Pergamum, 42

Galenic medicine, 5, 42–3, 45–6, 47, 55, 62, 78–80, 153–6

genitals, 8, 14, 22
  female, 47, 79

Gilbert, A.N., 64

Gillis, John, 31, 38

Gordon, Thomas, 73

Gothic, 83

Gowing, Laura, 97

Graham, James, *Lecture on Generation*, 50, 51

Gray, Elizabeth, 1

Griffin, William, 71
Griffiths, Ralph, publisher and
    pornographer, 21; *see also*
    censorship
Griffiths, Sarah, 97

Hardwicke's Marriage Act (1753),
    106–7; *see also* marriage,
    clandestine
Haynes, Sarah, 44
Heister, Ann (Lais), 35–6
Henderson, Anthony, 95
hermaphroditism, 79, 91
heterosexuality, 2, 5, 80, 111
    and lesbianism, 91–2
    and masturbation, 57
Hitchins, Charles, 68
Hollingsworth, Ralph, 78
homosexuality, 2, 58–75 *passim*,
    111, 156–9
    legal status of, 58, 59–63
homosociability, 34–5, 64
    and lesbianism, 86
houses of correction, 86
    Bridewell, London, 69
humour, sexual, 10–14
humours, *see* Galenic medicine
Hunt, Lynn, 3, 17, 18

identity, sexual, 2
illegitimacy, 10, 25, 26, 39, 87, 93,
    96, 104–5, 113; *see also* bastardy
    rate; marriage
infanticide, 53; *see also* abortion
Ingram, Martin, 97
inns, *see* alehouses
intolerance, sexual, 3

James I, 65
Jones, Richard, 93

kiss-in-the-ring, 10

L'Escole des filles, 18, 20
Ladies of Llangollen, 82–3; *see also*
    romantic friendship
Lake, Peter, 63, 99
Laqueur, Thomas, 27–8, 45–7, 57
Lawrence, Gabriel, 71

Le Vasseur, Therese, 39
leap frog, 9
Leeuwenhoek, Anton van, 47
lesbian/lesbianism, 2, 45, 61, 76–92
    passim, 111, 159–63
    attitudes towards, 77–8
    continuum, 77, 83
    historical denial of, 81
    legal position of, 77–8
    plebeian, 85–6
    slang, 84, 85
    subculture, 84
liberationist school of historical
    analysis, 3–4, 6
libertinism/libertine clubs, 8, 21–2,
    40
    French, 18
    masturbatory nature of, 22
    and molly culture, 64–5
    see also Beggar's Benison;
        Medmenham Monks
Lister, Anne, 84–5, 87
Lock Hospital, 96, 104, 106; *see also*
    venereal disease
Locke, John, 74
London Lying-In Hospital, 106
London pattern of courting, 39–40
luxury, 66
    and prostitution, 99
lying-in, 93

Maclean, Ian, 47
Madan, Martin, 105–6
Magdalen Hospital, London, 104,
    105–6
Manningham, Richard, 'artificial
    matrix', 13
marriage, 24–41 *passim*, 37–8,
    150–3
    age at, 25, 26
    clandestine, 37–8, 104, 106–7
    customary, 33
    role of betrothal in, 33
    role of consummation in, 38
    role of economics in, 26
    see also courting; Hardwicke's
        Marriage Act
Marrow, Ann, 77
Martensen, Robert, 46

masculinity, 48–9, 68–9, 74, 91,
    100–1, 108, 111–12
  and rape, 101
Masonic order, 75
masturbation, 11, 14, 17, 20, 45,
    50, 81, 153–6
  condemnations of, 29, 54–7
  consequences of, 55
  learning how to, 29
  literature as pornography, 14–15
  mutual, 32, 38, 91
  ritual, 8
  see also sex, non-penetrative
maternalisation of women's bodies,
    49
Maternity Hospital, London, 106
Mavor, Elizabeth, 82
McClure, Ruth, 104
McIntosh, Mary, 58
McLaren, Angus, 51, 52, 54
medicine, 29, 42–57 passim; see also
    Galenic medicine
Medmenham Monks, 22; see also
    libertinism
Meldrum, Tim, 97
mercantilism, 56–7
middling sort, 8, 12–17, 20
midwifery, 46, 47, 48
  man-midwife, 47, 48, 53
migragtion, 39
misogyny, 47
molly-house culture/mollies, 58, 59,
    65–75 passim
  age structure, 69
  attitudes towards, 73
  location of houses, 67–8
  Mother Clap's, 67–8, 71
  published accounts of, 72
  raids on houses, 71–2
  see also homosexuality
monster births, 62
Montagu, Lady Mary Wortley, 99
Muhlhahn, Margaretha, 61

nakedness, see nudity
Navy, British, homosexuality in, 58,
    59, 64
Needham, Mother, 95
novels, 17, 19, 27, 94, 100

nudity, 1, 22
nymphomania, 56

Old Bailey Sessions Papers, as
    pornography, 15
Old Poor Law, 113
Onania, or, The Heinous Sin of
    Self-Pollution, 14, 55, 79–80
'one body' model of sexual
    difference, 45–6, 47, 78, 111
oral sex, 32, 61
Ordinary of Newgate, His Account, as
    pornography, 15
orgasm, 43
  female, 45, 50
  male, 48
Osterwald, Jean-Frederic, The Nature
    of Uncleanness Consider'd, 55
ovaries, 43
Oxford, homosexuality in, 64

passionless woman, rise of, 81, 91
Payne, Mary, 97
Payne, William, 72
peer group, 11
  role in courting, 29–30, 31
penis, 43, 79, 81
Pepys, Samuel, 20
phallocentrism, 91, 111
pillory, 95
  treatment of lesbians, 77
  treatment of sodomites, 73
pimping, 95
Piozzi, Hester Thrale, 82–3, 84
Place, Francis, 10, 39, 50
plebeian sexuality, 9–12
Plowden, Francis, 16
policing of sexual offences, 62
polygamy, 105–6
Ponsonby, Sarah, 82
poor relief, 93
Poor Robin's Intelligence, 11–12
popular health texts, as
    pornography, 14–15
popular sex manuals, 110
population, see demography
pornography, 2–3, 8–23 passim, 56,
    94, 147–50
  definition of, 17

pornography-*contd.*
  French, 8, 18–19
  as source of sexual knowledge, 40
  visual, 18, 23
Porter, Roy, 14–15, 50, 51
poverty, as check to reproduction, 26
pregnancy, attitudes towards, 35
print culture, 112–13
Proclamation Society, 107
procuring, 95
professionalisation of medicine, 47
promiscuity, attitudes towards, 97
prostitutes/prostitution, 71, 94–8, 105–6, 107–8, 111
  as aggressors, 99
  and life-cycle, 95–6
  and marriage, 96
  perception of by social reformers, 98–101
  plebeian attitudes towards, 97–8
  in pornography, 17, 21
  punishment of, 99
  role in plebeian society, 96
  rural, 94–5
  and seduction, 99–100
  social origin of, 100
  see also brothels
proto-industrialisation, 26
prudery, 8–9
psychoanalysis, 2, 3, 6 59
punishment of sexual deviancy, 102

quacks, 13
quickening, 53; *see also* foetus, development of

rape, 15–16, 66, 101, 108, 163–6
  homosexual, 60, 61, 62
reformation of manners, 54, 67, 70–1, 72, 97–8, 99, 102–3, 107
reputation, sexual, 36; *see also* church courts
Rich, Adrienne, 77
Richardson, Samuel, *Clarissa*, 100
Ridgeway, John, 69
Rochester, Earl of, 19, 65
Roman Catholicism, 1, 19
  and prostitution, 99

romantic friendship, 76, 81–3, 87, 91, 111
Roper, Lyndal, 46
Rose, Mary, 32
Rousseau, J.-J., 11
running races, female, 8
Ryder, Dudley, 64

Sade, Marquis De, 18
scatological humour, 14
scrotum, 43
Sealy, Mary, 78
seduction, 99–101
  and rape, 101
  and social policy, 104, 105
semen, 43, 47, 80
sensibility, 83
sentiment and sex, 27
separate spheres, 49
sex
  consequences for men 44–5
  consequences for women, 44–5
  in courting, 30, 33, 35, 36, 38
  non-penetrative, 31, 34, 35, 38, 80
  penetrative, 29, 36, 38, 39, 57, 91, 110
  see also masturbation, mutual
sex manuals, popular, 49–51
sexology, 2, 59
sexual aggression, female, 80–1, 87
sexual control, 34
sexual desire, 4, 5
  female, 36, 48
  male, 48–9
sexual differentiation, 43–4, 46
sexual dysfunction, 51
sexual humour, 22–3
sexual metaphors, 12–14
  readership, 13
sexual pleasure, 3, 80
sexual revolution, 2, 3–4, 27, 40–1, 111–12
Shakespeare, William, 12
Sharp, Jane, 48, 50; *see also* midwifery
Shiebinger, Londa, 47
Shoemaker, Robert, 71
Shorter, Edward, 3–4, 27

Simpson, Antony, 58, 61, 62, 74, 77–8, 88, 101, 112
sin, 5, 63, 102–3
skeletons, sexual differentiation of, 45, 47
sleeping arrangements, 32, 86
sociability, new, 59, 75
social policy, 111, 113, 163–6
Society for Promoting Christian Knowledge, 54, 71, 103–4
Society for the Propagation of the Gospel in Foreign Parts, 71
Society for the Suppression of Vice, 107
sodomy, 15, 60–3
court and monarchical, 65–7
death penalty for, 60
elite, 65–6
and heresy, 61
and politics, 65–6
prosecuted as assault, 61
public character of prosecuted instances, 61–2
and Roman Catholicism, 61
tolerance of, 63
see also homosexuality
sperm, 46, 47, 111
spinster clustering, 76
spirituality, 43
Spufford, Margaret, 10
St Thomas's Hospital, London, 69
Sterne, Lawrence, Tristram Shandy, 50
Stone, Lawrence, 3, 20, 27, 40, 62
Stretser, Thomas, 12–13
stripping, 22; see also nudity

Tahiti, 23
tea drinking, 13
testes, 43
Thistlewayte, Robert, 64
thread-the-needle, 10
Tissot, Samuel, L'Onanisme, 56–7

Toft, Mary (Rabbit Woman of Godalming), 44
trial reports, as pornography, 15–16
tribady, 79–80, 91
Trumbach, Randolph, 58, 59, 70, 74
'two body' model of sexual differentiation, see 'one body' model of sexual differentiation

urbanisation, 4, 27

vagina, 45, 46, 47
van de Pol, Lotte, 90, 91
venereal disease, 53, 84, 113
Venette, Nicholas
Secrets of Conjugal Love, 14
Tableau de l'amour conjugal, 49, 50
Venus in the Cloister, 21
Verdion, Theodora, 89–90
virginity, 21, 34, 37

wages, 26
Wagner, Peter, 3, 14–15, 17
Watson, Sophia, 108–9
Weeks, Jeffrey, 59
Wellington, Duke of, Arthur Wellesley, masturbatory habits of, 20
Wheelwright, Julie, 88
Whig history, 3, 4
whore, as term of abuse, 97, 98, 99
widows' sexuality, 10–11, 45
William III, 65
Willis, Robert, 46
Wilson, Adrian, 39
Withers, Mary, 30
womb, 43, 44
Woodward, John, Rebuke of the Sin of Uncleanness, 54
workhouses, 10, 86, 103–4, 108–9
Wright, Thomas, 71
Wrigley, E.A., 26, 39